<musicdot.com>

<musicdot.com>
general editor: roger walton

<musicdot.com>

First published in 2001 by:
HBI, an imprint of HarperCollins Publishers
10 East 53rd Street
New York, NY 10022-5299
United States of America

Distributed in the United States
and Canada by:
Watson-Guptill Publications
770 Broadway, 8th Floor
New York, NY 10003-9595
Telephone: (800) 451-1741;
(732) 363-4511 in NJ, AK, HI
Fax: (732) 363-0338

ISBN: 0-8230-8347-0

Distributed throughout the rest
of the world by:
HarperCollins International
10 East 53rd Street
New York, NY 10022-5299
Fax: (212) 207-7654

ISBN: 0-06-018616-X

Conceived, created, and designed by:
Duncan Baird Publishers
6th Floor, Castle House
75–76 Wells Street, London W1T 3QH

Designer: 27.12 Design Ltd, NYC
Project Co-ordinator: Tara Solesbury
Editor: Carolyn Ryden

10 9 8 7 6 5 4 3 2 1

Typeset in Frutiger
Color reproduction by Colourscan, Singapore
Printed in China

NOTE
All caption material is based upon information received from the designers. Where there is no caption information, no information has been received despite all efforts to contact all parties. The term n/a (non-applicable) is used where a designer has felt that a category is not relevant.

<contents>

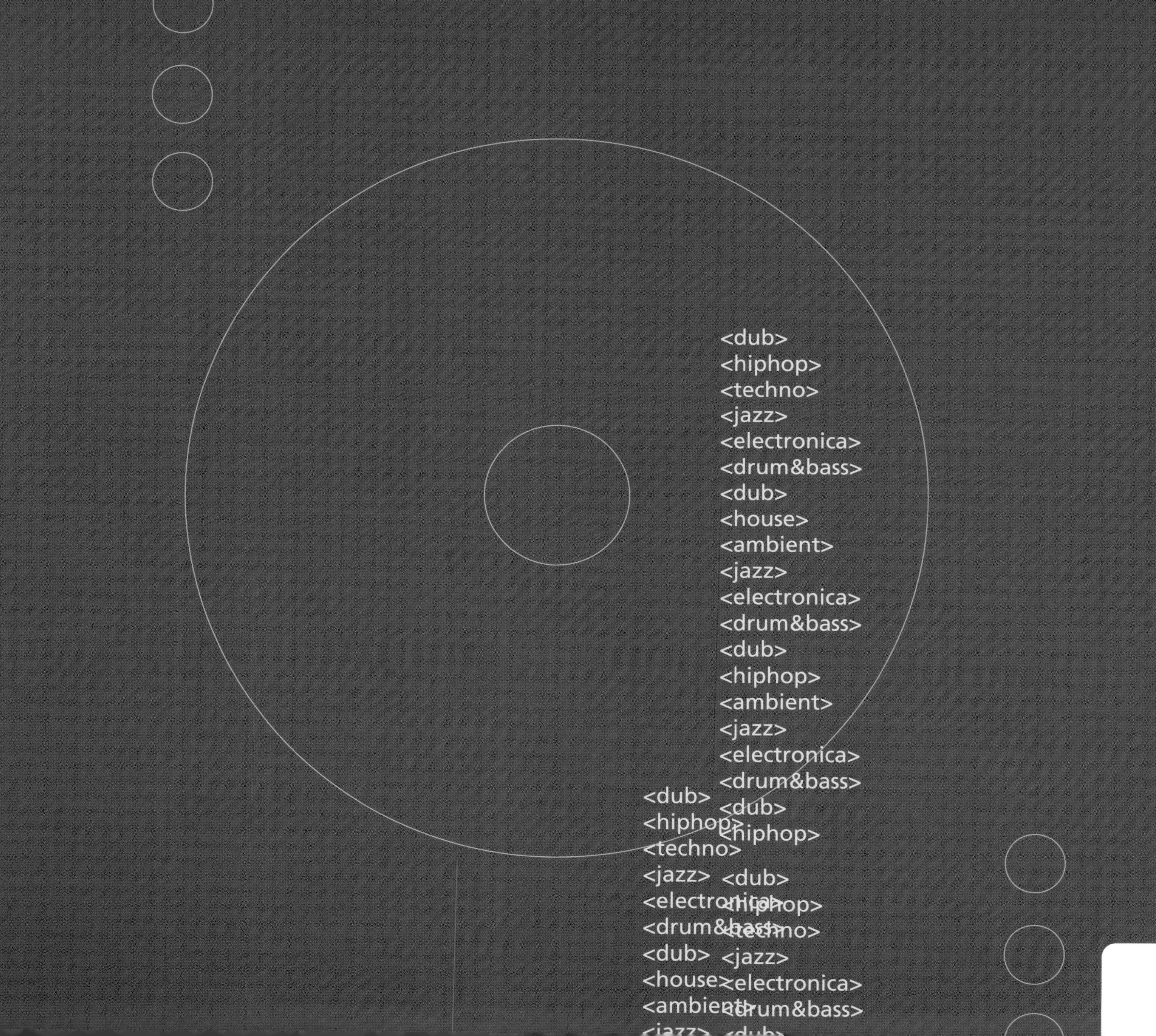
<dub>
<hiphop>
<techno>
<jazz>
<electronica>
<drum&bass>
<dub>
<house>
<ambient>
<jazz>
<electronica>
<drum&bass>
<dub>
<hiphop>
<ambient>
<jazz>
<electronica>
<drum&bass>
<dub>
<hiphop>
<dub>
<hiphop>
<techno>
<jazz>
<electronica>
<drum&bass>
<dub>
<house>
<ambient>
<dub>
<hiphop>
<techno>
<jazz>
<electronica>
<drum&bass>

<musicdot.com> is a State of the Union address for music website design at the beginning of the twenty-first century.

As use of the internet increases, and music promotion becomes ever more global in its ambitions, the website has become a highly versatile marketing tool. It can offer not only instant visual and aural information, but also digital downloads of original material not available elsewhere, calling traditional music marketing, copyrighting, and distribution systems into question. But commercial considerations have not prevented website designers and editors from concocting ever more striking, original, and sometimes downright bizarre music sites.

Here is the way things look today. Tomorrow it will change and <musicdot.com> will be the only permanent record of some of these fleeting visual pleasures.

Use this book as ready reference, or as a navigational tool to whet your appetite for the far points of web design. Check the web addresses and go exploring yourself. Travel in hope - it will be worth it.

r.w.

search...
<homepages>

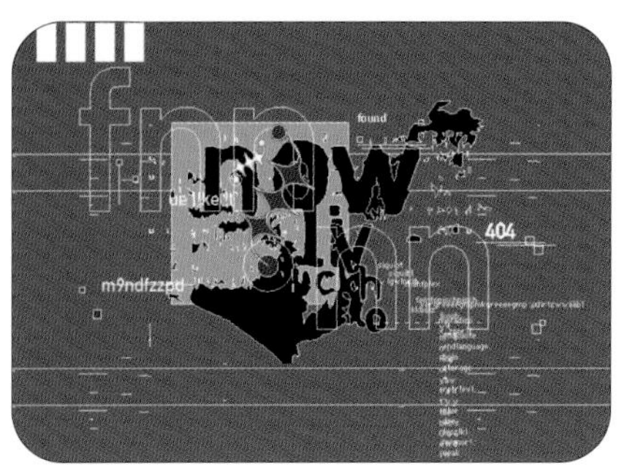

www.farmersmanual.co.at
148

www.gutterandstars.com
24

www.finleyquaye.com
40

www.max-ernst.de
84

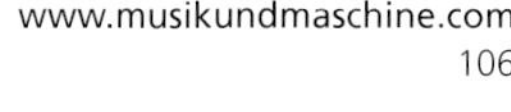
www.musikundmaschine.com
106

www.12k.com
102

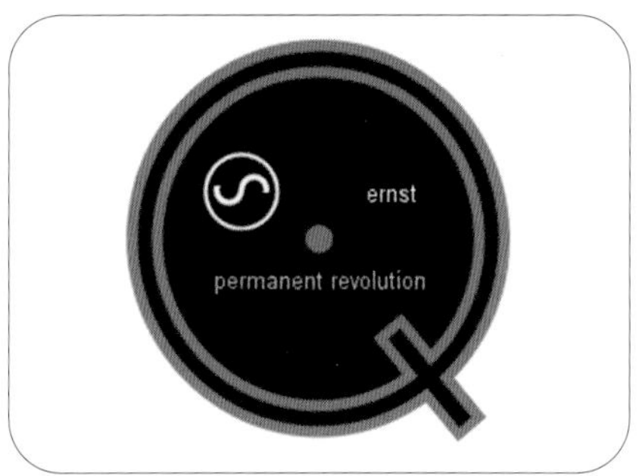

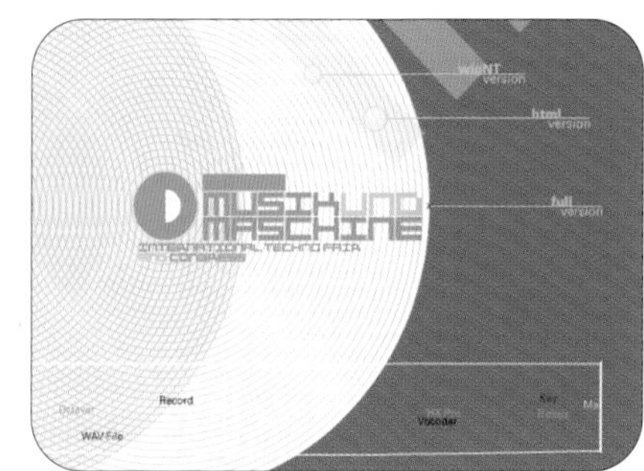

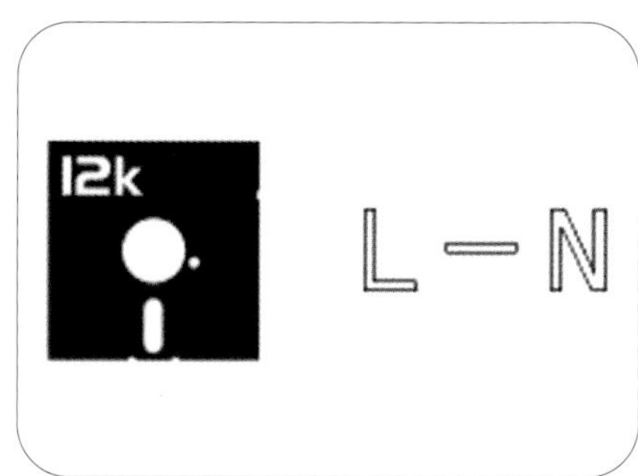

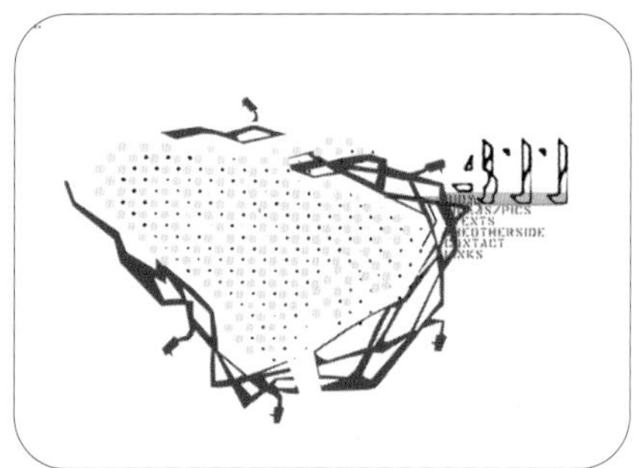

THE CINEMATIC ORCHESTRA

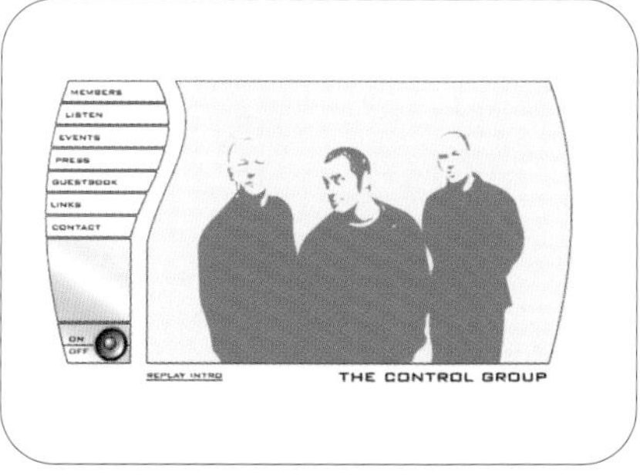

www.wordsound.com
130

www.cinematicorchestra.com
64

www.the-control-group.com
54

www.primaklimaclub.ch
98

www.mezzmusic.com
138

www.broadcast.uk.net
46

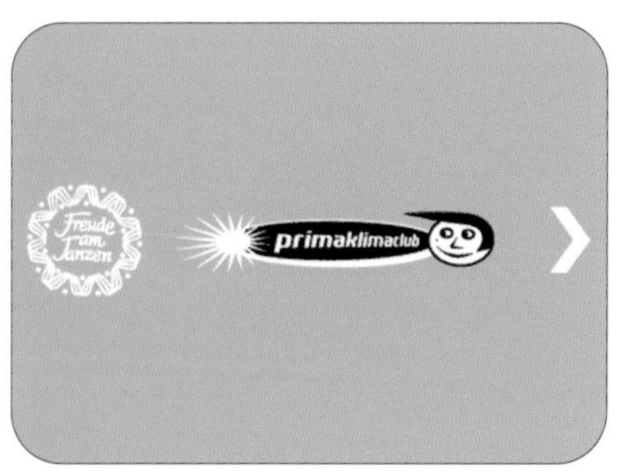

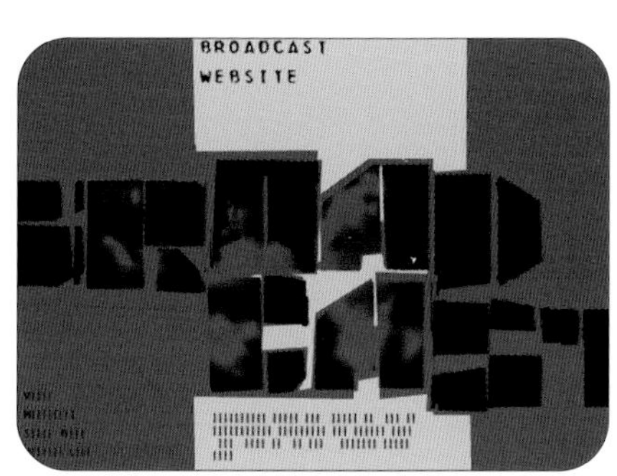

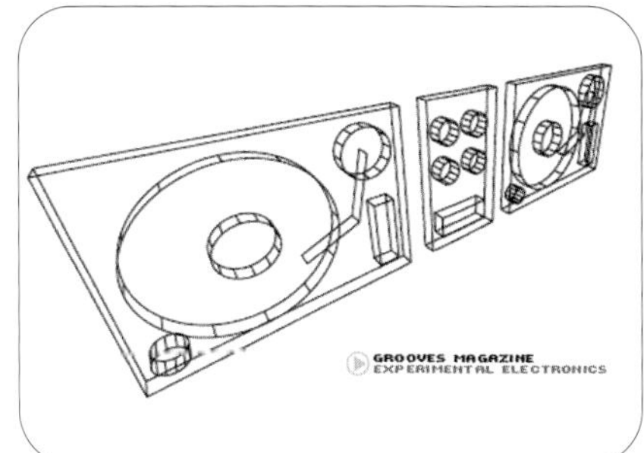

www.freestylers.net
42

www.groovesmag.com
120

www.luakabop.com
92

www.freude-am-tanzen.com
96

www.plugresearch.com
174

www.urbansounds.com
116

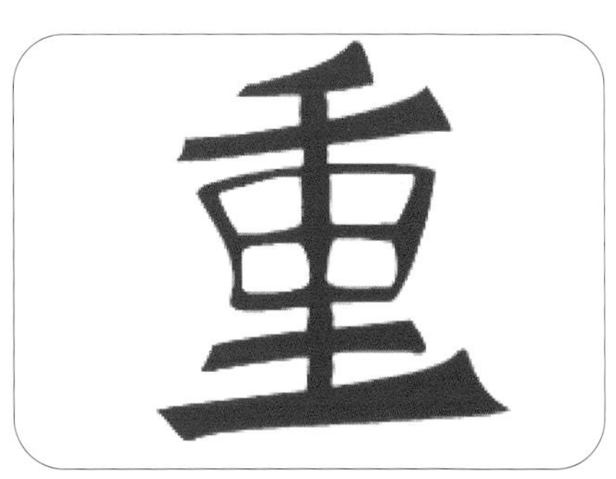

www.jamiroquai.co.uk
72

www.heavy.com
126

www.superfurry.com
32

www.olivemusic.net
18

www.pork.co.uk
152

www.maverickrc.com/solartwins
52

www.asiandubfoundation.com
50

www.airkingsound.com
121

www.badboyonline.com
104

www.heftyrecords.com
132

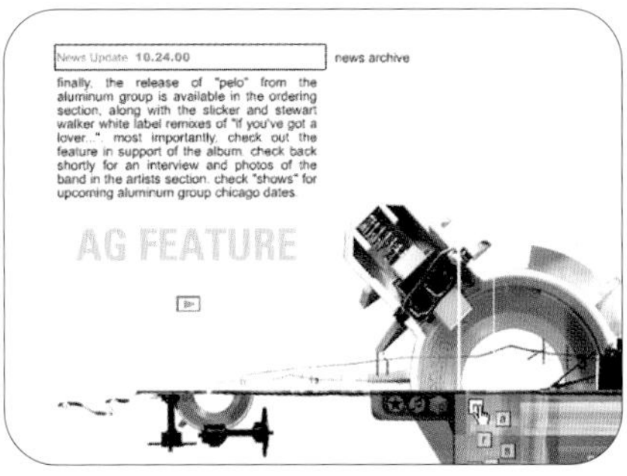

www.kracfive.com
90

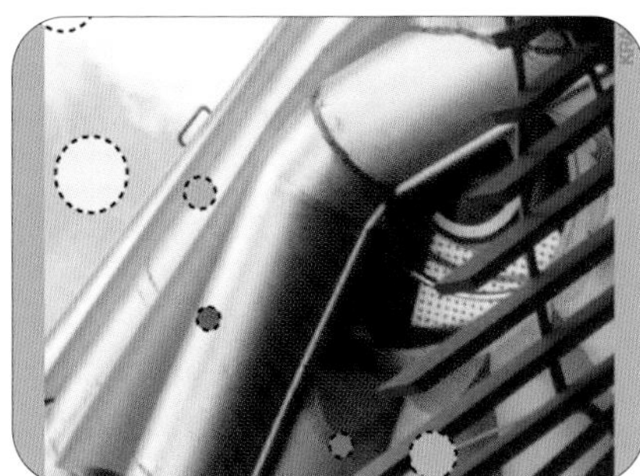

www.holzplatten.de
164

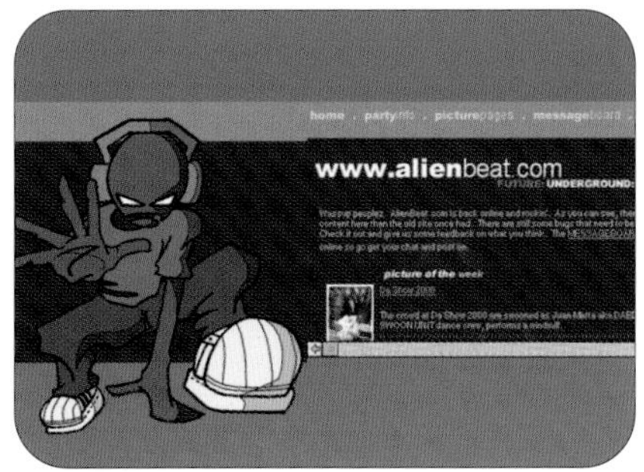

www.alienbeat.com
122

www.catcellular.com
142

www.hydrogendukebox.com
162

www.sonar.es
110

www.breakbeat.co.uk
101

www.heliozilla.com/propellerheads
20

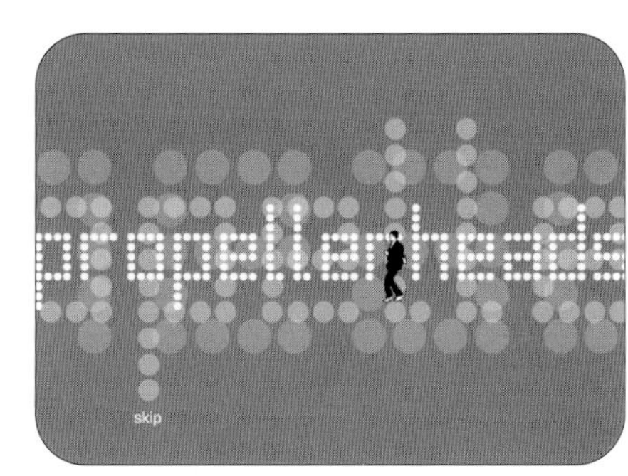

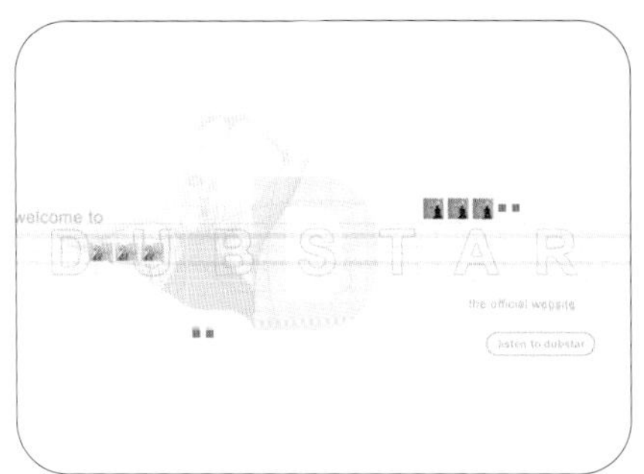

www.sanriot.com
154

www.blacklistonline.com
160

www.dubstar.com
74

www.kitty-yo.de
108

www.thelamp.demon.co.uk
166

www.lightspeed.co.nz
168

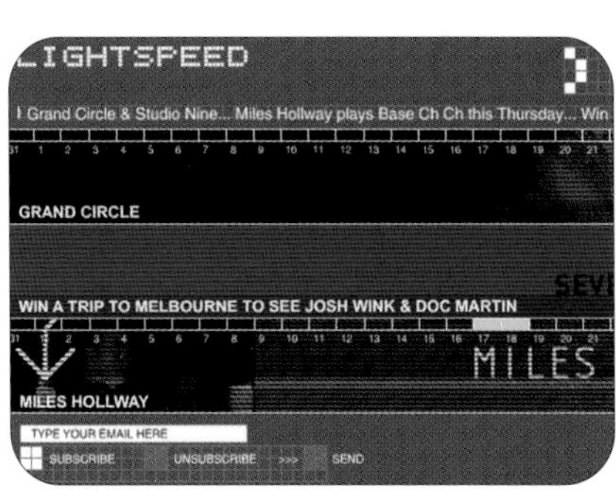

www.luakabop.com
92

www.dial-rec.de
94

www.surgeryrecords.com.au
134

www.quannum.com
86

www.thermalrecordings.com
100

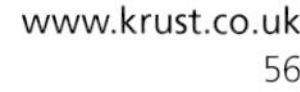

www.krust.co.uk
56

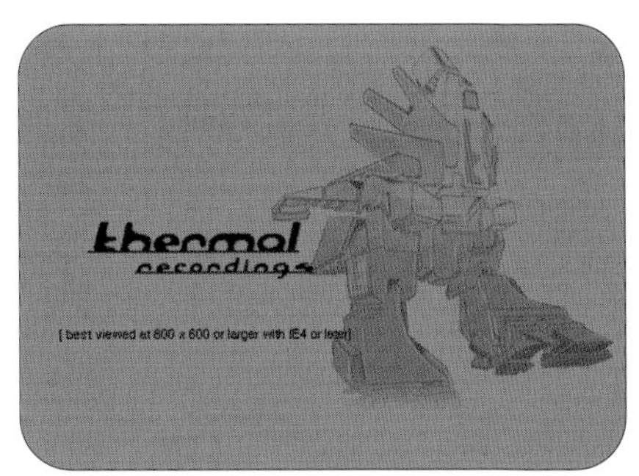

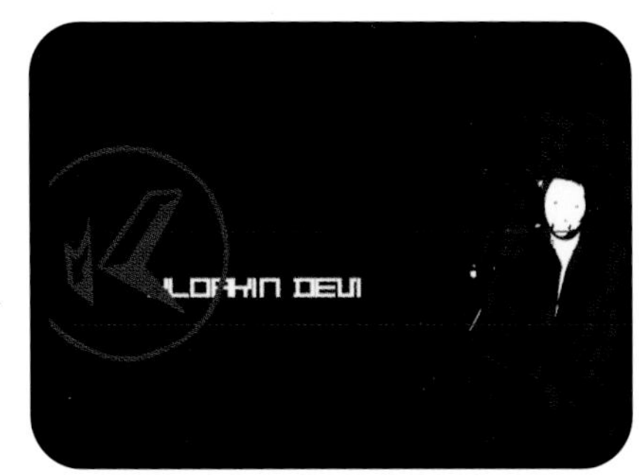

www.stereolab.com
60

www.strangeandbeautiful.com
38

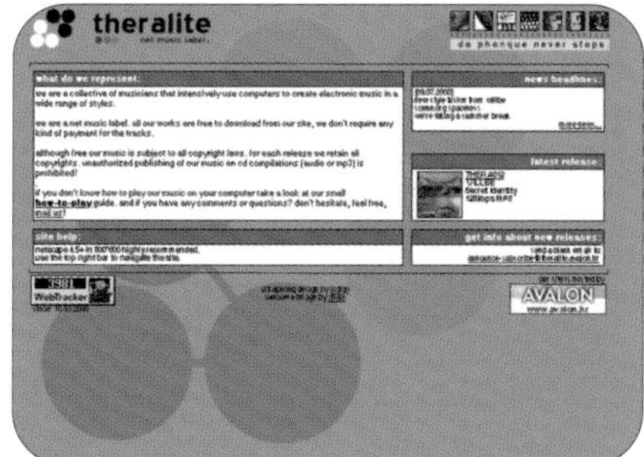

www.theralite.avalon.hr
172

www.positivarecords.com
170

www.sade.com
44

www.amontobin.com
58

www.lovestation.co.uk
45

www.touch21.com
80

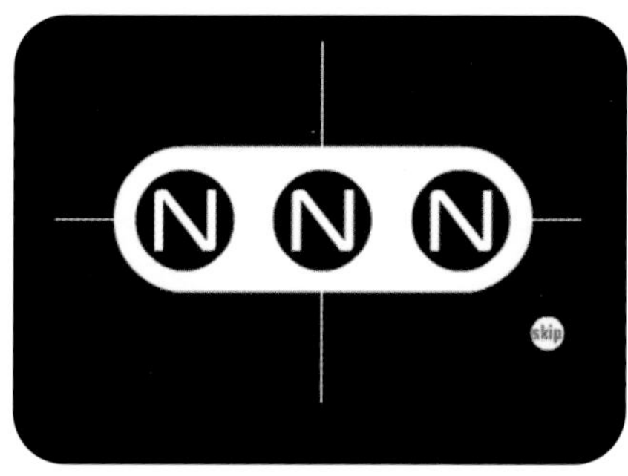

www.monocrom.de
176

www.m-nus.com
118

www.skam.co.uk
146

www.sleazenation.com
156

www.morcheeba.net
28

www.kompact-net.de
124

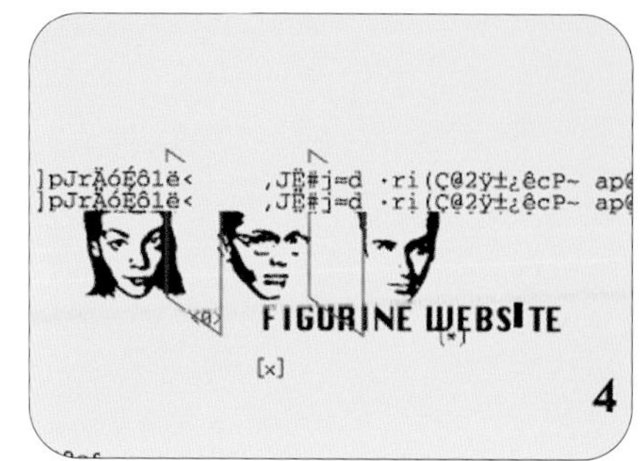

www.figurinedatacenter.co.uk
22

www.caipirinha.com
112

www.dublab.com
136

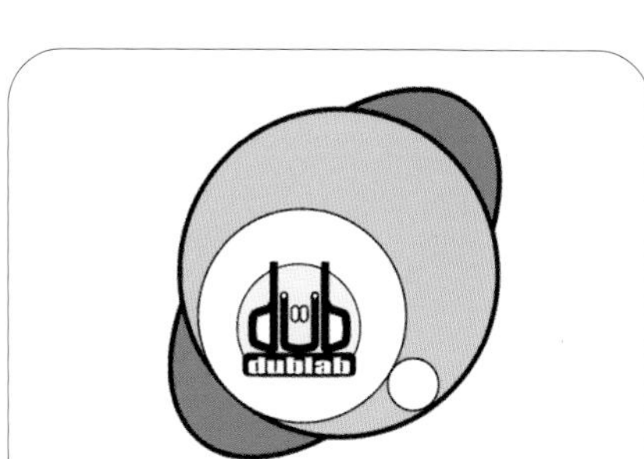

www.hookt.com
114

www.soulcontrollers.com
66

www.pressuredrop.co.uk
76

www.markusschultz.com
70

www.towatei.com
26

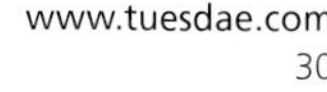
www.tuesdae.com
30

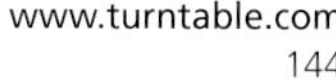
www.turntable.com
144

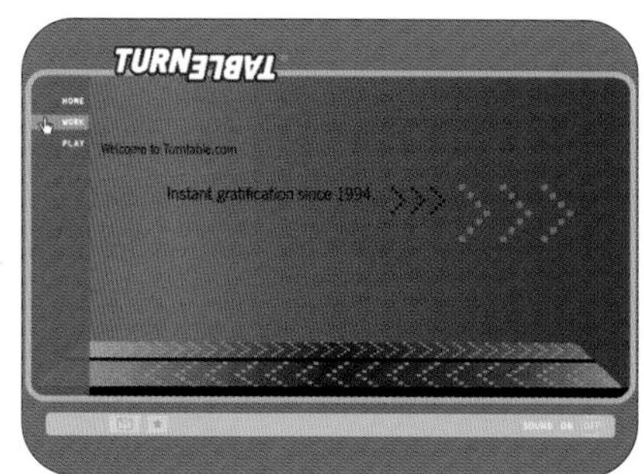

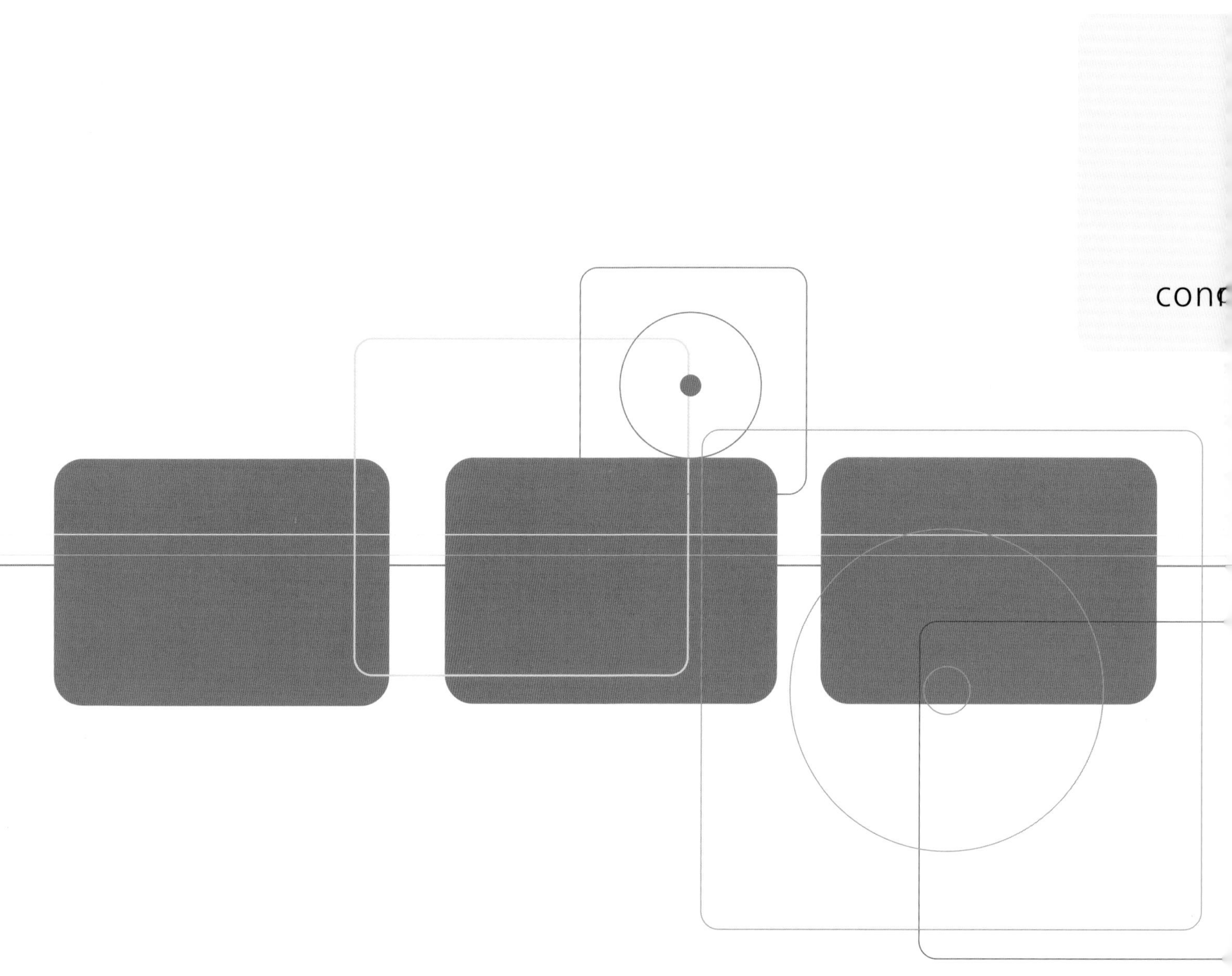

connect... connect... connect... connect... connect... connect... connect... connect... connect... connect...

connect...

<artists>

<title>
Olive

<web address>
www.olivemusic.net

<client>
Olive

<design company>
Popglory

<programs/software>
Illustrator, Flash, Photoshop

<number of pages>
n/a

<country of origin>
USA

<work description>
The official website for the band Olive offers news, information, discography, audio clips, photo gallery, and a mailbox.

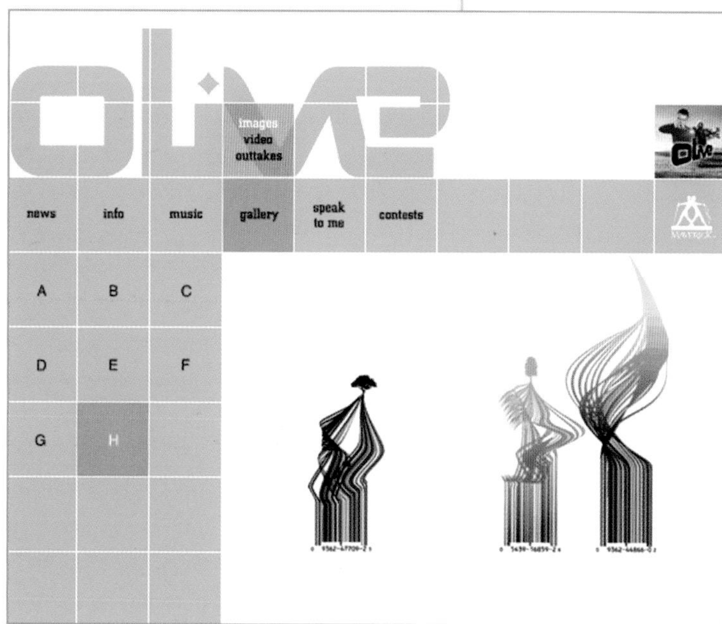

images
video
outtakes

music

A B C
D E

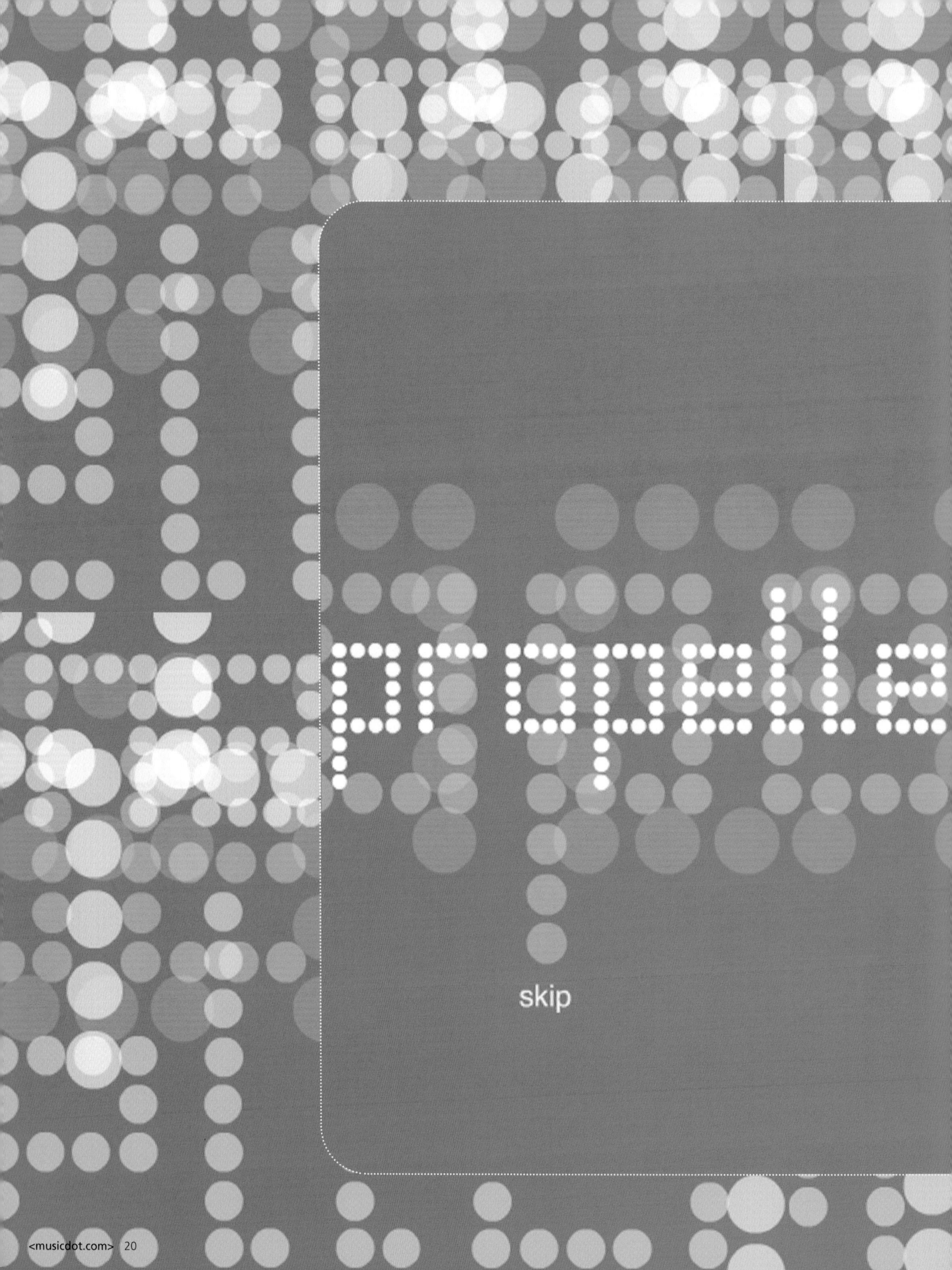
propelle
skip

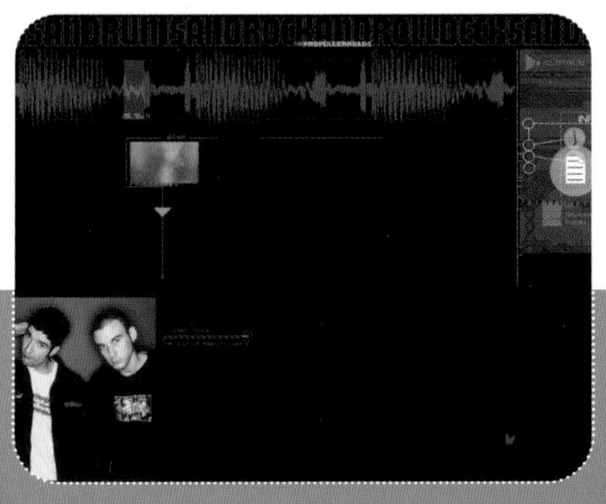

<title>
Propellerheads

<web address>
www.heliozilla.com/propellerheads

<client>
Dreamworks Records

<design company>
Helios

<programs/software>
n/a

<number of pages>
n/a

<country of origin>
USA

<work description>
The official website for DJ/electronic artists the Propellerheads features animation, audio clips, photos, news on tours and record releases.

<title>
Figurine Website

<web address>
www.figurinedatacenter.co.uk

<client>
Figurine

<design company>
David Figurine

<programs/software>
BBedit, Macromedia Fireworks,
Adobe Photoshop, Adobe Illustrator

<number of pages>
20+

<country of origin>
USA

<work description>
Figurine's overall design was approached organically and the site has been encouraged to grow in any direction needed. It includes animation, mp3s, information and diverse distractions.

SYSTEM FAILURE

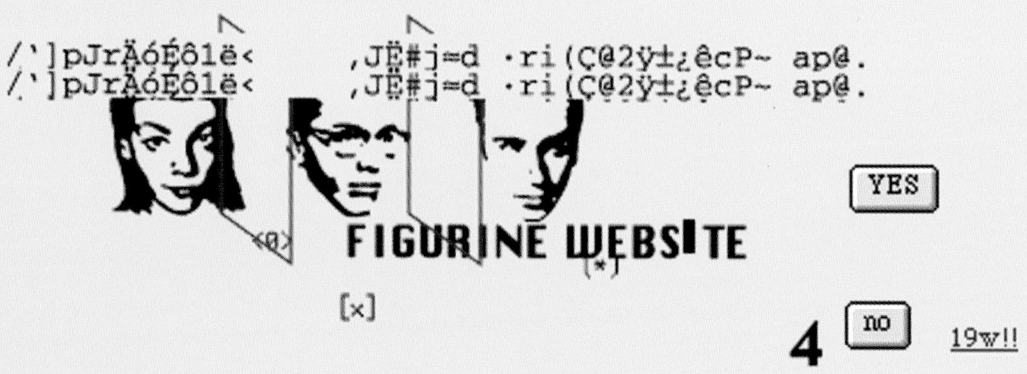

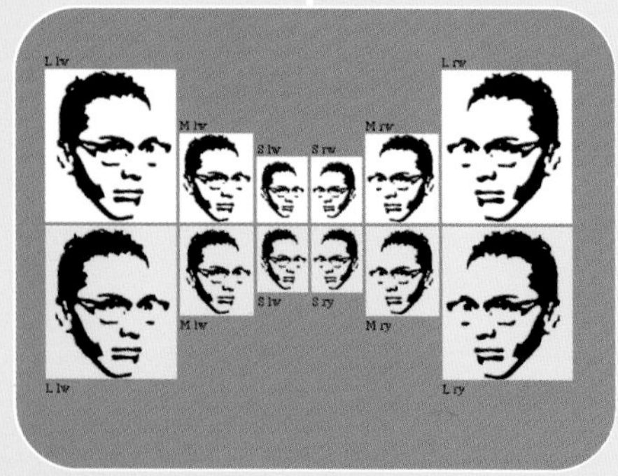

2 ~~SONG SEVEN INCH~~

I wait for you by the telephone |||||you (live in berlin)

figurine 7" #1

(more)

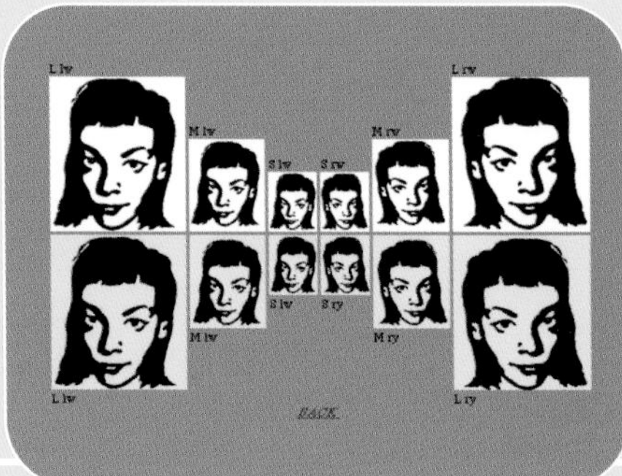

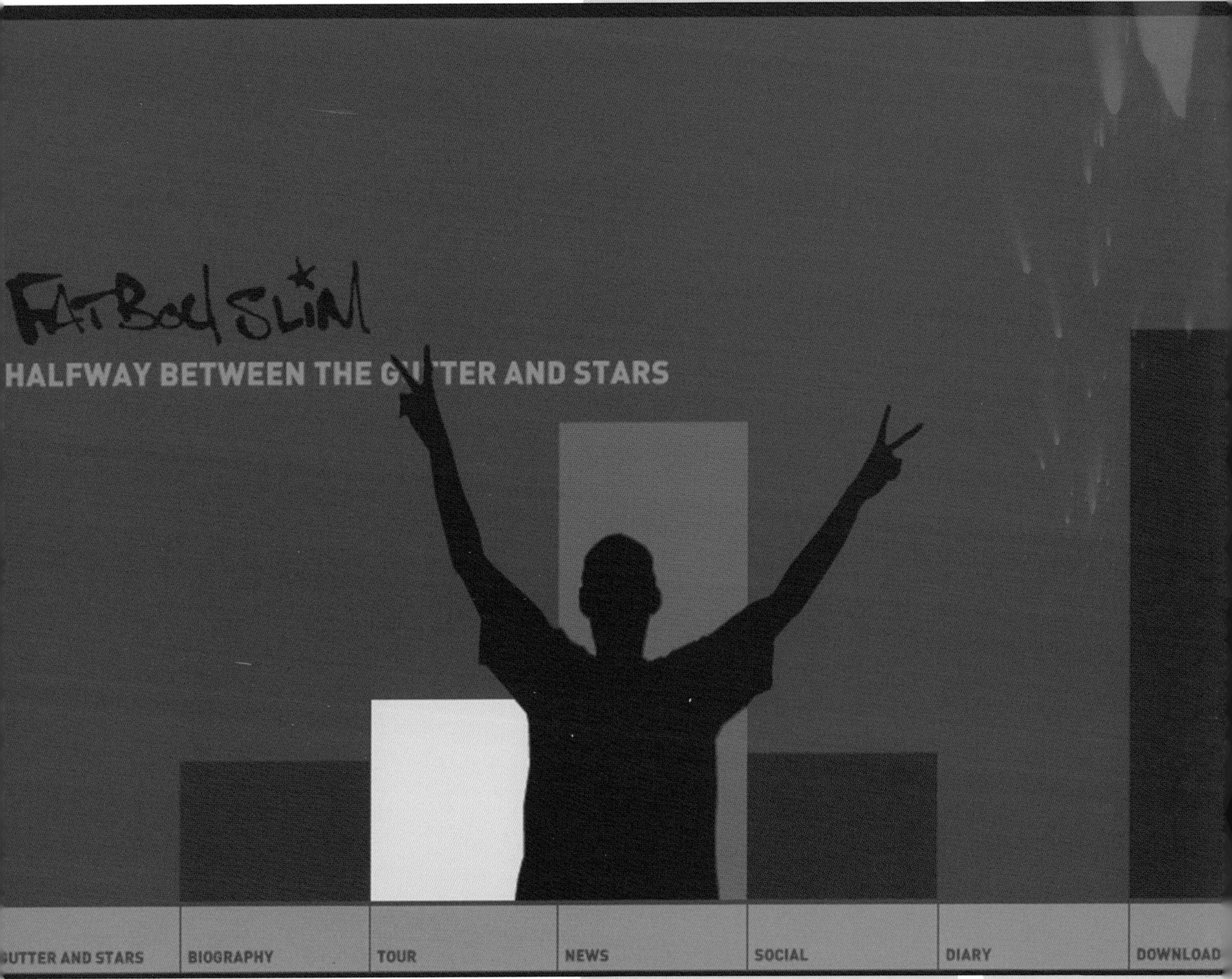

FATBOY SLIM*

HALFWAY BETWEEN THE G TTER AND STARS

UTTER AND STARS | BIOGRAPHY | TOUR | NEWS | SOCIAL | DIARY | DOWNLOAD

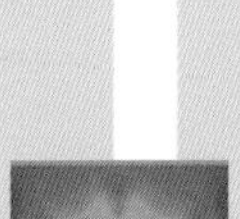

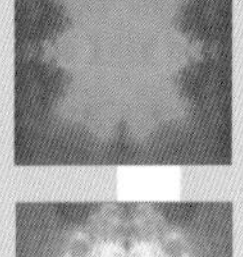

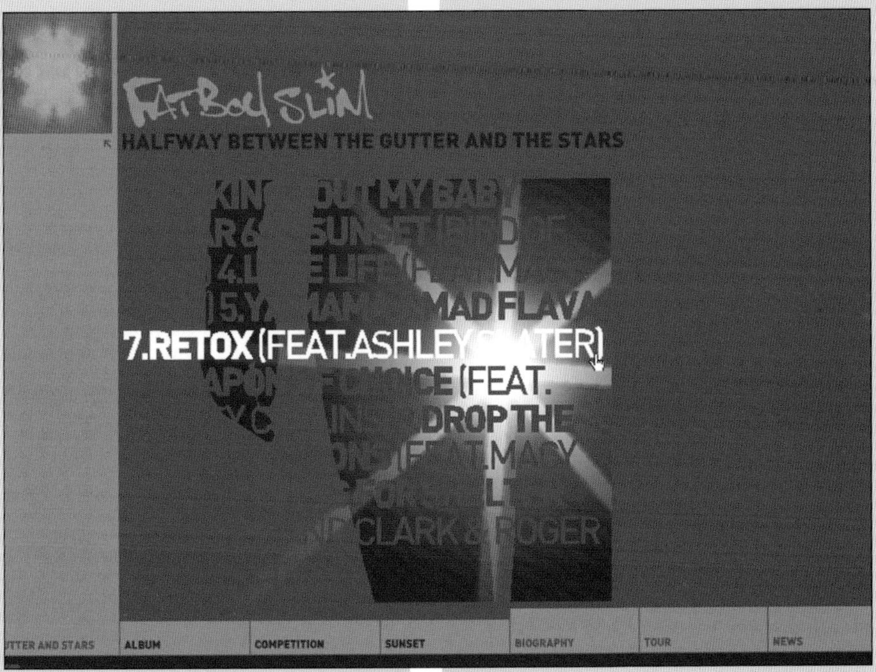

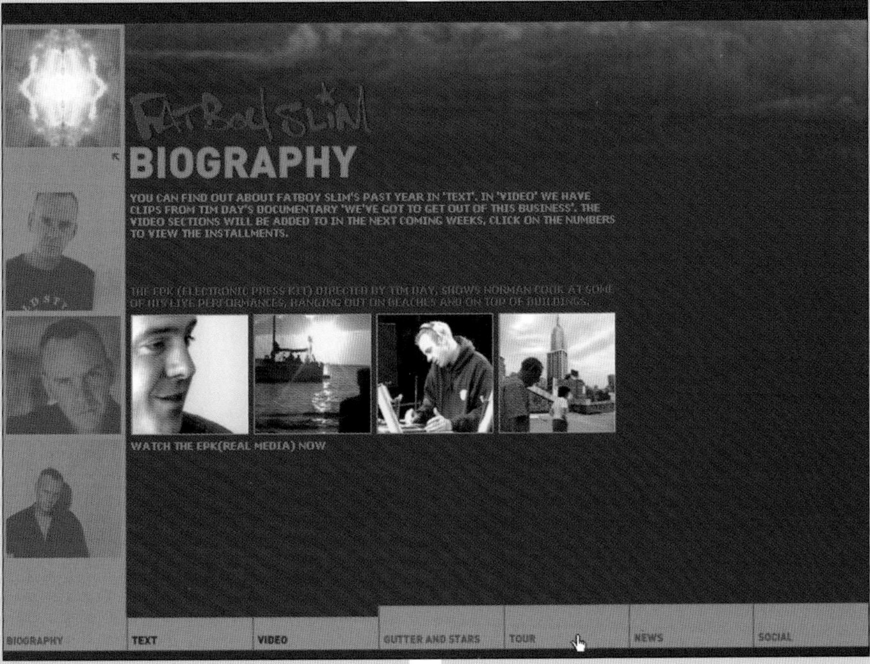

<title>
Fatboy Slim: Halfway between the Gutter and the Stars

<web address>
www.gutterandstars.com

<client>
Skint records

<design company>
Kleber Design Ltd

<programs/software>
Flash, BBedit, Photoshop, PHP, MYSQL, Freehand.

<number of pages>
n/a

<country of origin>
UK

<work description>
This site was designed to support the release of Fatboy Slim's album 'Halfway between the Gutter and the Stars'.

<title>
Towa Tei: Last Century Modern

<web address>
www.towatei.com

<client>
n/a

<design company>
n/a

<programs/software>
n/a

<number of pages>
n/a

<country of origin>
n/a

<work description>
The official website for the DJ/producer Towa Tei offers music samples, video clips, news, biography, and a photo gallery.

Last Century Modern

MORCHEEBA
NEWS
BIG CALM
DISCOGRAPHY
BIOGRAPHY
GALLERY
MORCHEEBA
BIG CALM
SAMPLER
01 THE SEA
02 SHOULDER HOLSTER
03 PART OF THE PROCESS
04 BLINDFOLD
05 LET ME SEE
06 BULLET PROOF
07 OVER & OVER
08 FRICTION
09 DIGGIN' A WATERY GRAVE
10 FEAR AND LOVE
11 BIG CALM
NEWS
BIG CALM
DISCOGRAPHY
BIOGRAPHY
GALLERY

<title>
Morcheeba

<web address>
www.morcheeba.net

<client>
China Records/Morcheeba

<design company>
Kleber Design Ltd

<programs/software>
Flash, Freehand, Photoshop, BBedit

<number of pages>
n/a

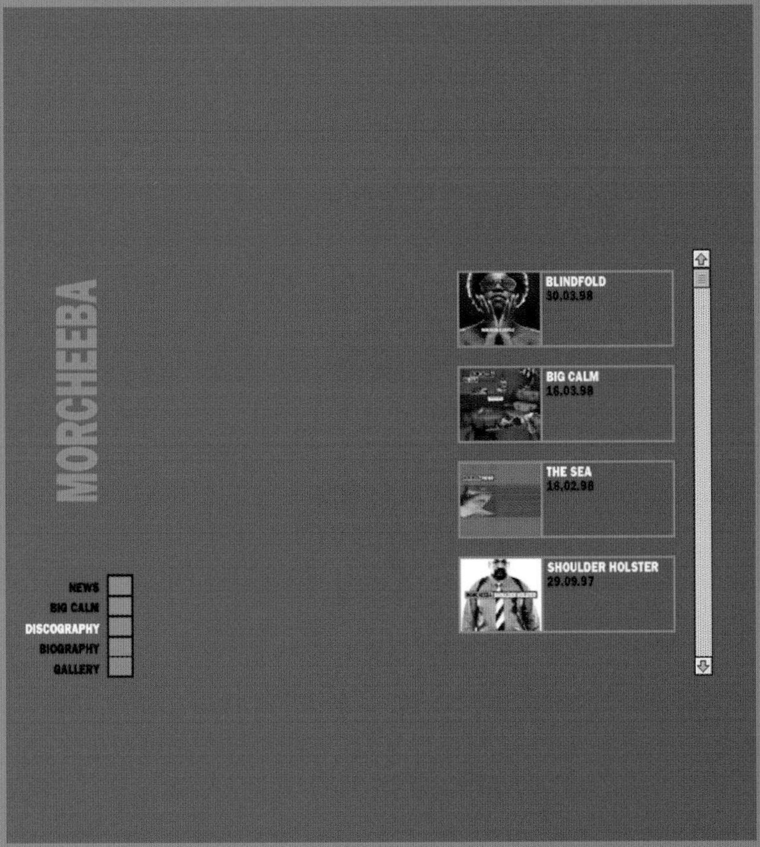

<country of origin>
UK

<work description>
The official website for the band Morcheeba offers videofootage, news, biography, discography, lyrics, and an interactive remix page.

TUESDAE

<title>
Tuesdae.com

<web address>
www.tuesdae.com

<client>
Tuesdae

<design company>
Agenda

<programs/software>
Macromedia Flash, Adobe Illustrator, Adobe Photoshop

<number of pages>
13

<country of origin>
USA

<work description>
The official website for the singer Tuesdae includes a biography, a photo gallery, and events listings, and offers mp3s of her latest songs.

TUESDAE
ZAP!!
girlfinder
GIRLFINDER

Love Struck
Tuesdae / Rowe, ©1999
stereo show
TUESDAE

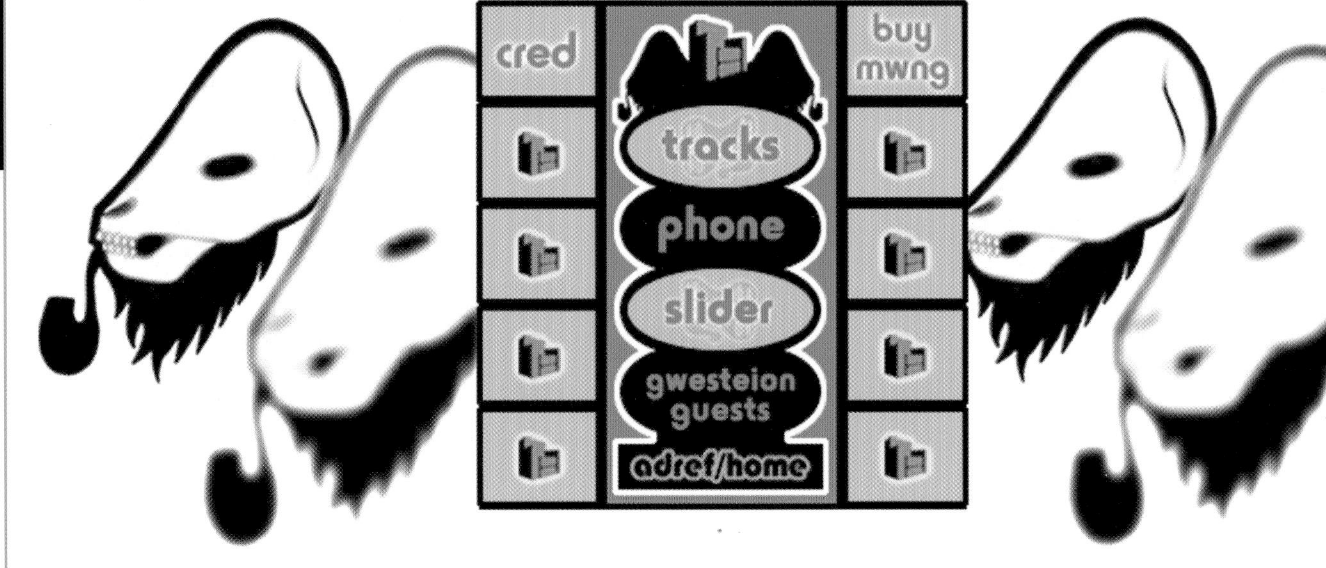

<title>
Super Furry Animals: Mwng

<web address>
www.superfurry.com &
www.mwng.co.uk

<client>
Super Furry Animals

<design company>
CoffeeCup New Media &
Iconmedia

<programs/software>
3D Studio, Photoshop, Hot Metal Pro

<number of pages>
50-70

<country of origin>
Wales

<work description>
This page features 'mwng' the band Super Furry Animals' first release in Welsh on their own new label, Placid Casual Recordings. The band's official website has grown organically over the years and now offers fan contributions, webcasts, record launches, media clips, an online shop, and a range of interactive areas.

placid™ casual

cd display stand

HOLDS 6 TO 8 CD'S AT A TIME!

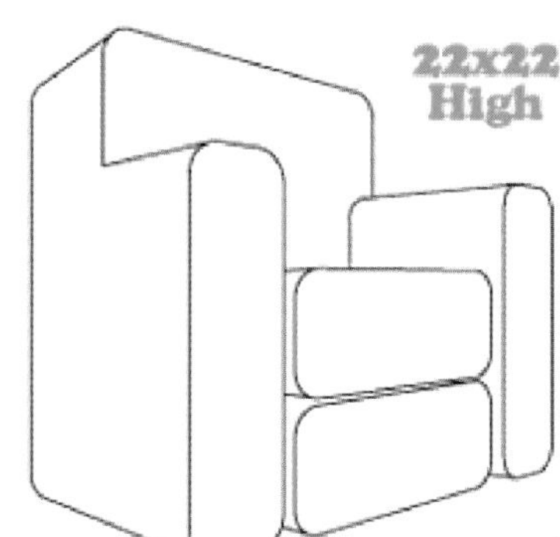

オーソフナ™
サリウナイ

オリナ ソトニ イス ノ マカレシ

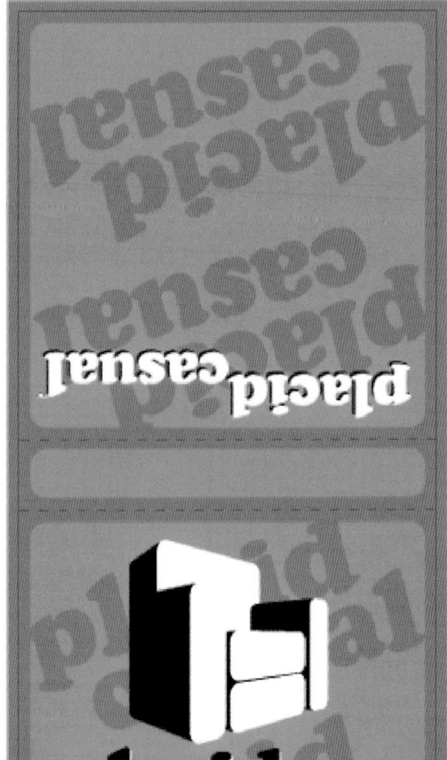

INSTRUCTIONS:
1. PUNCH OUT CHAIR AND CREASE ALONG SCORED LINES
2. ATTACH DOUBLE SIDED STICKY TAPE WERE INDICATED
3. LAY PRINTED SIDE DOWN
4. FOLD OVER BACK OF CHAIR fig.1
5. FOLD IN ARMS AND STICK FLAPS A,B,C & D fig.2
6. FOLD IN BASE AND STICK FLAPS E,F & G fig.3
NB: TRY OUT 4, 5, & 6 BEFORE STICKING

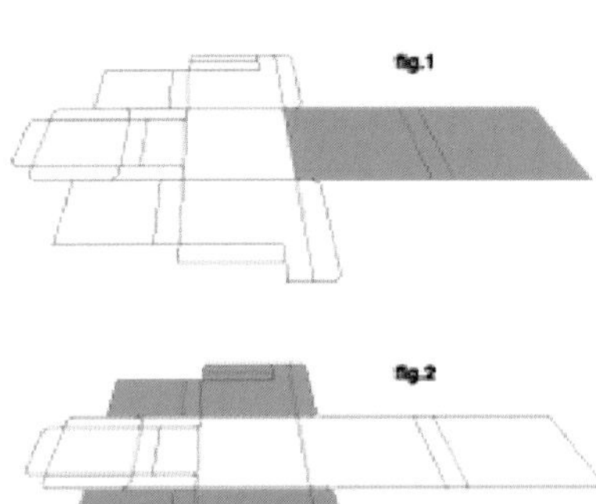

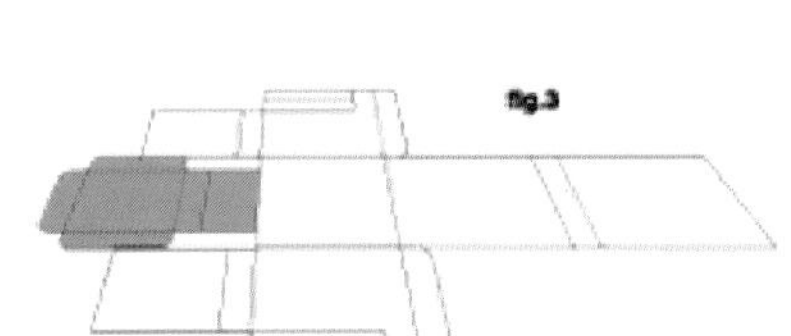

NEWS!

808

The Hour of Bewilderbeast

XL RECORDINGS TWISTED NERVE email

The Hour of
Bewilderbeast

Badly Drawn Boy
one
The Shining
Everybodys Stalking
Bewilder. Fall in a River
Camping Next to Water Stone on the Water
Another Pearl Body Rap
Once Around the Block
This Song.
TWO
Bewilderbeast Magic in the Air
Cause A Rockslide Pissing in the Wind
Blistered heart Disillusion
Say It Again Epitaph.

<title>
World of Badly Drawn Boy

<web address>
www.badlydrawnboy.co.uk

<client>
XL recordings/BIG LIFE

<design company>
PNOOM

<initial design>
PNOOM and Rick Meyers

<production and management>
PNOOM

<photography>
Bill Green

<programs/software>
Adobe Photoshop, BBedit, Debabalizer

<number of pages>
30

<country of origin>
UK

<work description>
The official website for the artist Badly Drawn Boy was designed using core html techniques to make it as widely accessible as possible. The site uses traditional design techniques such as model-making, still-frame animation, and hand-drawn type to give it its defining character.

english version - version française

© 2000 atome.fr - contact us

<title>
Atome

<web address>
www.atome.fr

<client>
n/a

<designer>
Xavier Bougouin

<programs/software>
Photoshop, Illustrator, 3D Studio Max, ImageReady

<number of pages>
10

<country of origin>
France

<work description>
Atome is a European-wide electronic music-related e-zine that promotes the techno scene with news and reviews of independent techno artists, record labels, and events.

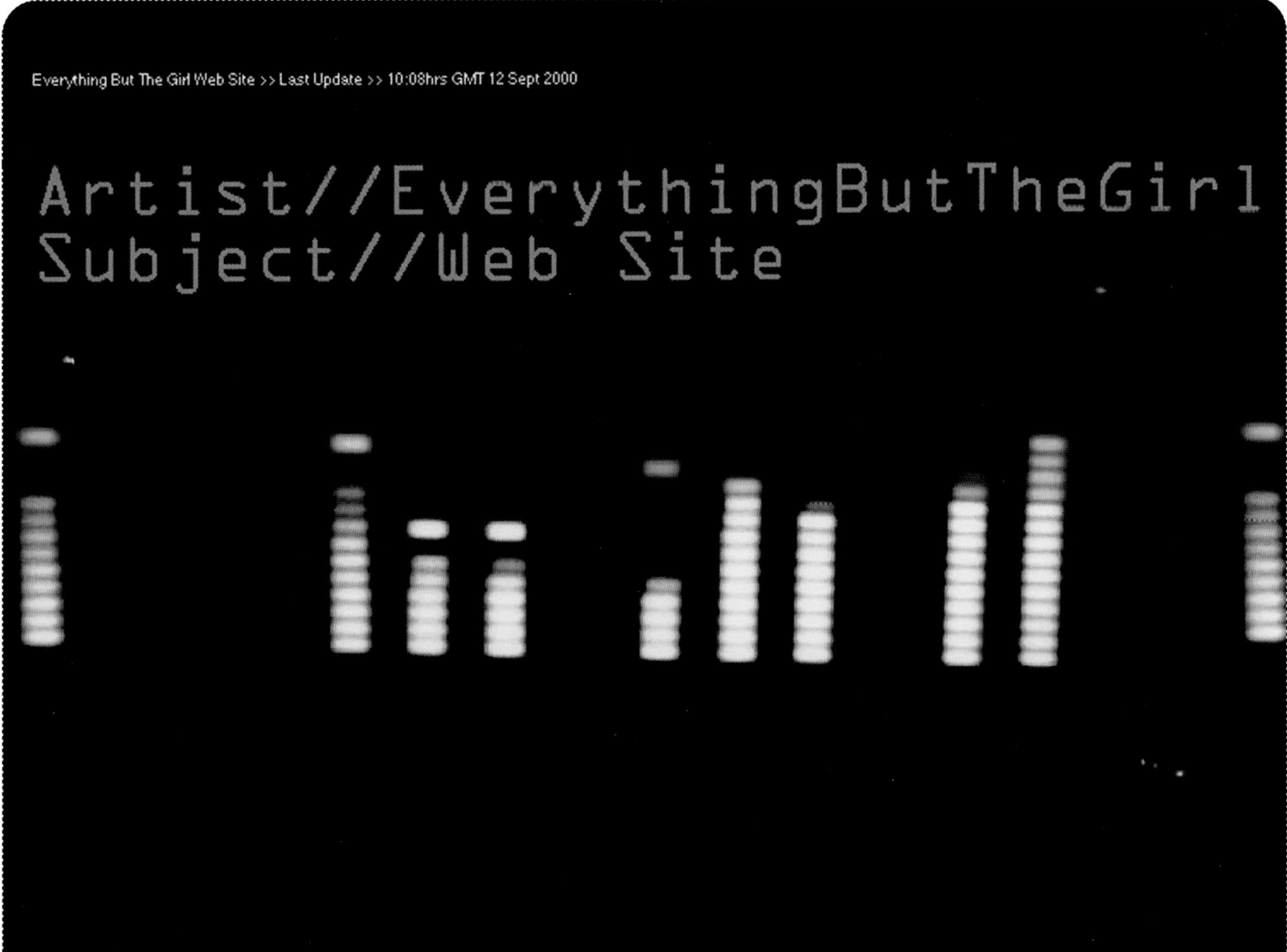

<title>
Everything But The Girl

<web address>
www.ebtg.com

<client>
Everything But The Girl

<designer>
Ben Watt

<programs/software>
Simpletext, Adobe Photoshop, Soundedit, Gifbuilder

<number of pages>
50

<country of origin>
UK

<work description>
Set up in 1994 and updated by Ben Watt of the band,the EBTG website is one of the earliest major UK band sites. It offers news, audio, personal insight, pictures, fan interaction and archives.

<title>
Strange and Beautiful Music

<web address>
www.strangeandbeautiful.com

<client>
John Lurie

<design company>
The Speared Peanut Design Studio

<programs/software>
Freehand, Photoshop, Quicktime, After Effects, Gifbuilder, Pixelspy, RealPlayer and Simpletext.

<number of pages>
25

<country of origin>
USA

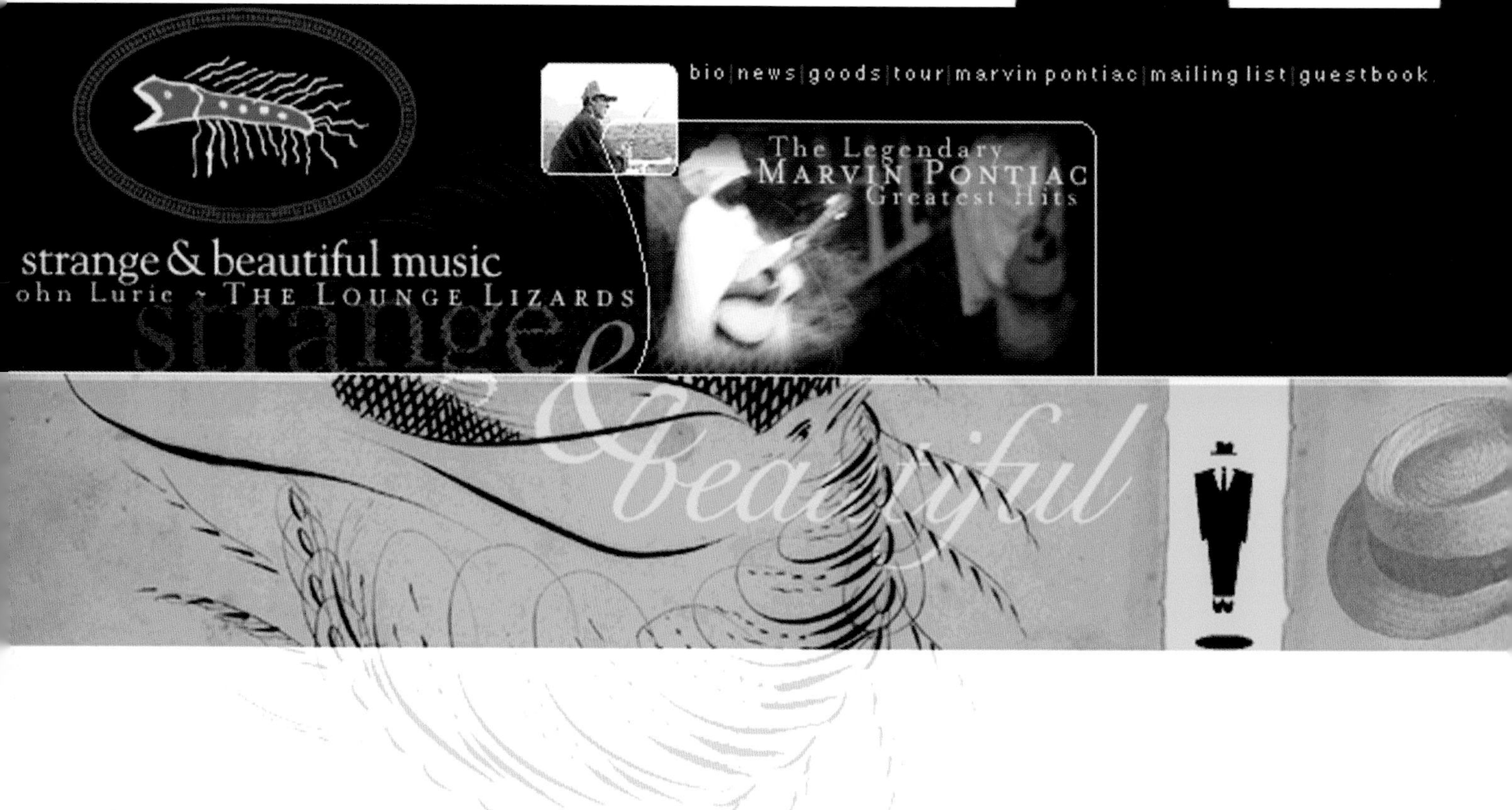

<work description>
This is the official website for avant-jazz bandleader/multi–instrumentalist John Lurie and his record label Strange and Beautiful Music.

strange & beautiful bio

BIO | news | tour | goods | marvin pontiac
mailing list | guest book | links

Strange and Beautiful Music...

Here's why Lounge Lizards leader John Lurie founded Strange and Beautiful Music: "I believe we've got some wonderful and moving records here and I want to protect them to the best of my ability," he says. "So I started my own record company to make these exquisite items available to the world."

Lurie considered a myriad of names for the label. "But every time I came in with a name that I was excited about, somebody in the office would say 'Eeewww, I don't like that,'" he says. "I became so exasperated that at one point I was going to call it I'm Naked Records so that the people who worked there would have to answer the phone, 'I'm naked, can I help you?' It came really close to that.

"Then I was on line to see Titanic and I'm looking at the people on the line and I thought, these are the people who have to buy your CD, John. If they heard your music, what would they think of it? They might think it's strange. They might think it's beautiful." Eureka!

This isn't the first time John Lurie has taken matters into his own hands. In 1989, he circumvented the usual major label shenanigans and direct-marketed the Lounge Lizards' brilliant Voice of Chunk via a TV commercial and an 800 number. New York Times critic Robert Palmer said the record "staked out new territory west of Charles Mingus and east of Bernard Herrmann." The album also garnered a three and a half star review in Rolling Stone, while Musician said "Lurie and the Lounge Lizards have carved their own musical niche...Voice of Chunk represents a very high order of musical miscegenation." Jazz arbiter Downbeat magazine said the music was "music of character played by a bunch of characters."

The Legendary Marvin Pontiac

Intro 1 2 3

bio | NEWS | tour | goods | marvin pontiac
mailing list | guest book | links

July 31, 2000. (source: Michelle Sonnstedt)

Steve Buscemi's film, *Animal Factory*, based upon the novel by Edward Bunker, premiered Sunday, July 30 on Cinemax. The film stars Willem Dafoe and Edward Furlong, and features another brilliant soundtrack by John Lurie. The film will repeat on Wednesday, August 2 at 10pm (ET).

Fishing with John is being re-run at 8:30pm & 11:30pm (ET), Monday, July 31, on the Independent Film Channel, repeating on Tuesday, August 1 at 3:45am and on Sunday, August 6 at 9:00am and 7:30pm.

February 29, 2000. (source: The Speared Peanut)

Nerve Radio will preview The Legendary Marvin Pontiac Greatest Hits this week. They are also broadcasting some pretty strange clips of a rare interview with Marvin. Go to www.nerve.com/radio and listen!

February 09, 2000. (source: Mohamed Alladin)

Coming soon from Strange and Beautiful Music...The Legendary Marvin Pontiac greatest hits available end of Feb, 2000 from our GOODS section.

December 20, 1999. (source: Mohamed Alladin)

The John Lurie National Orchestra will be performing at Joe's Pub on Tuesday December 28 and Wednesday December 29, 1999. Showtimes are 9:00 PM each night. Seating is limited. For reservations call (212) 539-8778. Tickets can also be purchased at the door if available. Joe's Pub is located at 425 Lafayette Street between 4th Street and Astor Place, New York City.

John Lurie National Orchestra is a trio featuring Lounge Lizards members:

John Lurie, saxophones

Questions or Comments??? ...e-mail Michelle@StrangeAndBeautiful.com

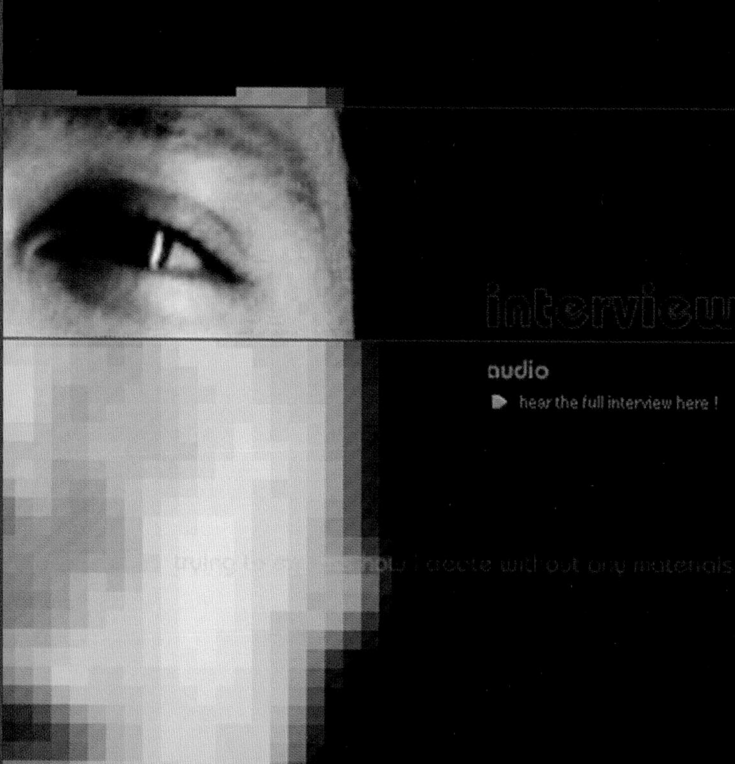

Interview with Finley Quaye

j: I'm joined now in the studio/picnic bench by Finley Quaye, welcome Finley

f: How are ya doing?

j: I'm well thank you, very well. So you've been away well its three years since Maverick A Strike came out. Why have you been away so long?

f: oooh, heinous crimes

j: fill us in a little bit on the last three years, what hav you been doing?

f: just been taking it really cool man, just trying to enjoy life.

j: were you suprised by the success that you came about, I mean you won a Brit, did that come as a suprise or were you like, yes I'm expecting this?

f: no, I certainly didn't expect to win the Brit, no. Looking back at it now, I suppose, it was a fantastic experience. I dunno what really merits winning that Brit.

f: I did put a lot of time into Britain, UK tours and regional promotion and sort of made an agreement basically, with the Americans not to go there.

j: Why was that?

f; Well because we just didn't want to spread ourselves too thinly really

<title>
Finley Quaye

<web address>
www.finleyquaye.com

<client>
Epic/Sony Music

<design company>
Hi-res!

<programs/software>
Flash, Photoshop, Cubase

<number of pages>
n/a

<country of origin>
UK

<work description>
The official site for the musician Finley Quaye offers webcasts, information, interviews, audio bites, and fan pages.

<title>
Freestylers

<web address>
www.freestylers.net

<client>
Fresh Records

<design company>
Curve Design

<programs/software>
Photoshop, GoLive, Illustrator, Flash, Streamline, Media Cleaning Pro, Soundedit

<number of pages>
10

<country of origin>
UK

<work description>
The official Freestylers' website has a gritty, graffiti look and offers band news, tour information, biographical details, lyrics, video and audio samples.

ORiGinal RUDEBWOYS
ORiGinal GANGSTAS

the stuff the media
e about, we don't personally think rocks the dance floor
OPPOSITE of when you go looking to have a dance,
end up enduring a saxophonist farting away for ages.

NEWS
BIOG
TOUR
SNAPZ
BEATZ
LYRICS
VID
MAIN
REPLAY INTRO

mammoth

JAY ROCK

TURNTABLES

BACK

<title>
Sade: 'Lovers Rock'

<web address>
www.sade.com

<client>
SZ/EPIC/Sony Music Entertainment UK

<design company>
Kleber Design Ltd

<programs/software>
Flash, BBedit, Photoshop, PHP, MYSQL, Freehand.

<number of pages>
n/a

<country of origin>
UK

<work description>
This website was created to support the release of Sade's 'Lovers Rock' album and offers biographical information, photos, video and audio clips, and an interactive fan base.

<title>
Lovestation

<web address>
www.lovestation.co.uk

<client>
Fresh Records

<design company>
Curve Design

<programs/software>
Photoshop, GoLive, Flash,
Illustrator, Streamline,
Media Cleaner Pro, Soundedit

<number of pages>
8

<country of origin>
UK

<work description>
The official Lovestation website offers animation, audio clips, discography, biographies, and photos.

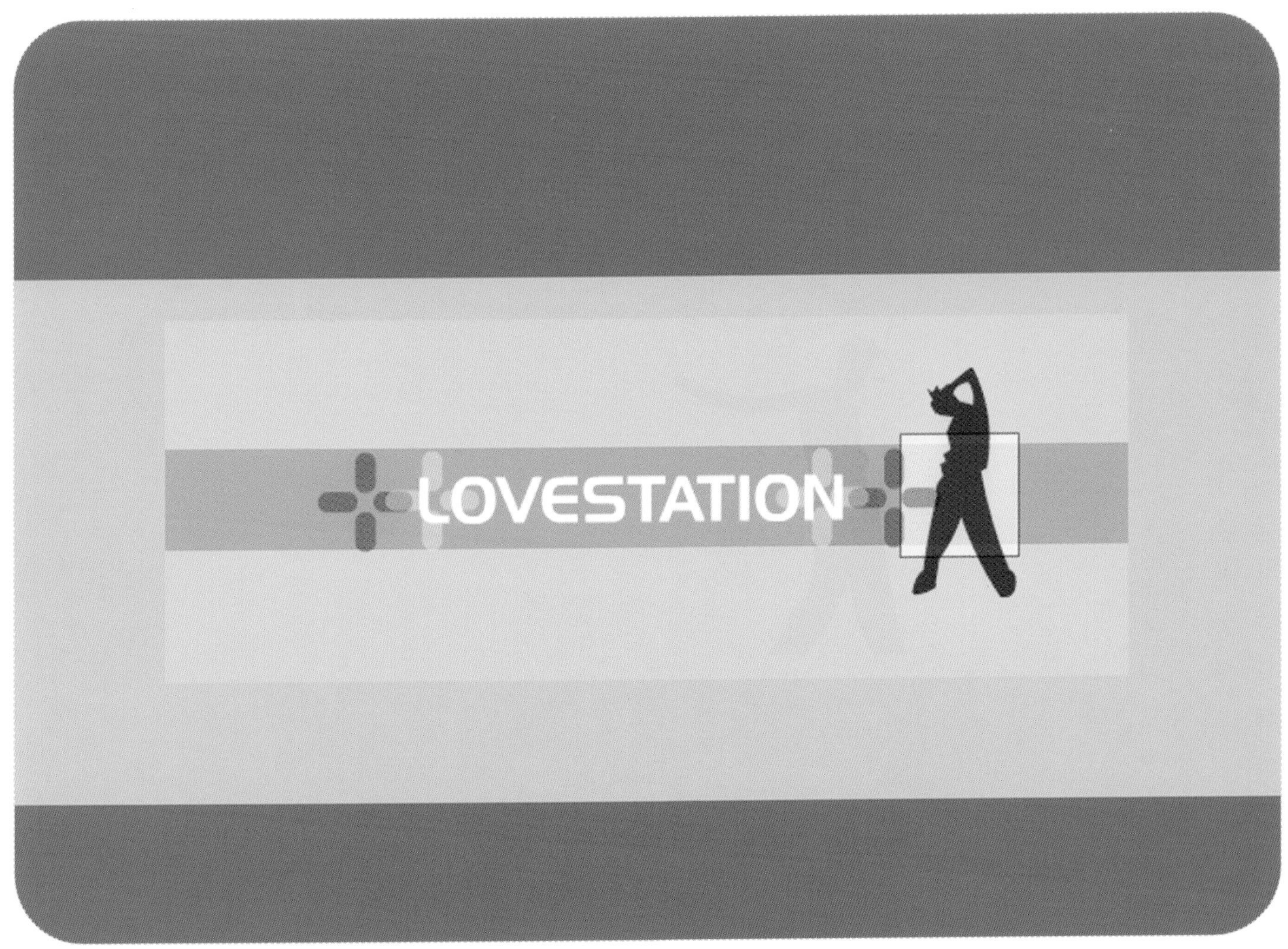

BROADCAST

WEBSITE

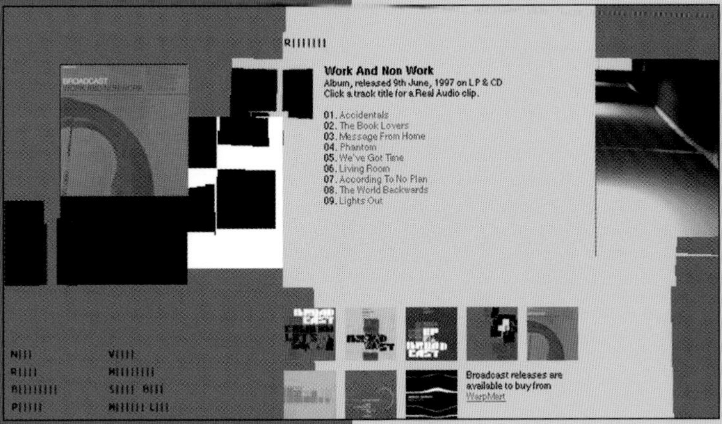

<title>
Broadcast

<web address>
www.broadcast.uk.net

<client>
Warp Records

<design company>
Kleber Design Ltd/Intro

<programs/software>
Photoshop, Flash, Freehand, BBedit.

<number of pages>
n/a

<country of origin>
UK

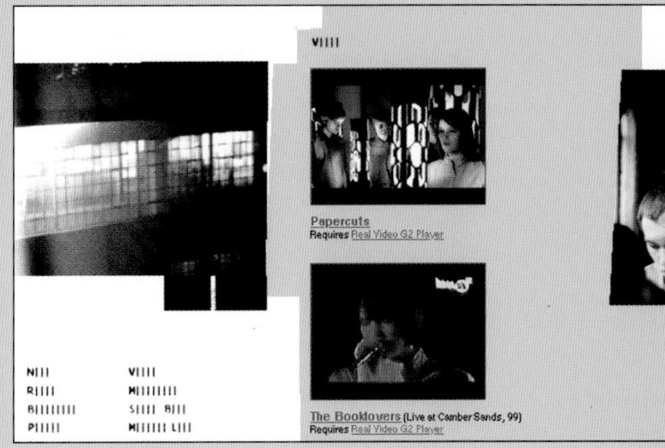

<work description>
This website, created for the Warp band Broadcast, offers band news, video and audio clips, webcasts, photos, discography, and interactive fan pages.

<title>
Swayzak: 'Himawari'

<web address>
www.swayzak.co.uk

<client>
Higherground/Sony Music Entertainment

<design company>
Kleber Design Ltd

<programs/software>
Flash, Photoshop, BBedit, SoundEdit, Real Producer Plus

<number of pages>
10

<country of origin>
UK

<work description>
The official website for the band Swayzak offers information on new releases, tours, discography, photos, and audio clips supplied by the band.

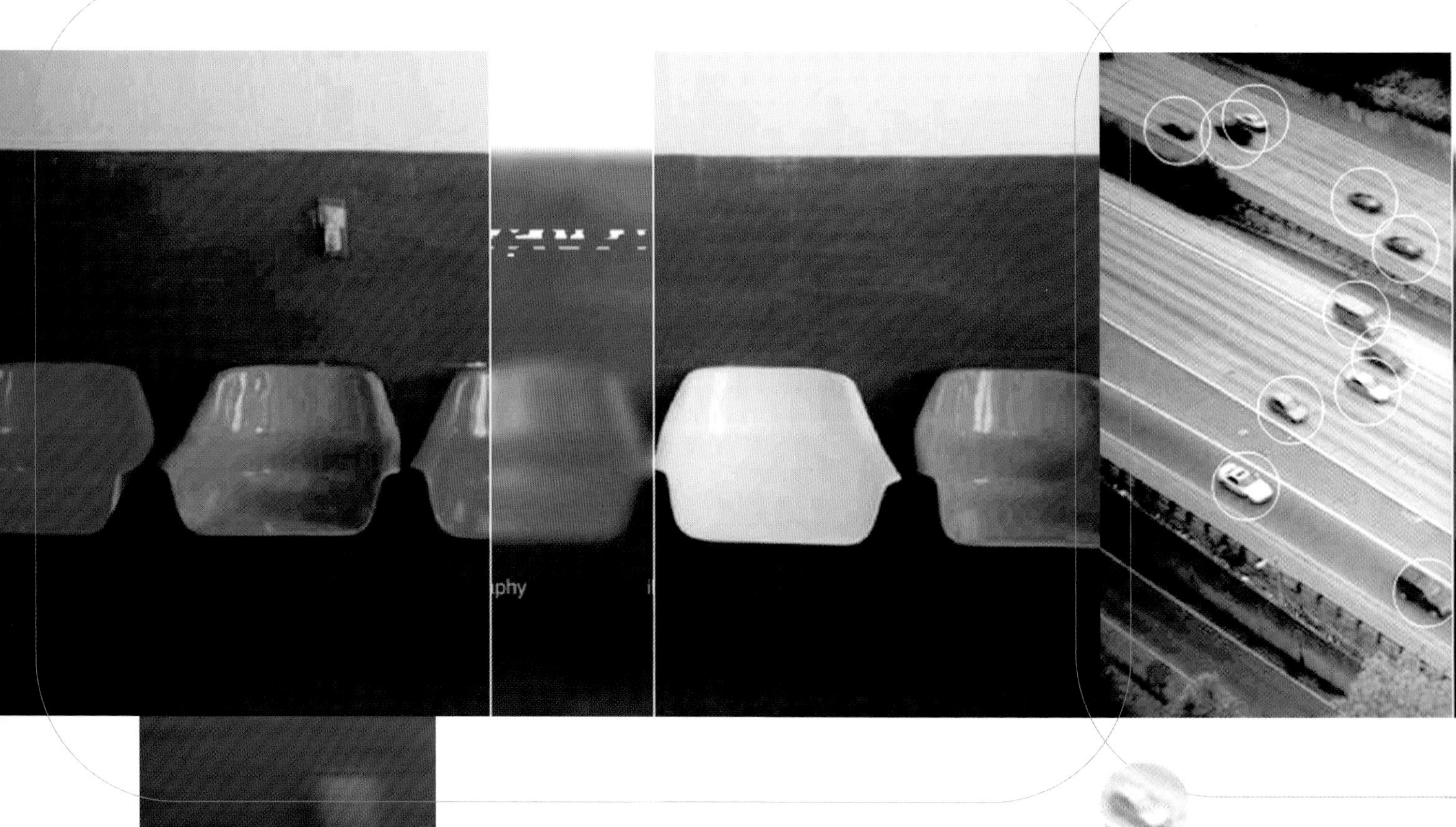

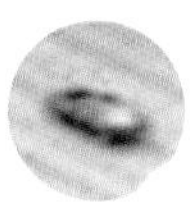

adfnews
biography
sounds
top10
adfed
satpal ram
ricky reel
articles
erchandise
links
gallery
guestbook
chat
credits

AsianDubFoundation

>

adfNews | Biography | Sounds | AdFed | Satpal Ram | Ricky Reel | Articles | Merchandise | Links | Gallery | Guestbook | Chat | Credits

ADF's new album "COMMUNITY MUSIC" is available now

SOUNDS

REAL GREAT BRITAIN SINGLE London Records, 2000

Real Great Britain
(Flash video)

RAFI'S REVENGE London Records, 1998

Naxalite
Buzzin'
Black White
Assassin
Hypocrite
Charge
Free Satpal Ram
Dub Mentality
Culture Move
Operation Eagle Lie

Check out ADF lyrics

tunes
sun-j
Click on one of the band to check their current listening and all-time favourites
chandrasonic
deedar

chandrasonic

CURRENT LISTENING

ALBUM	ARTISTS
KEEP IT REEL	VARIOUS
CAUGHT YOU OUT	KELIS
HIP HOP	DEAD PREZ
HEY HOWS YOUR GIRL	HANDSOME BOY MODELLING SCHOOL
SARGAM	TARUN BHATTACHARYA

TOP TEN

ALBUM	ARTISTS
IT TAKES A NATION OF MILLIONS	PUBLIC ENEMY
MOTOWN'S GREATEST HITS	TEMPTATIONS
HEART OF THE CONGOES	CONGOES
GREATEST HITS	JIMMY CLIFF
STRANGE CELESTIAL ROAD	SUN RA
METAL BOX	PUBLIC IMAGE
MOTHERSHIP CONNECTION	PARLIAMENT
PLAYING WITH A DIFFERENT SEX	AU PAIRS
UNKNOWN PLEASURES	JOY DIVISION
VERY BEST OF	CURTIS MAYFIELD

<title>
Asian Dub Foundation

<web address>
www.asiandubfoundation.com

<client>
Asian Dub Foundation

<designer>
Arun Kundnani

<programs/software>
Adobe GoLive, Photoshop

<number of pages>
about 50

<country of origin>
UK

<work description>
Asian Dub Foundation's official website offers fans the chance to chat to band members online, the latest news, biographies, audio clips, photos, and merchandise.

solar twins

racing truth infection

light radiator

vain electronic logic

wailing head sirens

smiling sonic hurricane

crazy desire temple

noise detector

fate oscillator

back to maverick

<title>
Solar Twins

<web address>
www.maverickrc.com/solartwins

<client>
Maverick Recording Co.

<designer>
Stefan Bucher

<design companies>
344 Design, LLC and Mischief New Media Inc

<programs/software>
Adobe Illustrator, Photoshop, GoLive, ImageReady

<number of pages>
10

<country of origin>
USA

solar twins

racing truth infection

light radiator

vain electronic logic

wailing head sirens

smiling sonic hurricane

crazy desire temple

noise detector

fate oscillator

back to maverick

Solar Twins will perform live
November 16, 1999 in Los Angeles

Austin Powers party at Tower Records on Sunset Blvd.

Date	City, State	Venue
Nov-16	Los Angeles, CA	Tower Records

<work description>
The Solar Twins' official site was designed as an on-line companion to the group's first major label release. It provides information about the duo, record and tour news, a photo gallery, and audio and video clips. Fragments from the band's lyrics form the site's menus.

MEMBERS
LISTEN
EVENTS
PRESS
GUESTBOOK
LINKS
CONTACT
COMING
ON
OFF
REPLAY INTRO
THE CONTROL GROUP
REPLAY INTRO
THE CONTROL GROUP

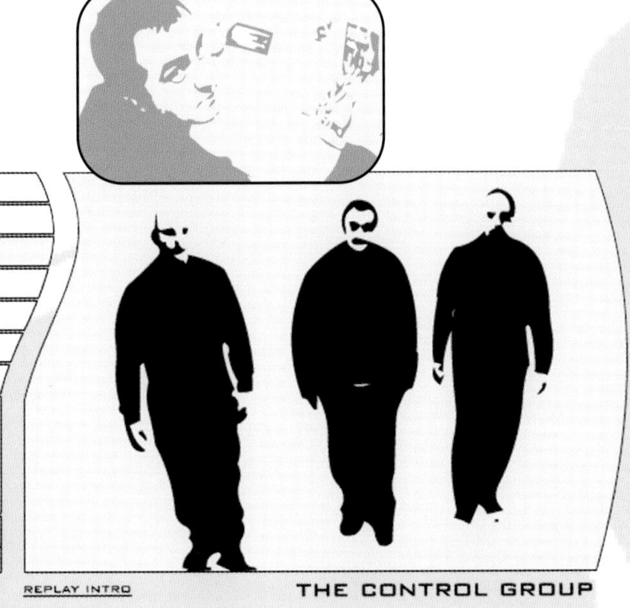

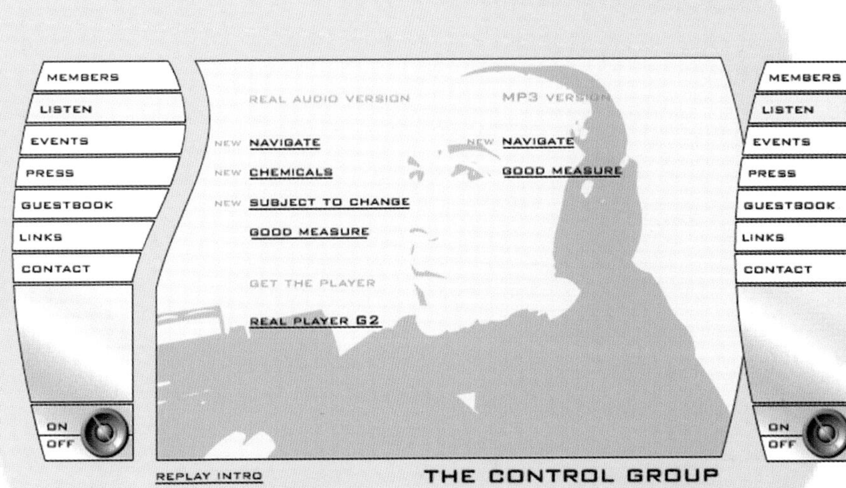

<title>
The Control Group

<web address>
www.the-control-group.com

<client>
The Control Group

<design company>
Squarewave interactive

<programs/software>
Macromedia Flash, Adobe Photoshop, Adobe Streamline

<number of pages>
n/a

<country of origin>
USA

<work description>
Official website for The Control Group with audio clips, mp3s, news, and features about the band.

LORKIN DEVI

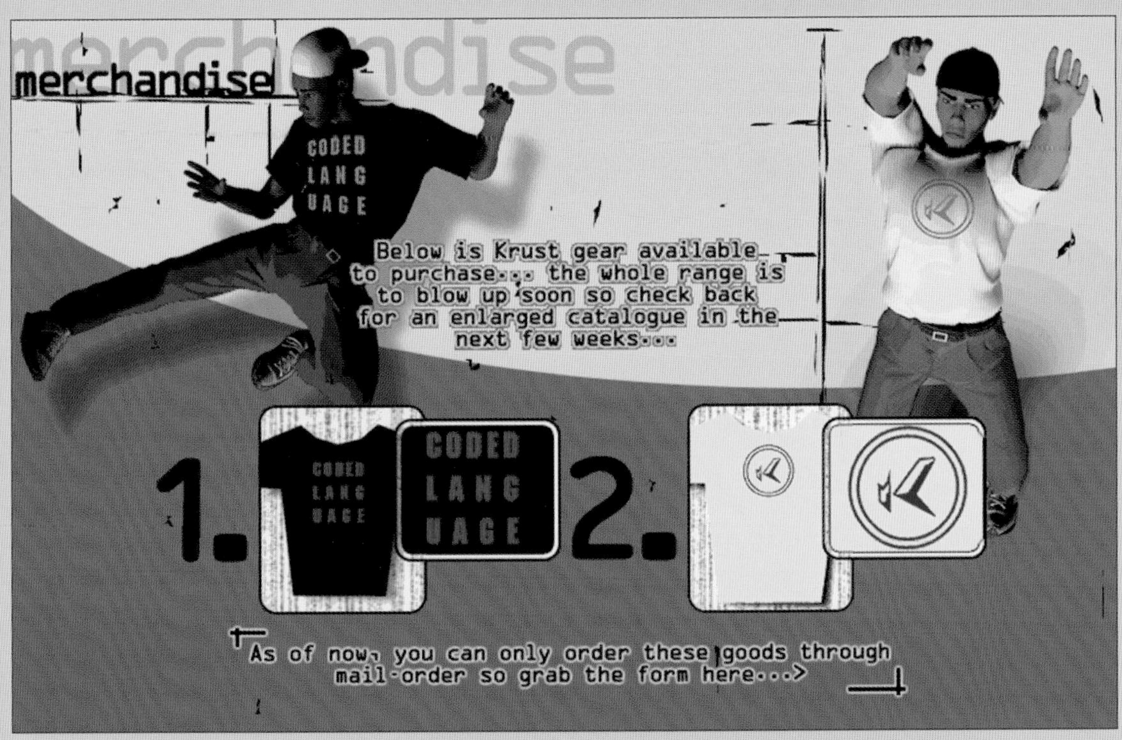

merchandise
CODED LANG UAGE
Below is Krust gear available to purchase... the whole range is to blow up soon so check back for an enlarged catalogue in the next few weeks...
1.
2.
As of now, you can only order these goods through mail-order so grab the form here...>

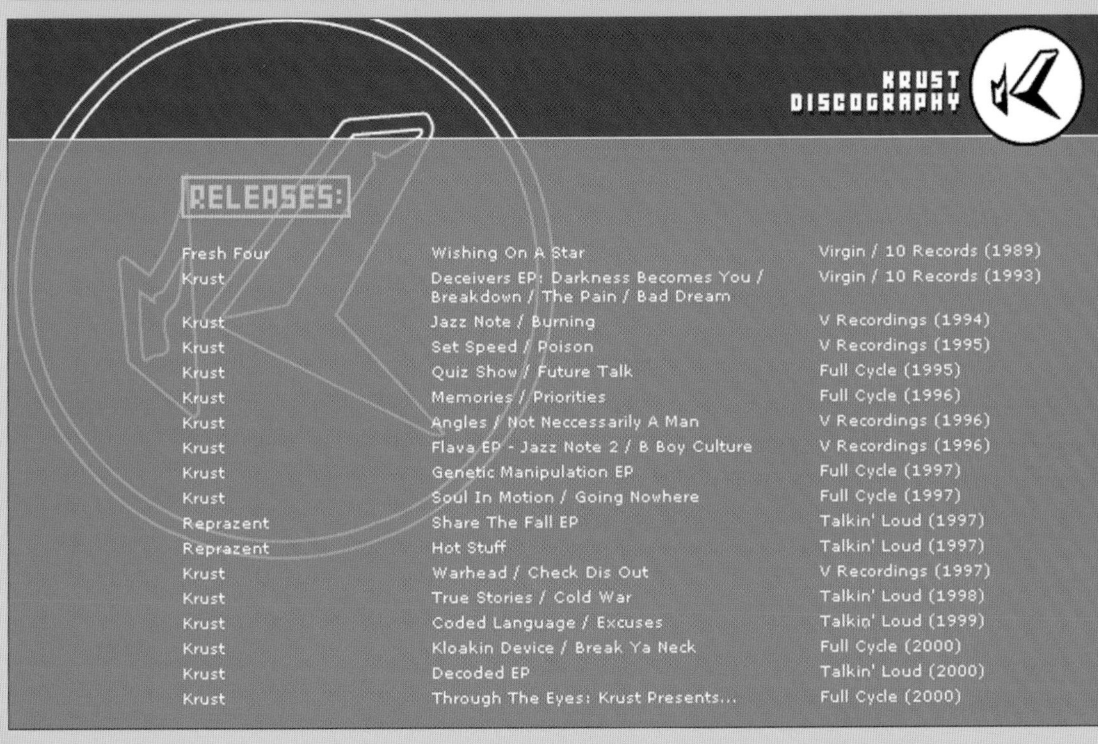

KRUST DISCOGRAPHY
RELEASES:
Fresh Four Wishing On A Star Virgin / 10 Records (1989)
Krust Deceivers EP: Darkness Becomes You / Breakdown / The Pain / Bad Dream Virgin / 10 Records (1993)
Krust Jazz Note / Burning V Recordings (1994)
Krust Set Speed / Poison V Recordings (1995)
Krust Quiz Show / Future Talk Full Cycle (1995)
Krust Memories / Priorities Full Cycle (1996)
Krust Angles / Not Neccessarily A Man V Recordings (1996)
Krust Flava EP - Jazz Note 2 / B Boy Culture V Recordings (1996)
Krust Genetic Manipulation EP Full Cycle (1997)
Krust Soul In Motion / Going Nowhere Full Cycle (1997)
Reprazent Share The Fall EP Talkin' Loud (1997)
Reprazent Hot Stuff Talkin' Loud (1997)
Krust Warhead / Check Dis Out V Recordings (1997)
Krust True Stories / Cold War Talkin' Loud (1998)
Krust Coded Language / Excuses Talkin' Loud (1999)
Krust Kloakin Device / Break Ya Neck Full Cycle (2000)
Krust Decoded EP Talkin' Loud (2000)
Krust Through The Eyes: Krust Presents... Full Cycle (2000)

<title>
Krust: Through the Eyes

<web address>
www.krust.co.uk

<client>
Krust

<design company>
Chris Design

<programs/software>
Photoshop, GoLive, Illustrator, Flash, Streamline, Media Cleaning Pro, Soundedit, Poser, Cinema 4DxL, Fireworks, After Effects.

<number of pages>
25+

<country of origin>
UK

<work description>
This is the official website for Krust - exponent of experimental electronic music. It offers information on new releases with audio and video clips, flash-animated lyrics, a discography, online merchandise, and a guestbook for fans.

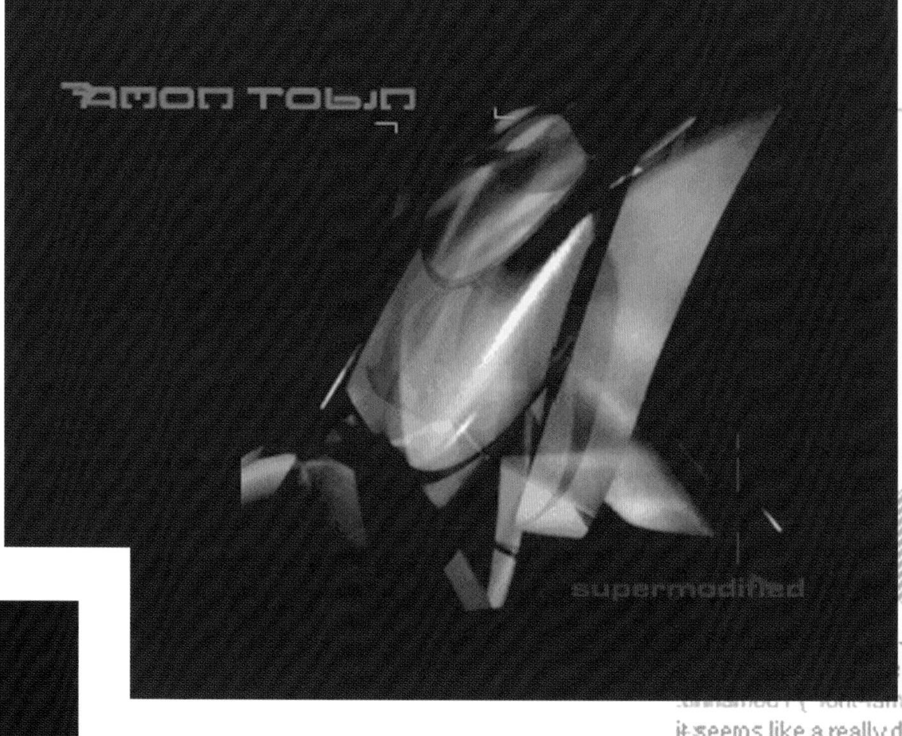

it seems like a really di
by adopting and incorp
context, something th
something new you're
all traditional musician
just more direct.
the whole idea of maki
make really strong ass

<script language="Jav
<!--
function MM_displaySt
status=msgStr;
like music that will pro
new musical context..
and it's quite good for
</script>
</head>

</html>

<title>
Amon Tobin

<web address>
www.amontobin.com

<client>
Ninja Tune Records

<design company>
Hi-res!/Openmind

<programs/software>
Flash, Photoshop, Cubase

<number of pages>
n/a

<country of origin>
UK

<work description>
Official website for the musician Amon Tobin.

```
<html>
<head>
<title></title>
<meta http-equiv="Content-Type" content="text/html; charset=iso-8859-1">
<style type="text/css">
the abuse of sampling has been around for a lot less time actually and that's all i'm interested in.

it's not just taking a sound and going - well, now i can use a guitar because i don't have a guitar...
it's really all about the sound.
.unnamed1 {  font-family: Verdana, Arial, Helvetica, sans-serif; font-size: 10pt; font-weight: normal}
it seems like a really direct way of making music, the way music has always been traditionally made
by adopting and incorporating things that influence you into something of your own with your own
context, something that's part of all the things you've heard and think are good... but it's also part of
something new you're making.
all traditional musicians make music like that as well in the same way the sampler does that - it's
just more direct.
the whole idea of making references in your music, that are recognizable, some sounds that people
make really strong associations with.

<script language="JavaScript">
<!--
function MM_displayStatusMsg(msgStr) { //v2.0
  status=msgStr;
like music that will produce certain images in peoples heads and you just put that into a completely
new musical context... it's all about saying : i took this from there - look where it is now.
and it's quite good for people to look where these samples come from...
</script>
</head>


</html>
```

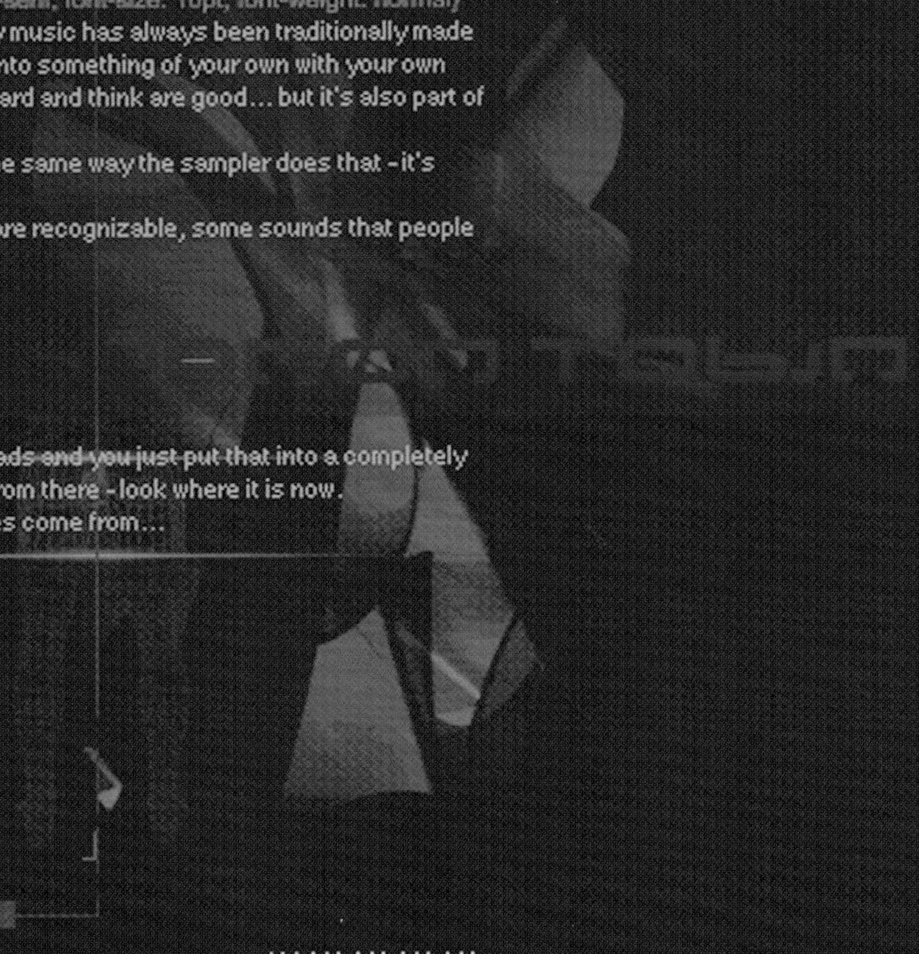

<title>
Stereolab

<web address>
www.stereolab.com

<client>
n/a

<design company>
n/a

<programs/software>
n/a

<number of pages>
n/a

<country of origin>
n/a

<work description>
Official site for the band Stereolab.

office
on tour
studio
news

stereolab

COBRA AND PHASES GROUP PLAY
VOLTAGE IN THE MILKY NIGHT

AVAILABLE FROM
21/27. SEPTEMBER

If you want to be updated
about additions to the site or
stereolab events, enter your
email address:

SEND →

office
on tour
studio
news
ALBUM
cobra phases group play voltage in the milkynight
AUDIO
14 the emergency kisses
15 come play in the milky night
VIDEO
the free design
the samples require RealPlayer G2
office
on tour
studio
news
usa
japan
confirmed tour dates 05.dec.99
[aust, nz, south america and second usa tour soon to be confirmed]
japan
13.feb.00 osaka, big cat
14.feb.00 nagoya, club quattro
16.feb.00 tokyo, liquid room
17.feb.00 tokyo, liquid room
18.feb.00 tokyo, club quattro
transrapid

<title>
Achtung Spitfire Schnell Schnell - Tellylounge

<web address>
www.achtung-spitfire.de

<client>
Achtung Spitfire Schnell Schnell

<design company>
n/a

<programs/software>
Windows, Macromedia, Flash, Notepad

<number of pages>
varies

<country of origin>
Germany (site language is English)

<work description>
Homepage for the official band website for Achtung Spitfire Schnell Schnell. The site is updated regularly by band members and offers mp3s as well as news and information.

Achtung Spitfire
Schnell Schnell!!
MEET THE BAND
DOWNLOADS
CONTACT
GIGS
NEWS
LINKS
REVIEWS
GUESTBOOK

Achtung Spitfire
Schnell Schnell!!
news gigs band reviews downloads guestbook contact links
MEET THE BAND
Sir Ana Achtung
KidKadaver
X-Ray Rumble
King Klabauter

THE CINEMATIC ORCHES

BIOGRAPHY
J.Swinscoe presen

Most eight year olds
clarinet or the violin.
classical guitar, not
learnt to play it like
youive told your pa
the bin. For the first
game.

long player

THE CINEMATIC ORCHESTRA

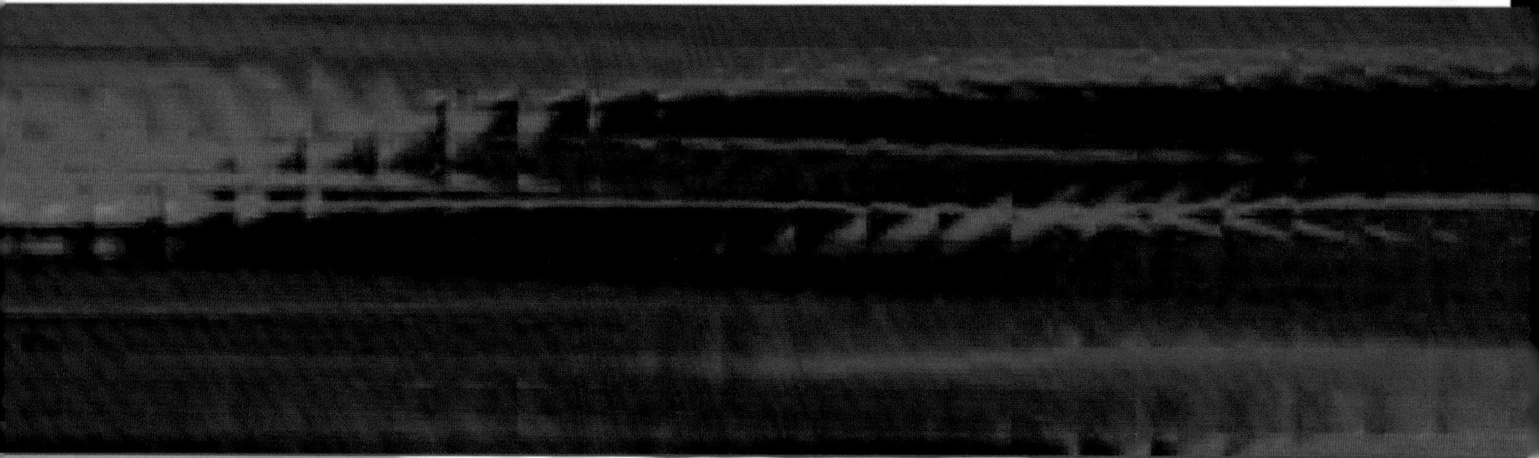

long player
TRA
The Cinematic Orchestra
re forced by their parents to take up the
Swinscoe learned to play guitar. Not
y fiddle-de-dee John Waters schtick. J
u do when youire a teenager. When
nts to fuck off and shoved the clarinet in
e, maybe, he was a little ahead of the
The Cinematic Orchestra
download [coming soon]
The Cinematic Orchestra
download [coming soon]

<title>
The Cinematic Orchestra

<web address>
www.cinematicorchestra.com

<client>
Ninja Tune Records/
Jason Swinscoe

<designers>
James Gibson and Robbie Tingey

<design company>
J-Buyers

<programs/software>
Photoshop, Illustrator, BBedit, Quicktime, Peak

<number of pages>
5

<country of origin>
UK

<work description>
Promotional site for the band The Cinematic Orchestra.

THIS SITE COMES IN 3 DIFFERENT VERSONS : : MAKE YOUR CHOICE BELOW : : :

FLASH FULLSCREEN [adventurous mode] : : FLASH REGULAR [fearful mode] : : TEXT [get to the point mode] : :

note : this site was created with fullscreen in mind : :

THIS SITE IS POWERED BY FLASH. IF YOU DO NOT ALREADY HAVE THE PLUG-IN, PLEASE DOWNLOAD IT FROM HERE : :

MESSAGEBOARD

GUESTBOOK

SOUL CONTROLLERS

power

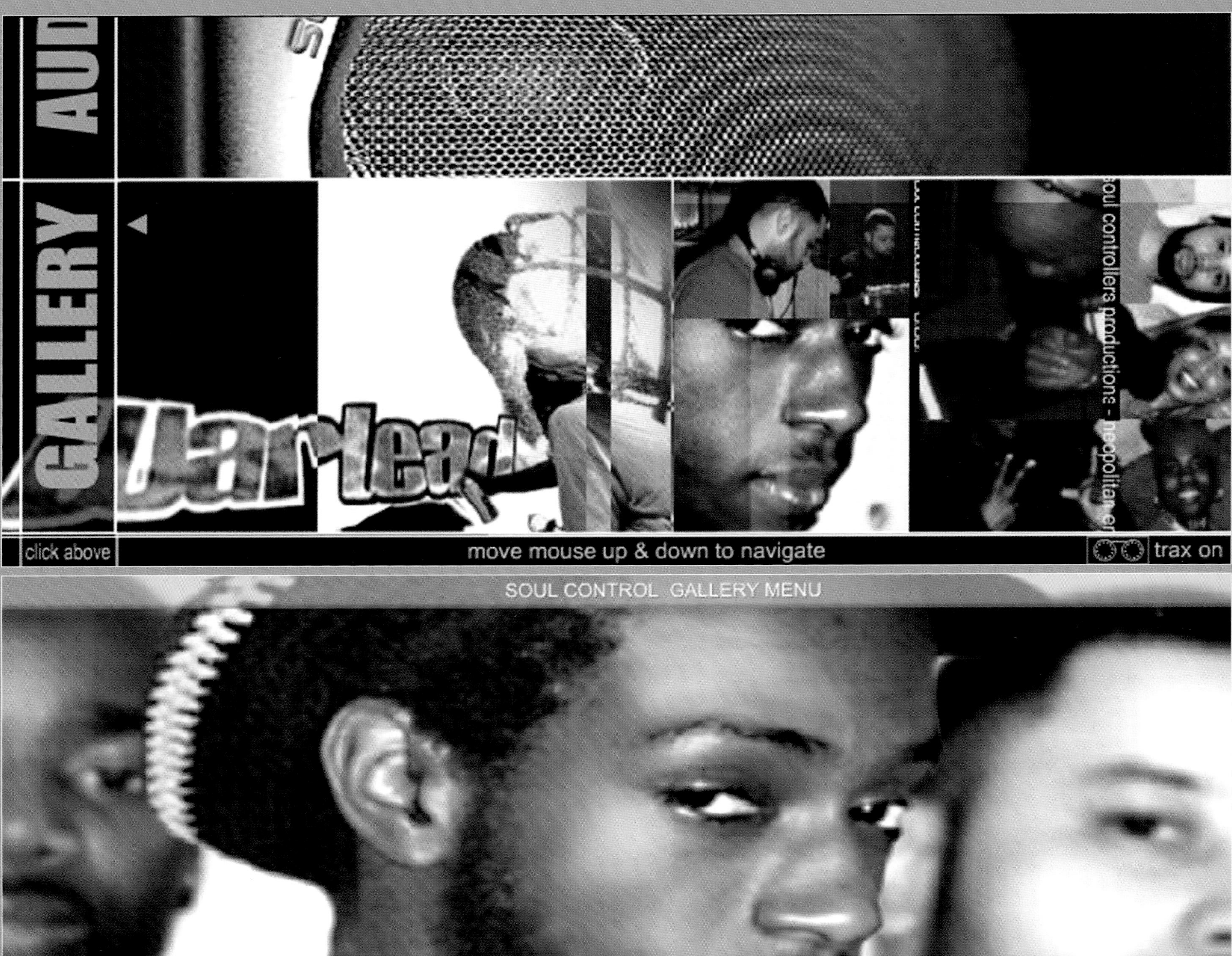
AUD
GALLERY
soul controllers productions - neopolitan en
click above
move mouse up & down to navigate
trax on
SOUL CONTROL GALLERY MENU

<title>
The Soul Controllers: the world's revolutionary sound crew

<web address>
www.soulcontollers.com

<client>
The Soul Contollers

<design company>
Riad (Neopolitan Entities)

<Programs/Software>
Adobe Photoshop, Flash, Dreamweaver, RealProducer, Gold Wave.

<number of pages>
21

<country of origin>
Canada

<work description>
The official website for DJ crew The Soul Controllers offers news, a photo gallery, video and audio clips as well as real-time mp3 streaming for ardent club fans.

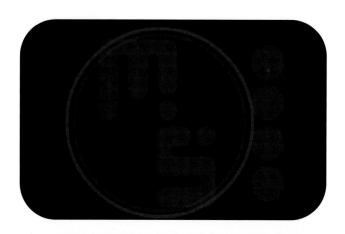

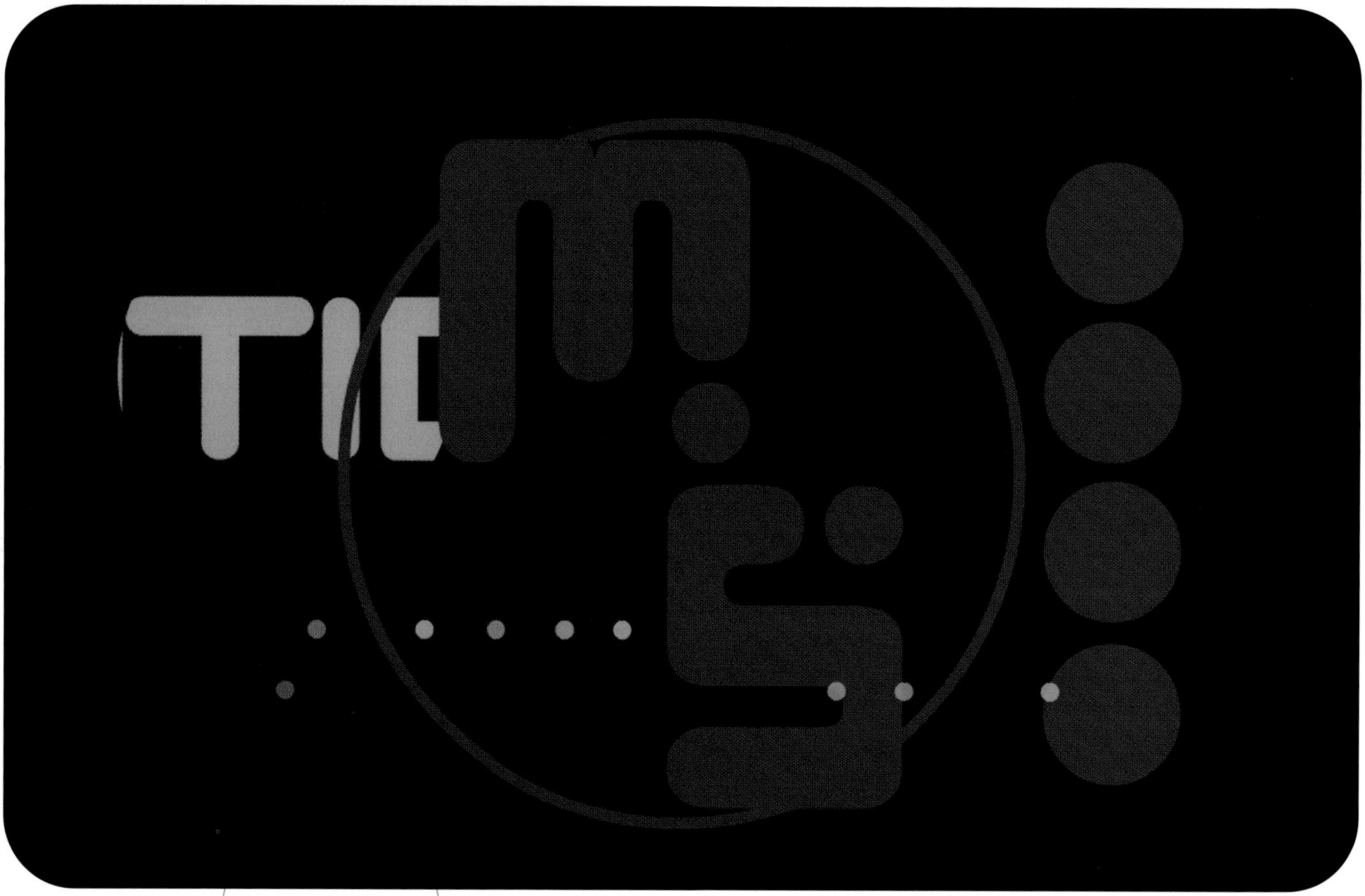

<title>
Markus Schulz

<web address>
www.markusschulz.com

<client>
Markus Schulz

<design company>
BaDDa b00m! Creative Media

<programs/software>
Macromedia Flash, Dreamweaver

<number of pages>
18

<country of origin>
USA

<work description>
The official website for DJ Markus Schulz offers downloadable audio clips, news, information, merchandise, and links.

I grew up listening to early hip hop. Artists like Grandmaster Flash, Dr. Jeckel and Mr. Hyde, Tom Tom Club, Man Parish, Kraftwerk, Soulsonic Force and Planet Patrol were always playing on my box.
As I started collecting records, my taste consisted of funky beats, with electronic keyboards. Tracks like "System" by Mel & Kim, and "Musique Non Stop" by Kraftwerk excited me. Funky baselines like ones you heard in "I'll be good" by Rene & Angela and "Encore" by Evelyn King, kept me interested in the mid-eighties R & B style. It wasn't until 1987 that I started getting interested in *House* music.
I'll never forget the feeling I got from looking at this wall of speakers in a small dive of a club in Boston called "The Haymarket" -pumping out "May Foom Bay" by Cultural Vibe. I remember looking up at the speakers as the baseline penetrated into my bones. It gave me an itch. One that I still have to this day. Shortly after, I first heard "Love Can't Turn Around" by J.M. Silk and my musical passion had forever changed. *House* music has been a passion ever since.

I am very excited about the scene here in America. With Production teams like Fade and Deepsky, and American Producers like Christopher Lawrence, Joshua Ryan, Lenny Bertoldi, Inertia, and C.L. McSpadden making waves...*the future is looking bright for American trance!*

back

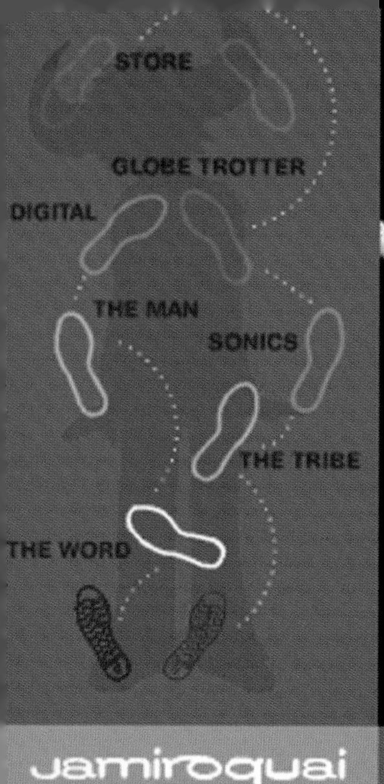
STORE
GLOBE TROTTER
DIGITAL
THE MAN
SONICS
THE TRIBE
THE WORD
jamiroquai

CREDITS
JAPANESE VERSION

<title>
Jamiroquai

<web address>
www.jamiroquai.co.uk

<client>
Sony Music UK

<designer>
Russell Newell

<design company>
The Real

<programs/software>
n/a

<number of pages>
n/a

<country of origin>
UK

<work description>
This promotional site for the band Jamiroquai offers music, videos, news, and interactive fan pages.

REGISTER
FORUM
REVIEWS
LINKS
MAILINGL
THE TRIB
ON THIS DAY IN HISTORY . . .
The single Deeper Underground was released this week in the UK in 1998.
WHY NOT RAP ABOUT SOME OF JK'S FAVORITE SUBJECTS OR VOTE TO START A NEW DISCUSSION, HERE ARE SOME IDEAS TO GET YOU ALL STARTED:

SYNKRONIZED ALBUMS SINGLES

SONICS

HERE YOU CAN FIND THE FULL JAMIROQUAI DISCOGRAPHY ALONG WITH SOUND SAMPLES OF EACH TRACK AND CLIPS FROM THE VIDEOS. YOU CAN ALSO SEE ARTWORK EXCLUSIVE TO THIS WEB SITE TO ACCOMPANY EACH TRACK FROM THE NEW ALBUM SYNKRONIZED.

<title>
Dubstar

<web address>
www.dubstar.com

<client>
n/a

<design company>
n/a

<programs/software>
n/a

<number of pages>
n/a

<country of origin>
UK

<work description>
The official website for the band Dubstar offers band and tour news, music from latest releases, a photo gallery, and press reviews.

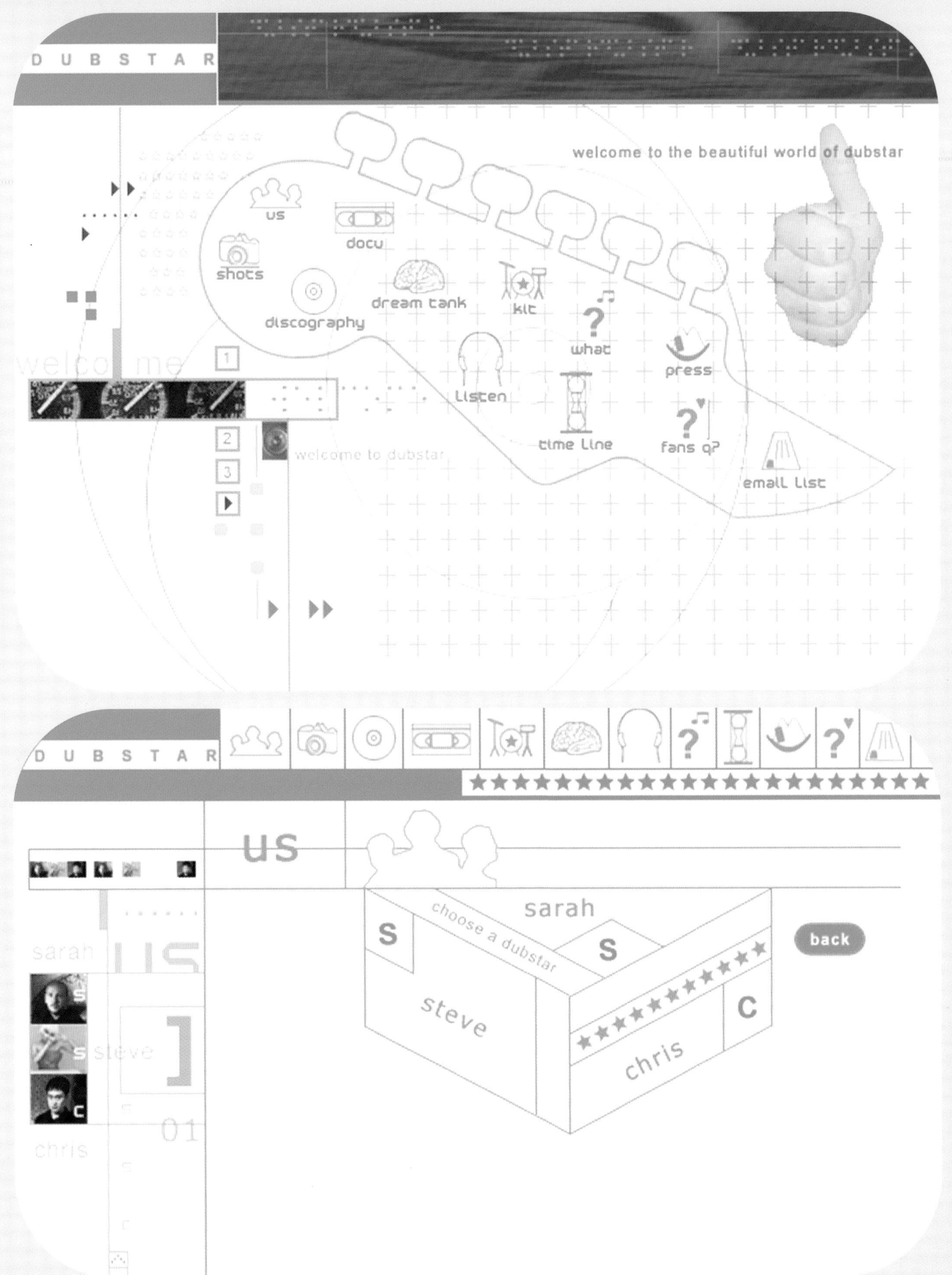

DUBSTAR
welcome to the beautiful world of dubstar
us
docu
shots
discography
dream tank
kit
what
press
listen
time line
fans q?
email list
welcome
welcome to dubstar
DUBSTAR
us
sarah
steve
chris
choose a dubstar
back
01

PD:TR#003

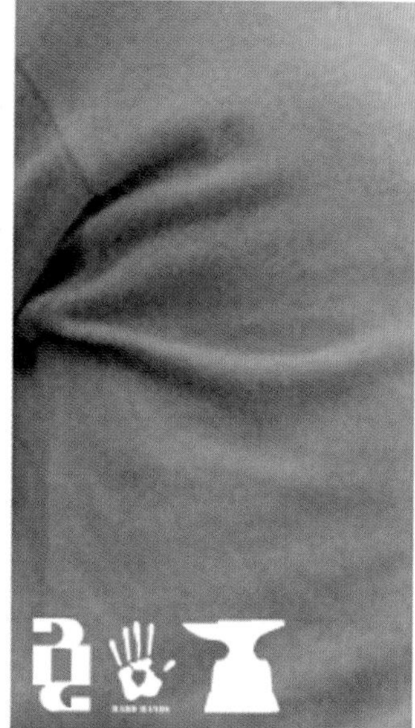

PRESSURE DROP

HOME

LATEST NEWS WARRIOR SOUND
WARRIOREMIX BIOGRAPHY INFLUENCES
TREAD SERIES CONTACT

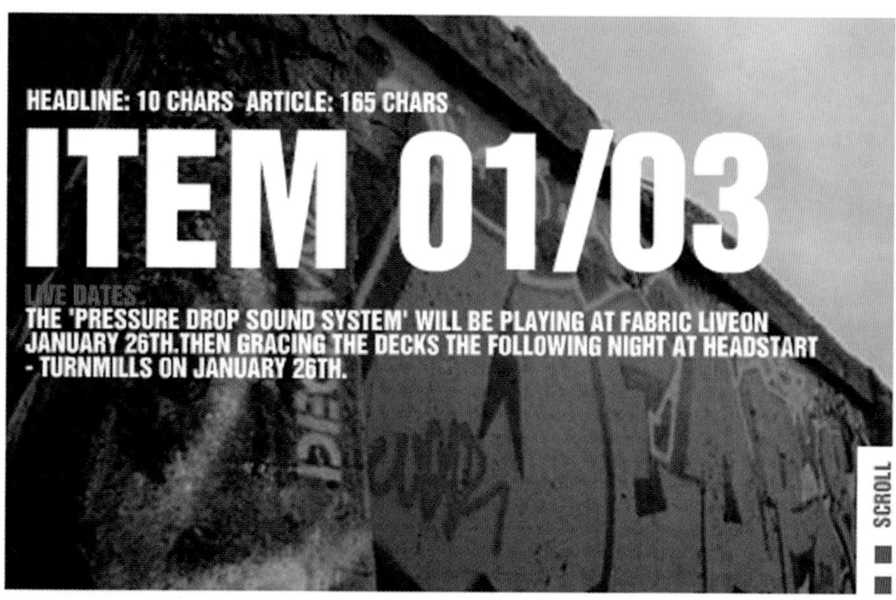
HEADLINE: 10 CHARS ARTICLE: 165 CHARS
ITEM 01/03
LIVE DATES
THE 'PRESSURE DROP SOUND SYSTEM' WILL BE PLAYING AT FABRIC LIVEON JANUARY 26TH.THEN GRACING THE DECKS THE FOLLOWING NIGHT AT HEADSTART - TURNMILLS ON JANUARY 26TH.
SCROLL

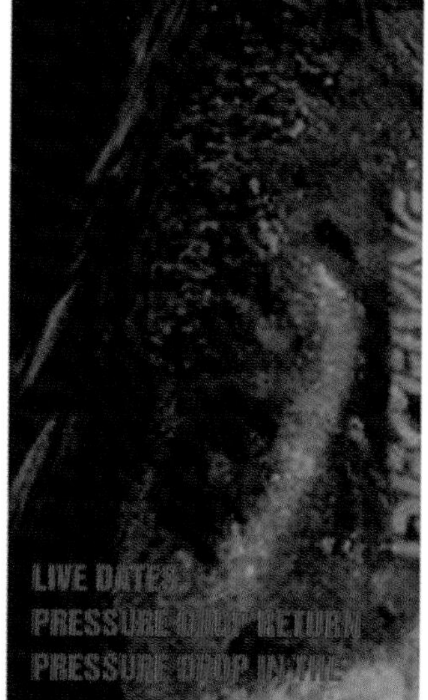
LIVE DATES

LATEST NEWS

HOME

LATEST NEWS WARRIOR SOUND
WARRIOREMIX BIOGRAPHY INFLUENCES
TREAD SERIES CONTACT

THE FIRST SINGLE TO BE TAKEN FROM THE NEW PRESSURE DROP ALBUM IS THE MIGHTY 'WARRIOR SOUND'. THE SINGLE WILL NOT BE RELEASED UNTIL THE NEW YEAR BUT THERE WILL BE A COUPLE OF 12" PROMOS AVAILABLE FEATURING THE FOLLOWING MIXES:
12" #1. WARRIOR DANCE
DEE KLINE VOCAL
ADAM FREELAND MIX
12" #2. ED CASE FULL VOCAL
ED CASE DUB MIX
ALBUM MIX
WARRIOR DRUMS
THERE WAS ALSO A VERY LTD NUMBER OF TEST PRESSINGS FOR 12" #1 BUT THESE ARE RARE SO YOU MAY NEED TO SHOP AROUND.
FORMATS
REAL VIDEO CLIP
ALBUM VERSION
DEE KLINE VOCAL
ED CASE VOCAL
WARRIOR DANCE
ADAM FREELAND MIX
MIKEY DREAD MIX
REALAUDIO MIXES

HOME

LATEST NEWS WARRIOR SOUND
WARRIOREMIX BIOGRAPHY INFLUENCES
TREAD SERIES CONTACT

PD:TR#001 PD-ON-SEA
PD:TR#002 WARRIOR SOUND 12" WHITE LABEL NO #1
PD:TR#003 WEBSITE
PD:TR#004 WARRIOR SOUND 12" WHITE LABEL NO #2
PD:TR#005 WARRIOR SOUND 12" PROMO NO #1
PD:TR#006 WARRIOR SOUND 12" PROMO NO #2
PD:TR#008 2 TRACK RADIO CD PROMO
PD:TR#009 WARRIOR SOUND VIDEO
PD:TR#010
PD:TR#011 TREAD CD ALBUM SAMPLER
PD:TR#012 WARRIOR COMMERCIAL CD
PD:TR#025 TREAD COMMERCIAL CD
PD:TR#026 TREAD COMMERCIAL VINYL
THROUGHOUT THE TREAD PROJECT EACH PRESSURE DROP ITEM - BE IT A 12" PROMO, CD SINGLE OR STICKER - WILL RECEIVE A NUMBER WHICH READS PD:TR#00...

TREAD SERIES

HOME

LATEST NEWS WARRIOR SOUND
WARRIOREMIX BIOGRAPHY INFLUENCES
TREAD SERIES CONTACT

<title>
Pressure Drop: 'Warrior Sound'

<web address>
www.pressuredrop.co.uk

<client>
Higherground/Sony Music Entertainment UK

<design company>
Kleber Design Ltd

<programs/software>
Flash, BBedit, Photoshop, PHP, MYSQL, Freehand.

<number of pages>
n/a

<country of origin>
UK

<work description>
Promotional website to support the release of Pressure Drop's 'Warrior Sound' album.

THE TITLE SAYS IT ALL, ALTHOUGH YOU DON'T NEED MUCH PERSUADING. THIS IS COCKTAIL MUSIC FOR THOSE BARMY BONGO PARTIES.

ENOCH LIGHT AND THE COMMAND ALL-STARS
PERSUASIVE PERCUSSION VOLUME 3
COMMAND

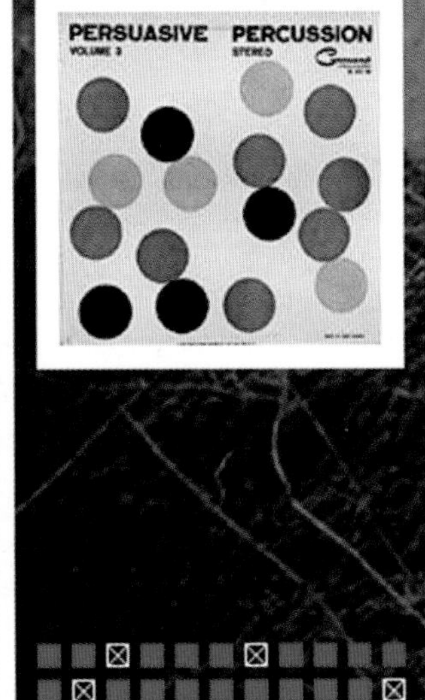

INFLUENCES

LATEST NEWS WARRIOR SOUND
WARRIOREMIX BIOGRAPHY INFLUENCES
TREAD SERIES CONTACT

download...

<labels/magazines/promotions>

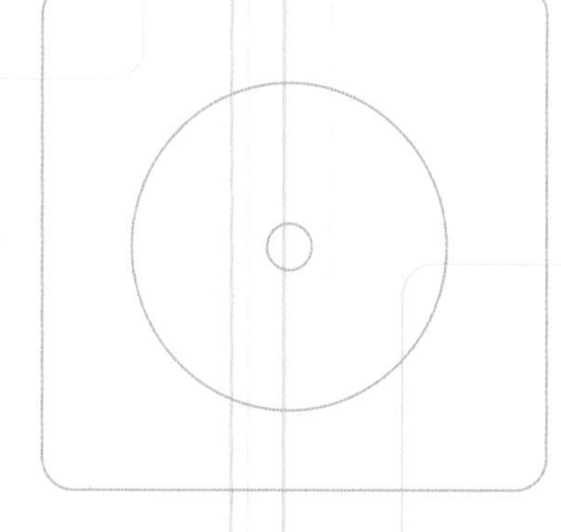

<electronica>
<drum&bass>
<dub> <hiphop>
<house> <techno>
<ambient> <jazz>
<jazz> <electronica>
<electronica> <drum&bass>
<drum&bass>
<dub> <house>
<hiphop> <ambient>
<ambient> <jazz>
<jazz> <electronica>
<electronica> <drum&bass>
<drum&bass>
<dub> <hiphop>
<hiphop> <ambient>
<drum&bass> <jazz>
<dub> <electronica>
<house> <drum&bass>
<ambient> <dub>
<jazz> <hiphop>
<electronica>

SKIP INTRO

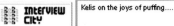

INTERVIEW CITY
REVIEWS
FEATURE
FASHION

Kelis on the joys of puffing....

Mary J Blige, The Wideboys, Non Phixon....and more

The all time Best Booty Bouncing Videos.....

People who wear clothes that look nice....

Play Intro Again

TOUCH

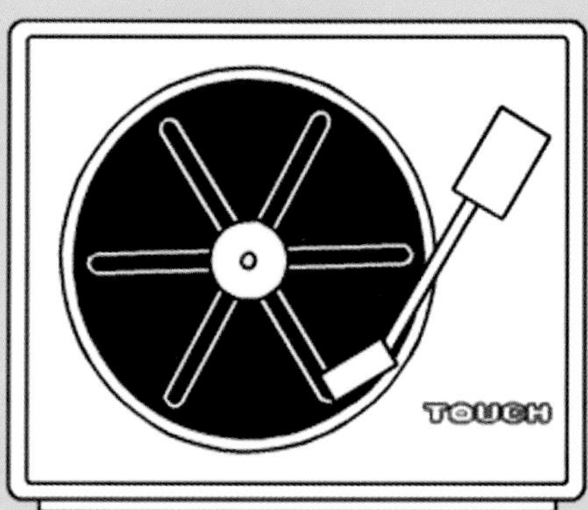

Kelis Kaleidoscope (Virgin LP)

She seems to be everywhere at the moment this young lady - top five of the national chart, all over the TV, even on the cover of Touch - and this is the reason why. Make no mistake, her uncompromising and outspoken personality (not to mention appearance) make her an instantly marketable commodity and media fodder in the extreme. However, such attributes can only get you so far and Kelis has an album that, musically, is as captivating as the flaming locks, eyebrows and... I'll leave the rest to your imagination. Suitably entitled 'Kaleidoscope', this is a truly original and imaginative album, combining a variety of styles and moods but maintaining quality throughout. And you can stop shielding your packets fellas, the lady dubbed 'Thunder Bitch' does reveal her more mellow side.

RORY BATHO

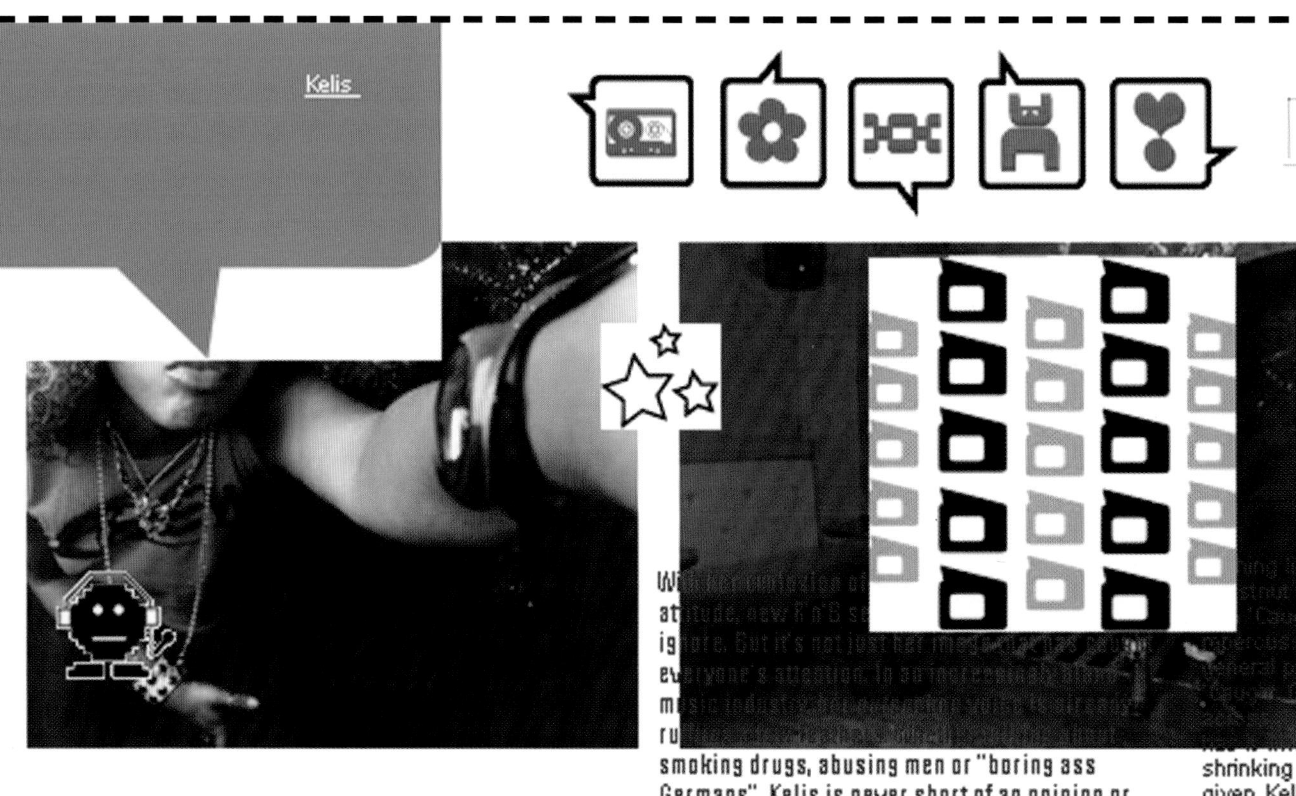

smoking drugs, abusing men or "boring ass Germans", Kelis is never short of an opinion or three...

shrinking could be h
given Kelis a bit of a
devours men for bre
'Thunder Bitch' one
name but it seems t

Loud And Proud

Text Lynda Cowell

HOUSE & GARAGE

omed, eh? Men used to laugh at that old
ers came along and blew everything apart
- a cautionary tale about the
ty. Perhaps better known amongst the
you so much right now, Aaarggghhh!',
ured the imagination of wronged women
n the other hand, ran for cover. Rumour
k was played, the sound of testicles
for miles. Unsurprisingly, the track has
utation as a man-hating monster who
st and spits them out when she's done.
alist called her. She doesn't like the
ve stuck.

"I get everyone to smoke weed with me. I've smoked with CEOs of companies." - Kelis on the joys of puffing

<title>
Touch Magazine

<web address>
www.touch21.com

<client>
Touch magazine

<design company>
Beer Davies

<programs/software>
Flash, Pagemaker,
Illustrator, Quark Express

<number of pages>
16

<country of origin>
UK

<work description>
This magazine site represents the UK black music environment and features music, clubs, fashion, and lifestyle issues.

<title>
Ernst-strom

<web address>
www.max-ernst.de

<client>
Thomas Brinkmann

<design company>
Max Kahlen Design
(MK. Design)

<programs/software>
Macromedia, Dreamweaver,
Adobe, Image Ready

<number of pages>
10

<country of origin>
Germany

<work description>
This is the promotional site for the labels max ernst, ernst and strom. The minimal design and structure of the site is intended to reflect the labels' music.

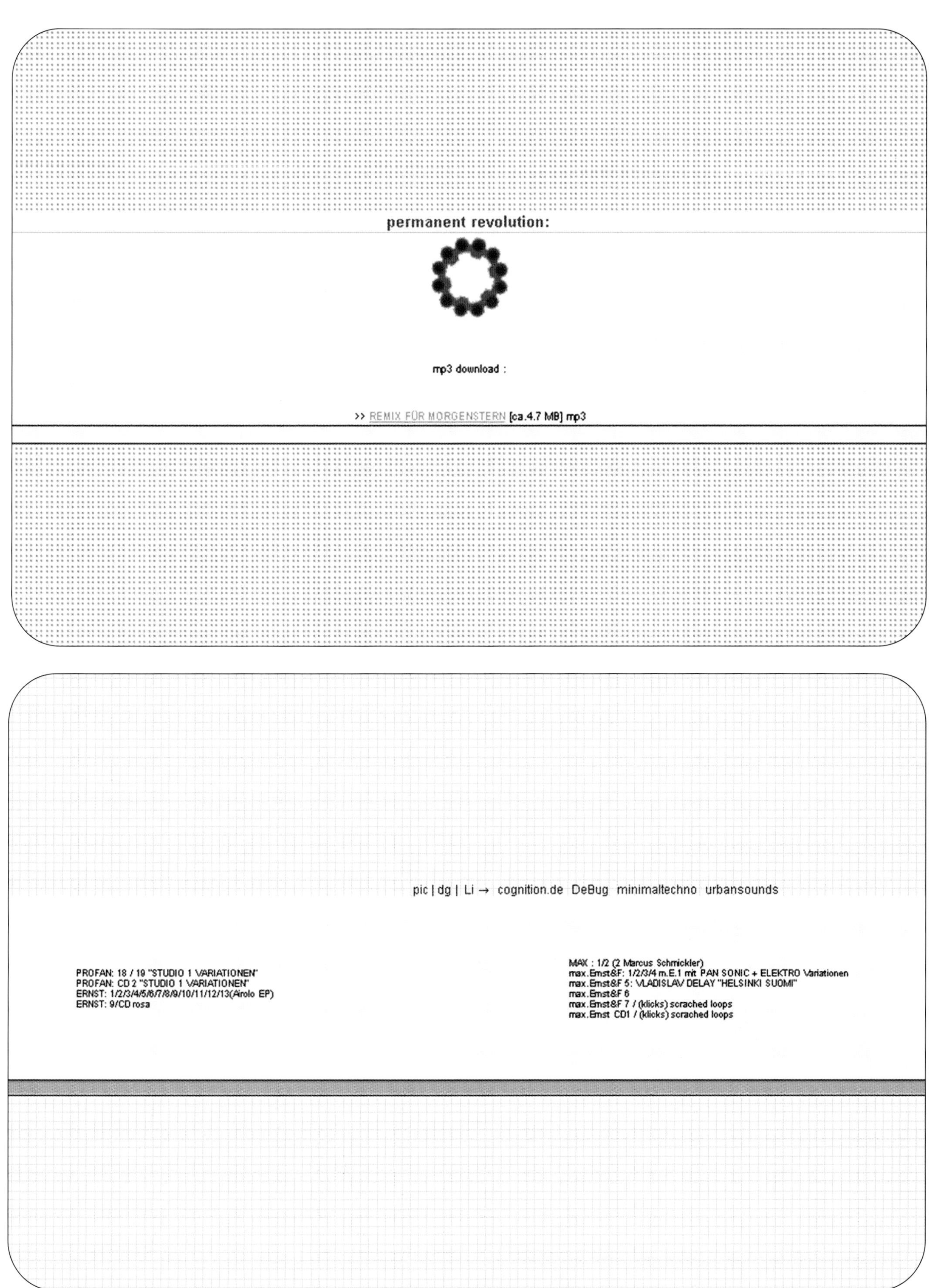

permanent revolution:
mp3 download :
>> REMIX FÜR MORGENSTERN [ca.4.7 MB] mp3
pic | dg | Li → cognition.de DeBug minimaltechno urbansounds
PROFAN: 18 / 19 "STUDIO 1 VARIATIONEN"
PROFAN: CD 2 "STUDIO 1 VARIATIONEN"
ERNST: 1/2/3/4/5/6/7/8/9/10/11/12/13(Airolo EP)
ERNST: 9/CD rosa
MAX : 1/2 (2 Marcus Schmickler)
max.Ernst&F: 1/2/3/4 m.E.1 mit PAN SONIC + ELEKTRO Variationen
max.Ernst&F 5: VLADISLAV DELAY "HELSINKI SUOMI"
max.Ernst&F 6
max.Ernst&F 7 / (klicks) scrached loops
max.Ernst CD1 / (klicks) scrached loops

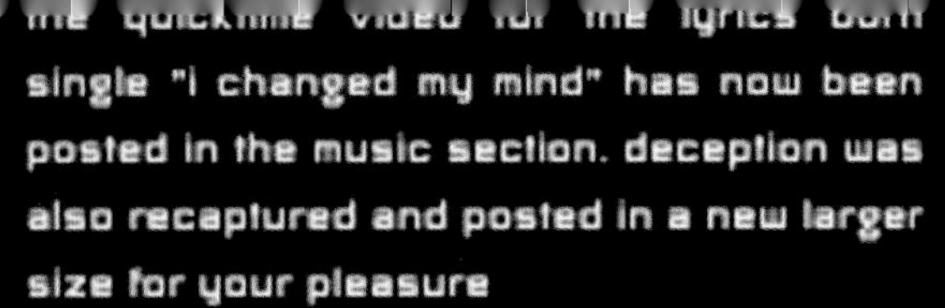

- the quicktime video for the lyrics born single "i changed my mind" has now been posted in the music section. deception was also recaptured and posted in a new larger size for your pleasure

- the muzappers remixes are available for your listening pleasure in the music section

news quannum bio music photos feedback buy

114345

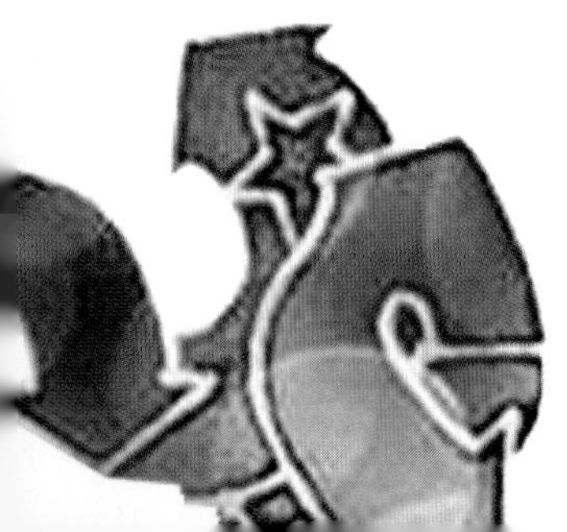

quannum projects
news
quannum bio
music
photos
feedback
buy
CURRENT NEWS
November
01 Detroit/State Theatre (Opening for Ben Harper)
02 Detroit/State Theatre (Opening for Ben Harper)
03 off
04 Chicago/Aragon Ballroom (Opening for Ben Harper)
05 Minneapolis/Roy Wilkens Auditorium (Opening for Ben Harper)
06 Madison/Oscar Meyer Th. (Opening for Ben Harper)
We are pleased to announce the first of what will be many Solesides Reunion shows, bringing together all of the original crew onstage, performing both classics and new material. What songs will they play? Who will be there? Is Lyrics Born

<title>
Quannum Projects

<web address>
www.quannum.com

<client>
n/a

<design company>
n/a

<program/software>
n/a

<number of pages>
n/a

<country of origin>
n/a

<work description>
The Quannum website offers news, biography, music, photos, webcasts, and online shopping.

<title>
Plastic Raygun

<web address>
www.plasticraygun.com

<client>
Plastic Raygun Ltd

<designer>
Leigh Smith

<design company>
Six Forty

<programs/software>
Freehand, Photoshop, Flash, Dreamweaver, PHP, HTML, Javascript

<number of pages>
n/a

<country of origin>
UK

<work description>
This is the core site of Plastic Raygun, intended as an experimental launcher for Plastic Raygun artists, music, and media projects.

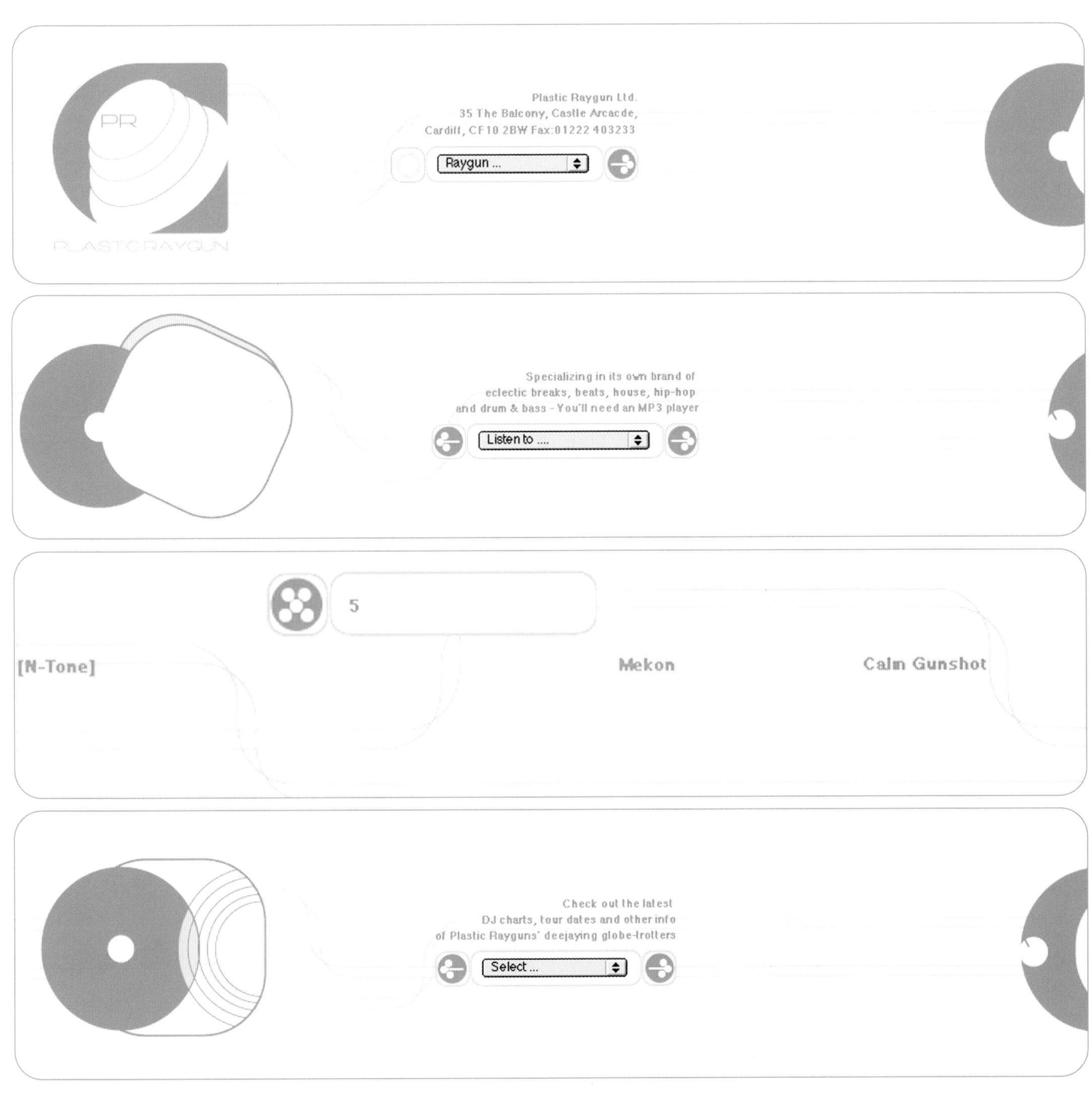
PR
PLASTICRAYGUN
Plastic Raygun Ltd.
35 The Balcony, Castle Arcade,
Cardiff, CF10 2BW Fax:01222 403233
Raygun ...
Specializing in its own brand of
eclectic breaks, beats, house, hip-hop
and drum & bass - You'll need an MP3 player
Listen to ....
5
[N-Tone]
Mekon
Calm Gunshot
Check out the latest
DJ charts, tour dates and other info
of Plastic Rayguns' deejaying globe-trotters
Select ...

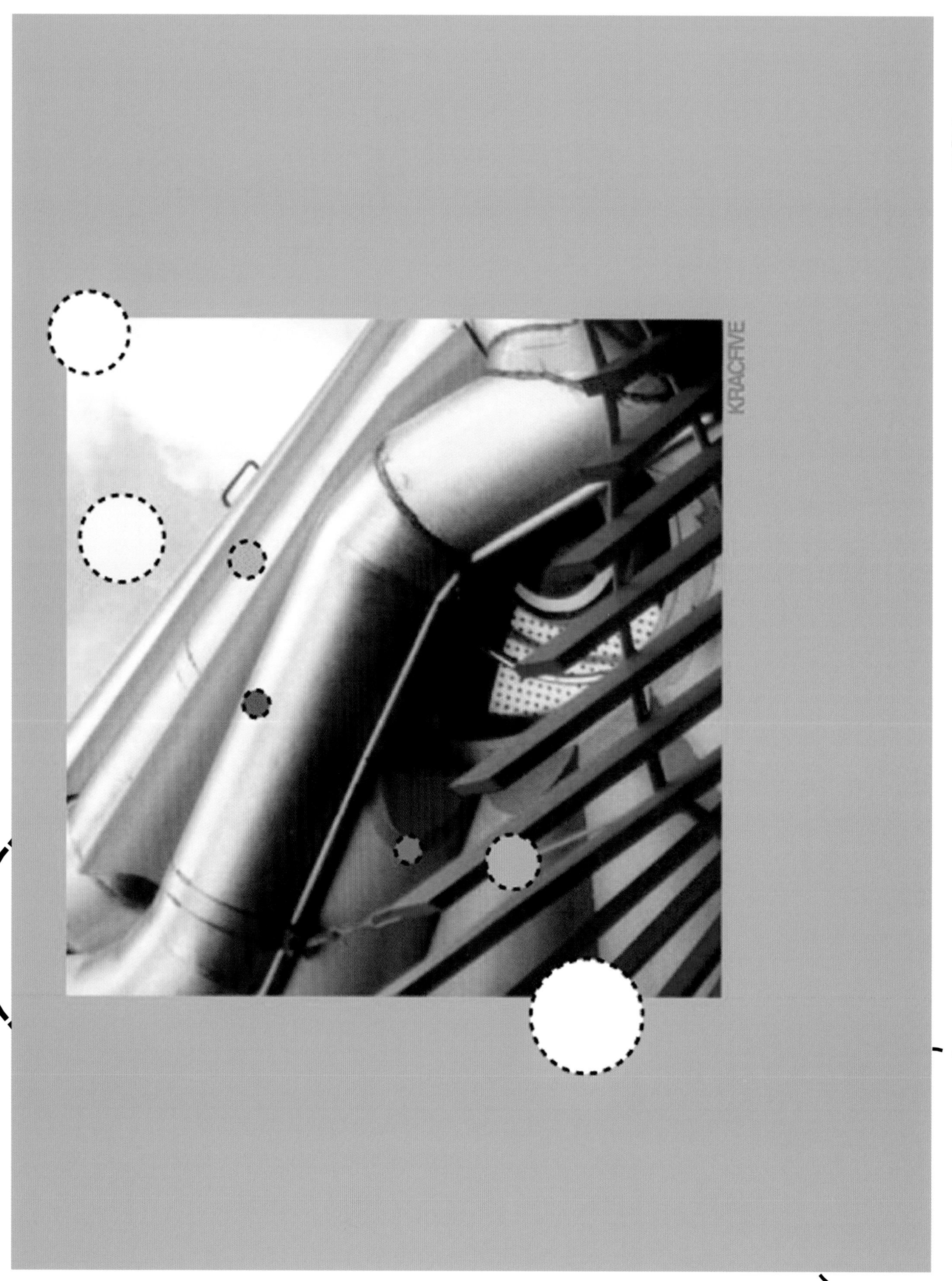
KRACRVE

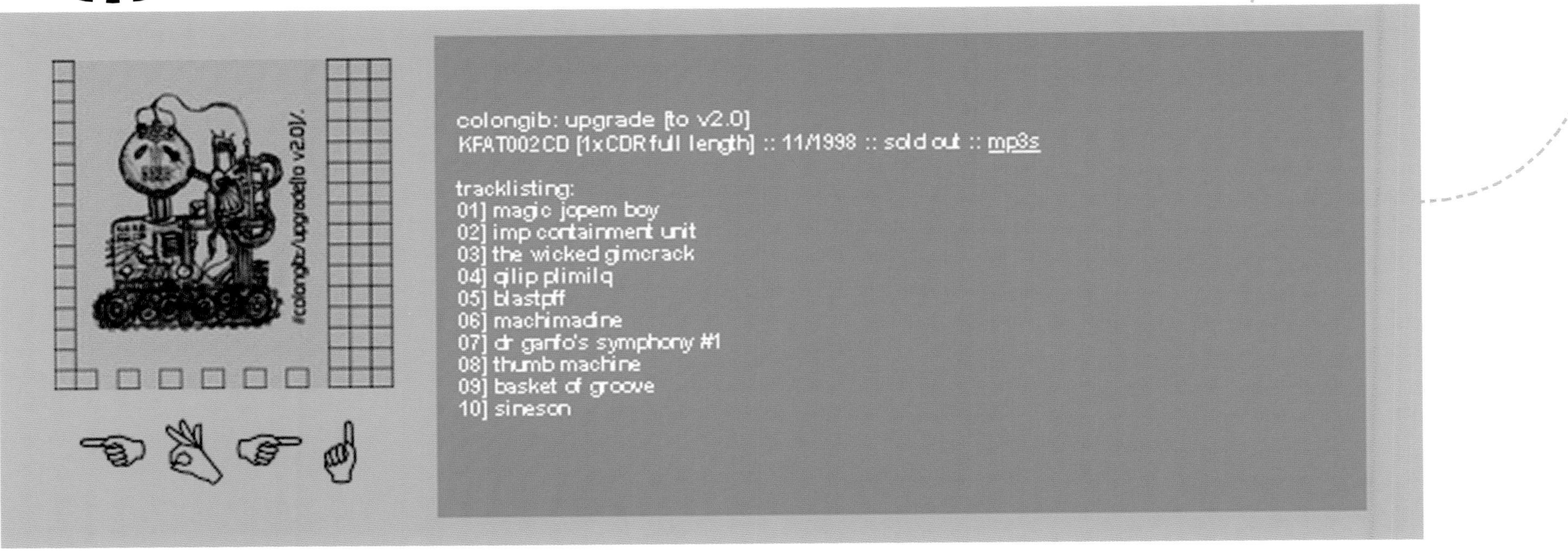

#colongib/upgrade[to v2.0]/.
colongib: upgrade [to v2.0]
KFAT002CD [1xCDR full length] :: 11/1998 :: sold out :: mp3s
tracklisting:
01] magic jopem boy
02] imp containment unit
03] the wicked gimcrack
04] qilip plimilq
05] blastpff
06] machimadine
07] dr garfo's symphony #1
08] thumb machine
09] basket of groove
10] sineson

<title>
Kracfive Musics

<web address>
www.kracfive.com

<client>
n/a

<design company>
Kracfive

<programs/software>
Photoshop, Illustrator,
GIF Movie Gear, Notepad

<number of pages>
n/a

<country of origin>
USA

<work description>
This site represents the Kracfive record label for experimental electronic music fans.

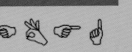

COLONGIB MAPPING MUSIC
colongib: mapping music
KFAT004CD :: [1xCD full length] :: 05/1999.
tracklisting / mp3 & realaudio samples:
01) buckshot [mp3]
02) dr. garfo and cousin dextah chillin' in the basement
03) giraffunkedgazz - colongib & miragliuolo
04) canoli kick [mp3]
05) fat_mat
06) retrigger
07) lolli seed [mp3]
08) lonely analog dog
09) sinedaddy
10) what map [mp3]

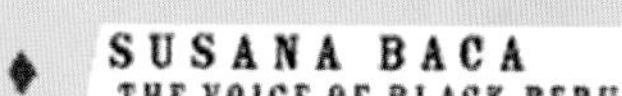

LABEL
ALL OUR DISCS
ARTISTS
COMPILATIONS
NEWS / TOURS
TOYBOX
SEARCH
ARTISTS
SUSANA BACA
THE VOICE OF BLACK PERU
WALDEMAR BASTOS
PRETALUZ
BLOQUE
PSYCHOTROPICAL FUNK FROM COLUMBIA
DAVID BYRNE
THE MAN WITH THE PLAN
CORNERSHOP
WESTERN ORIENTALS GOING FULL CIRCLE
GEGGY TAH
SOUTHERN CALIFORNIA'S ALTER-POP SCAVENGERS
KING CHANGO
HOUSE BAND OF THE URBAN PLANET
LOS AMIGOS INVISIBLES
THE NEW SOUND OF THE VENEZUELAN GOZADERA

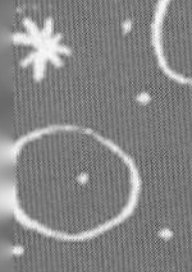

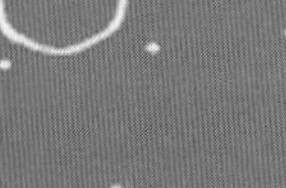

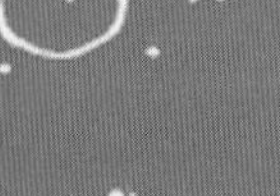
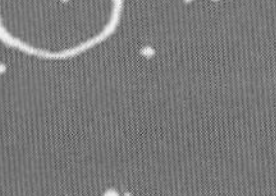
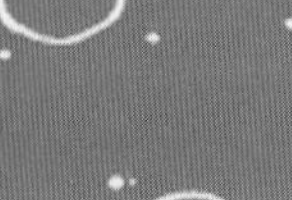
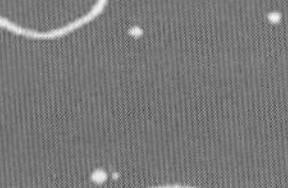

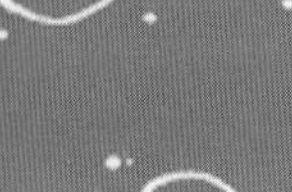
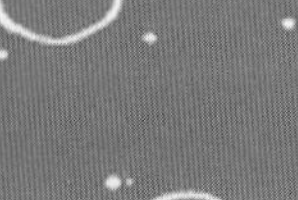
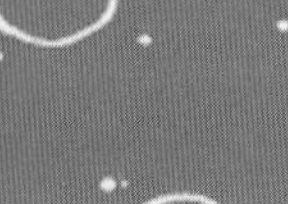
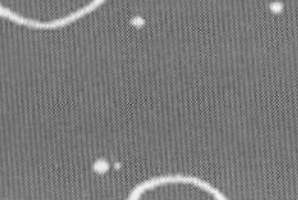
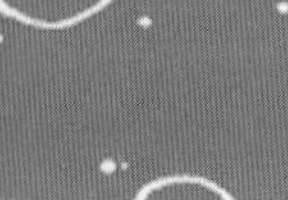
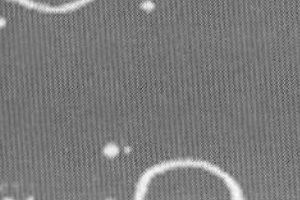

TOY BOX
LUAKA BOP
RADIO
LATIN MIX
BRAZILIAN MIX
LUAKA MIX
AFRICAN MIX
Do not attempt to adjust the horizontal. We have taken control of the vertical. Prepare to receive direct transmission from Luaka Bop radio — a 40-song stream of Luaka Bop artists, all killa, no filla. Tune in your Real Audio Player here. Your Real Audio panel will display the artist and song title. For all Luaka, all the time, start Real Audio and quit your browser. The entire Luaka Bop transmission will play while you get on with your life.
MP3
IS HERE!
LUAKA BOP PROUDLY PRESENTS: TEN FRESH TRACKS FROM OUR NEW SAMPLER, WE COME IN PEACE. SOME OF THESE

<title>
LuakaBop.com

<web address>
www.Luakabop.com

<client>
Luaka Bop

<design company>
Funny Garbage Inc.

<programs/software>
Photoshop, Illustrator, Streamline, GoLive, Dreamweaver, BBedit, Quicktime, Real Media Encoder

<number of pages>
540

<country of origin>
USA

<work description>
Luakabop.com is David Byrne's world music label website. It offers news, tours, and a discography for each of the Luaka Bop artists, as well as information about the label and a 'toy box' featuring Luaka Bop radio, mp3 downloads, comics and cool links. The site is designed to mirror Luaka Bop's quirky yet tasteful image.

<title>
Dial Rec

<web address>
www.dial-rec.de

<client>
Dial Rec

<design company>
www.sayimsorry.de

<programs/software>
Photoshop, Flash, Dreamweaver

<number of pages>
5

<country of origin>
Germany

<work description>
This site features the work of the Hamburg-based electronic music label Dial Rec. It contains an mp3 download section as well as news, links, and reviews of the latest releases.

made by sayimsorry.de

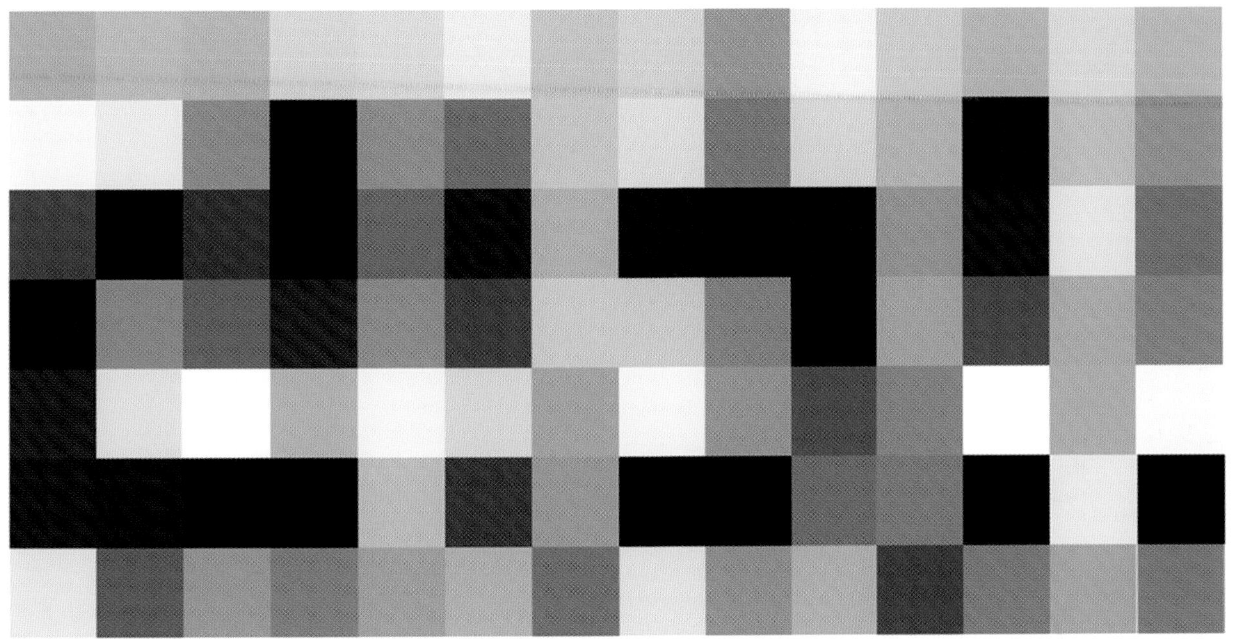

2000 © DIAL REC

HERE WE ARE NOW. COME IN AND FIND OUT. >

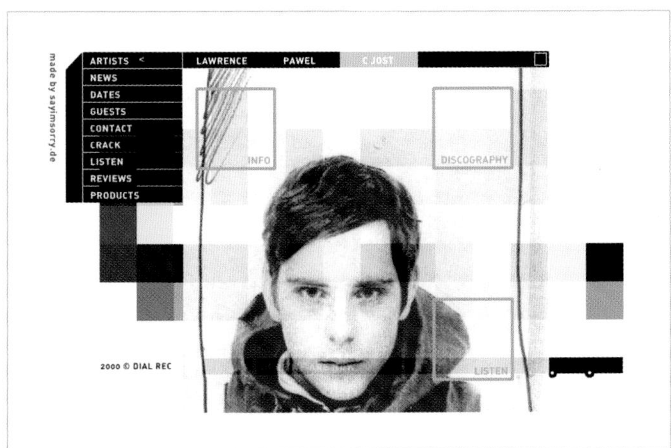

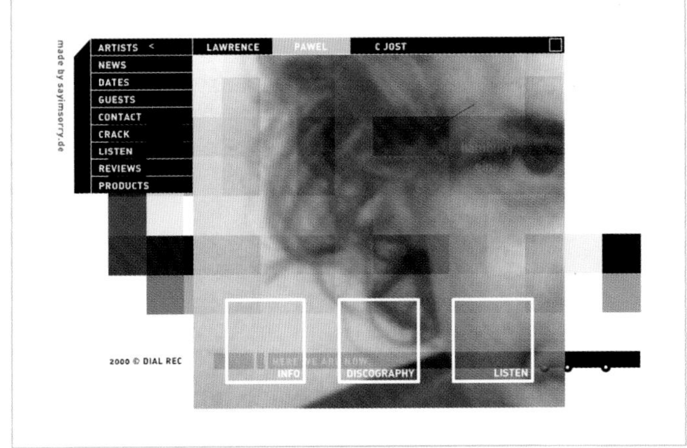

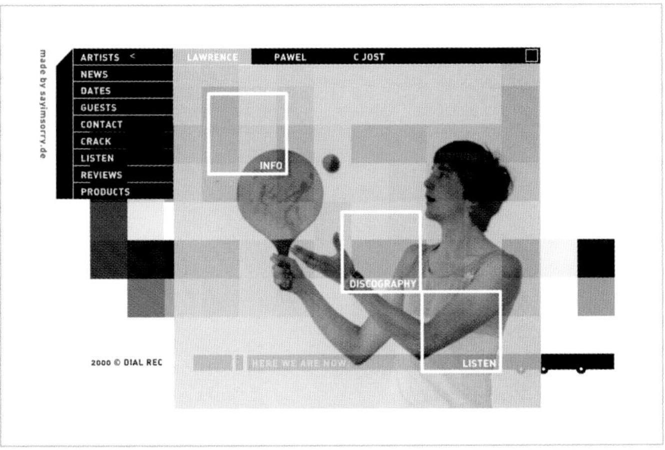

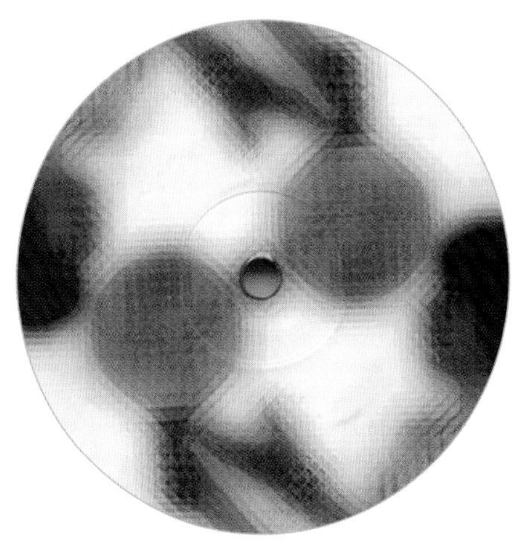

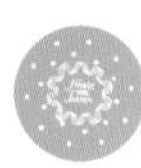

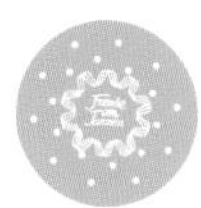

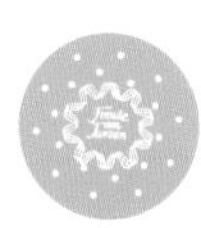

Freude am Tanzen

primaklimaclub

› GO

<title>
Freude am Tanzen

<web address>
www.freude-am-tanzen.com

<client>
Freude am Tanzen Kooperative

<design company>
Timespin GmbH

<programs/software>
Macromedia Freehand, Flash

<number of pages>
10

<country of origin>
Germany

Freude am Tanzen
wir feiern weiter

- FAT Philosophy
- FAT Booking
- FAT Events
- FAT Download
- FAT Contact

Our Guestbook

sessions | label | 12inch | merchandising | pictures | friends

<work description>
This site promotes the FAT music label and showcases all its music output.

Freude am Tanzen

FAT Philosophy

Freude am Tanzen - Wir schreiben das Jahr 5 nach -FAT-Kalender. Es ist Geburtstag! Aus einer dreieckigen Papiereinkaufstüte wurde vor Jahren ein Name ins Leben gerufen, der nun mehr fester Bestandteil anspruchsvoller Techno-House-Deep-Bass Veranstaltungen in Thüringen ist. Lasst uns erfreuen, denn eine gewisse Rafinesse, gepaart mit musikalischen Charme, charakterisieren seit Jahren -FAT-, bei der Umsetzung akustisch optischer Techno-House Präsentationen. Aus vielen kreativen Synonymen entstand eine Symbiose kreativen Schaffens, die heute aus -FAT- ein elektronisches Energiebündel, Partyorganisationsmotor und Finest DeepHouse Label gemacht haben. Wir feiern natürlich nicht alleine, sondern Ihr seit herzlich eingeladen, wenn es heisst: Party On und Spot an!

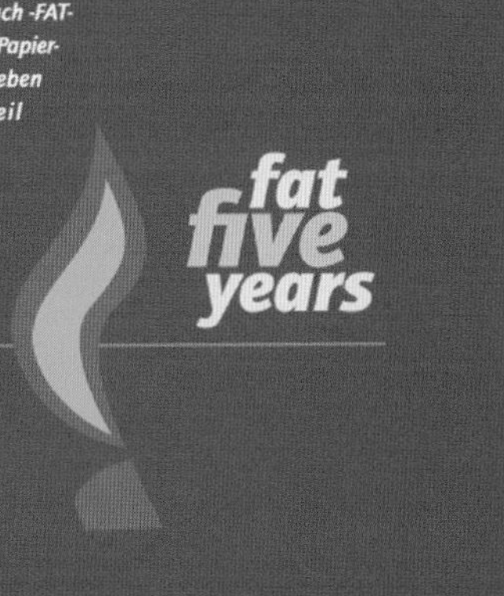

fat five years

<title>
Primaklimaclub

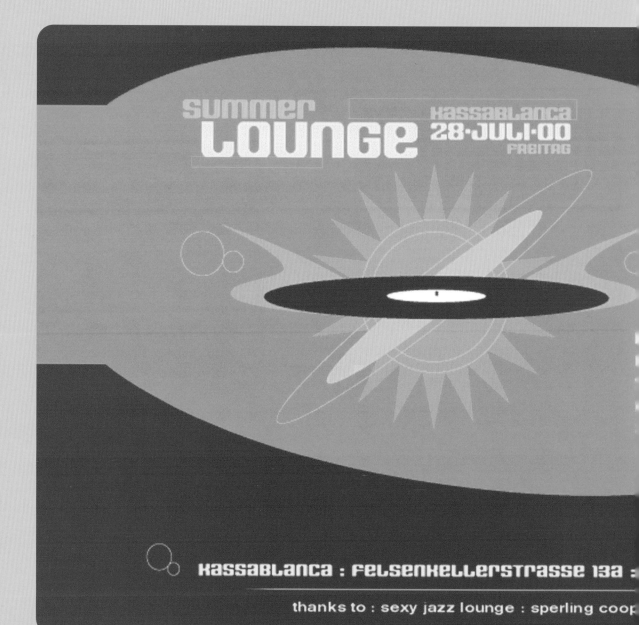

<web address>
www.primaklimaclub.ch

<client>
Primaklimaclub

<design company>
Timespin GmbH

<programs/software>
Macromedia Freehand, Flash

<number of pages>
6

<country of origin>
Germany

<work description>
This site promotes a small club in Jena, Germany. The flyer style includes dates, DJ details, and music.

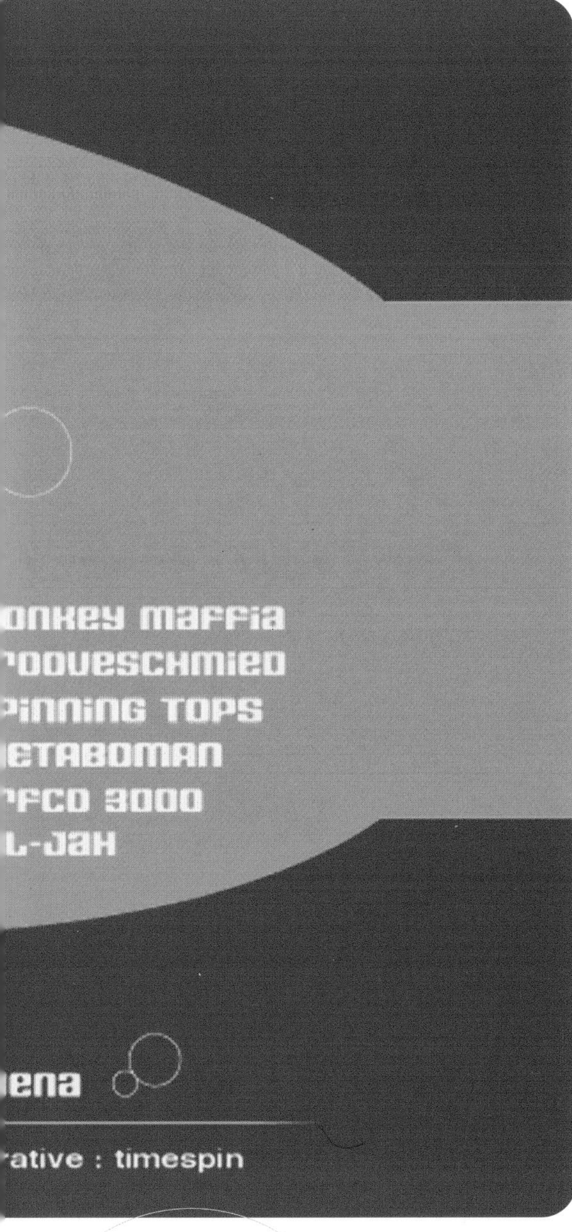
onkey maffia
roodueschmied
pinning tops
etaboman
fcd 3000
l-jah
ena
rative : timespin

primaklimaclub
freestile cowboys [berner oberland/ch]
elektro gabor
Freitag 22.00 Uhr
16[06]2000
die kleine quelle jena
triphop-sessions with sunshine ---- contact us ▶▶▶▶
primaklimaclub
royal downbeat heroes [nizza:cote.d.azur]
johannisstrasse 11
die kleine quelle jena

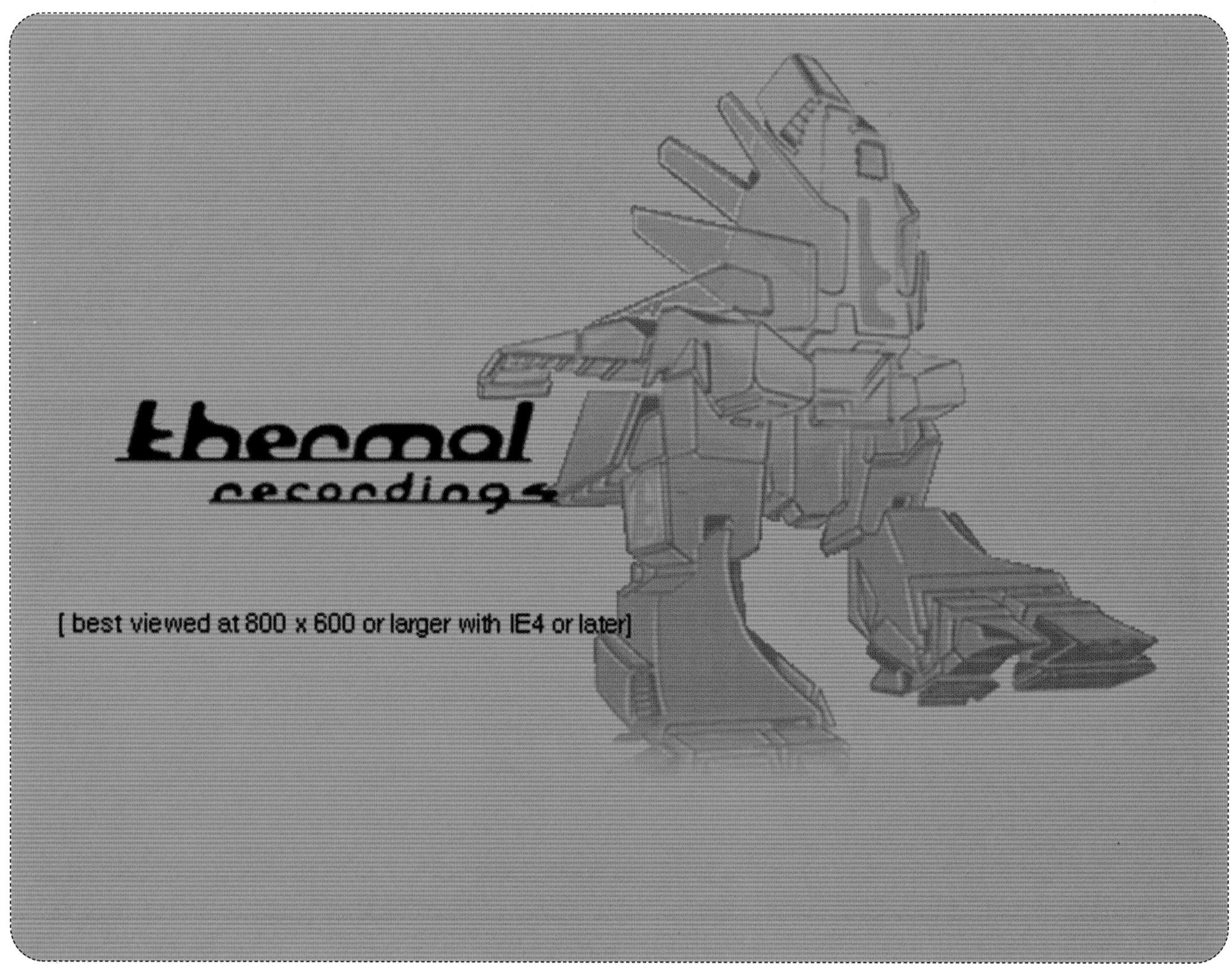

thermal
recordings
[best viewed at 800 x 600 or larger with IE4 or later]

<title>
Thermal Recordings

<web address>
www.thermalrecordings.com

<client>
Thermal Recordings

<designer>
Ian Loyd

<programs/software>
Flash, Homesite,
Photoshop, Fireworks

<number of pages>
106

<country of origin>
USA

<work description>
This site promotes the Thermal record label and acts as a showcase for all its products.

DRUM&BASSARENA
ESTABLISHED 1996_UPDATED DAILY
>>click here to step into the arena <<

<title>
Drum & Bass Arena

<web address>
www.breakbeat.co.uk

<client>
Art Empire Industries Ltd

<design companyr>
The Designers Republic

<programs/software>
Freehand, Photoshop, Dreamweaver, PFE, Fireworks

<number of pages>
600+

<country of origin>
UK

<work description>
The most up-to-date drum and bass site on the web featuring video and audio clips, live web-casts, and a host of interactive dialogs and forums.

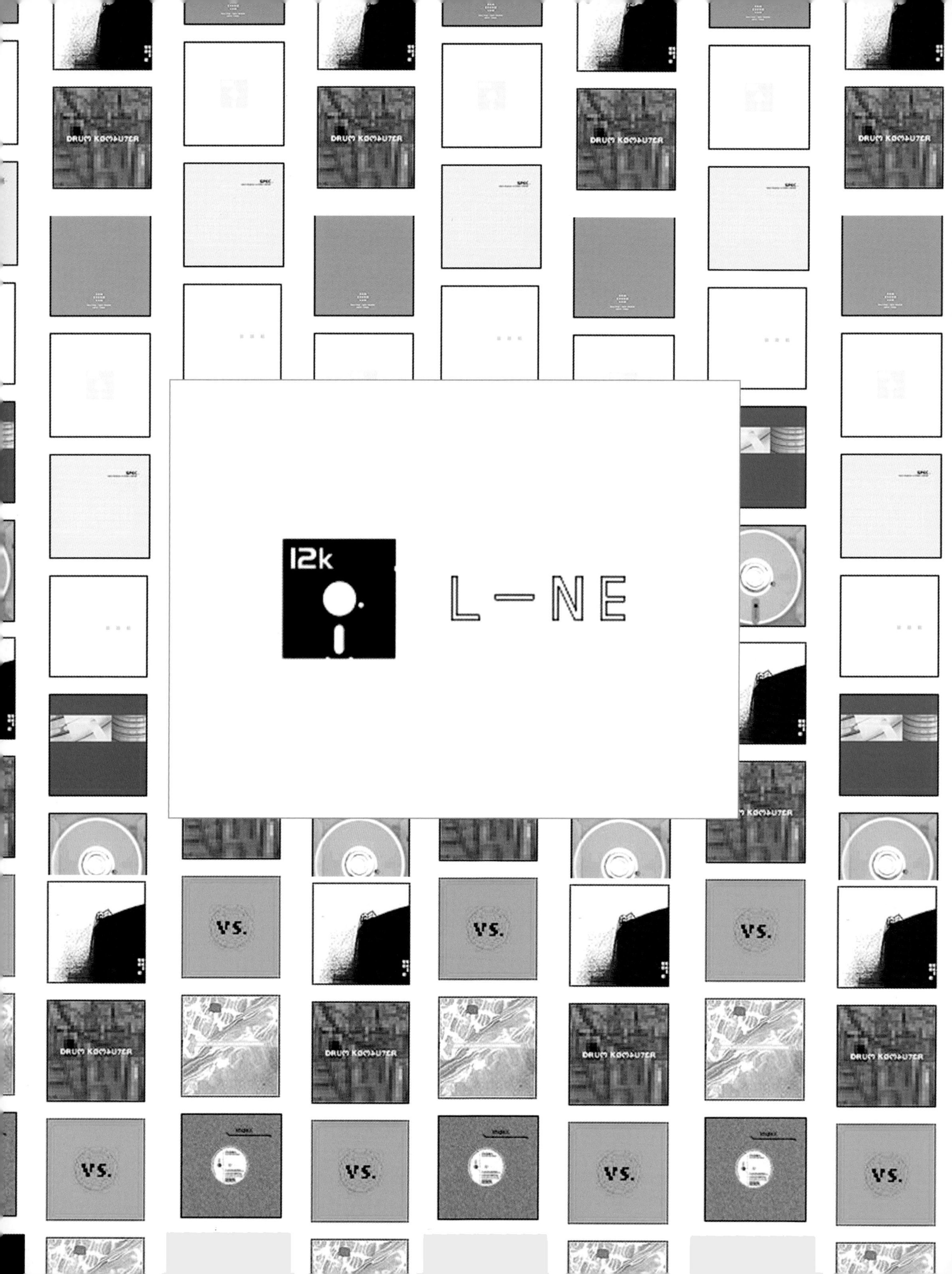
12k
L—NE
DRUM KOMPUTER
VS.

CATALOG
CONTACT
EVENTS
FEEDBACK
LINKS
MISSION
NEWS.ARCHIVE
PRESS
SOUND
STUDIO
WHERE.TO.BUY

●●●

TAYLOR DEUPREE:
BIO
DISCOGRAPHY

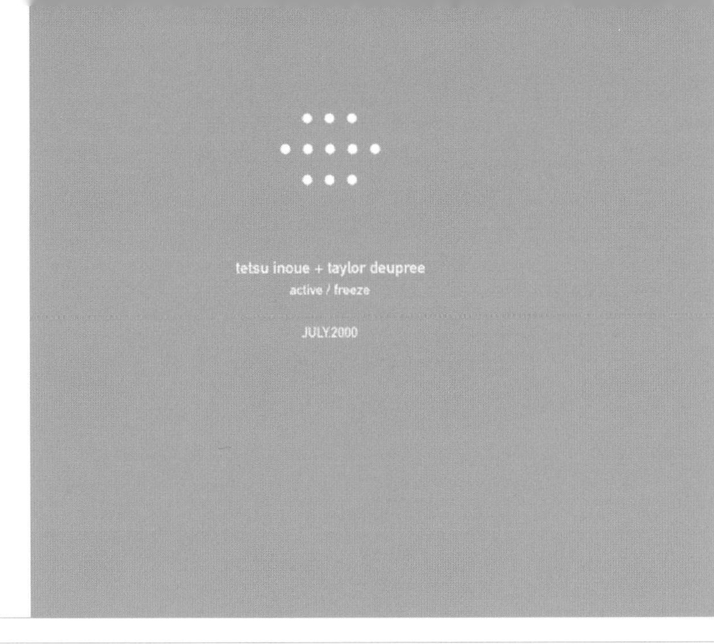

tetsu inoue + taylor deupree
active / freeze
JULY.2000

CATALOG
CONTACT
EVENTS
FEEDBACK
LINKS
MISSION
NEWS.ARCHIVE
PRESS
SOUND
STUDIO
WHERE.TO.BUY

●●●

TAYLOR DEUPREE:
BIO
DISCOGRAPHY

taylor deupree:
taylor deupree is a 29 year-old musician and graphic designer residing in brooklyn, new york. on january 1st, 1997 he founded his label, 12k, and now uses it as the home-base and focus for his creative energy. in the course of the last 3 years taylor and 12k's increasingly refined sonic mission has been to push the boundaries of minimal, ultrasynthetic sound art. he coined the term "microscopic sound" to describe these tonal experiments in frequency and rhythm and carries out his sound design and compsing using a mixture of analog modular synthesizers and the latest software audio programs.

besides releasing music on 12k taylor records for a number of other labels including ritornell/mille plateaux, raster music (germany), föllt (ireland), and audio.nl (netherlands). in addition, over the past 7 years he has recorded albums for instinct records, caipirinha music, plastic city (usa), disko b (germany), and dum (finland).

taylor has received much critical acclaim and recognition for his past musical projects including the techno and ambient sounds of prototype 909, SETI, human mesh dance, and futique and has many recording accomplishments and a substantial discography under his belt. he now, however, focuses his energy on 12k, solo productions under his own name, networking with a family of like-minded sound artists, and the furthering of his tiny sound experiments.

CATALOG
→ CONTACT
EVENTS
FEEDBACK
LINKS
MISSION
NEWS.ARCHIVE
PRESS
SOUND
STUDIO
WHERE.TO.BUY

●●●

TAYLOR DEUPREE:
BIO
DISCOGRAPHY

aquasphere
THE AQUASPHERE IS THE 12K RECORDING
IT IS LOCATED IN BROOKLYN, NEW YORK
THE LOGO IS THE CHINESE CHARACTER FOR 'WATER'

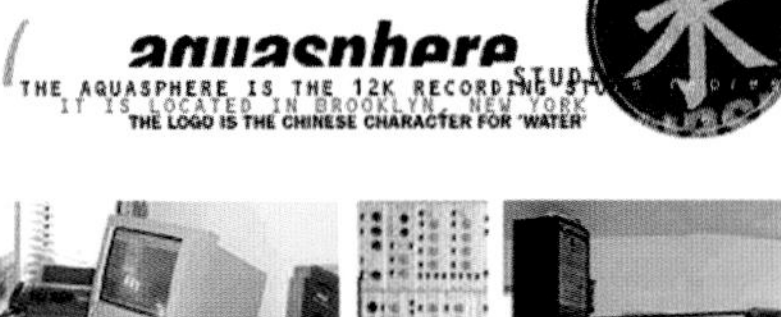

<title>
12K

<web address>
www.12k.com

<designer>
Taylor Deupree

<programs/software>
Cyberstudio, Homepage, Fireworks, Photoshop

<number of pages>
20+

<country of origin>
USA

<work description>
This is the official homepage for the 12K label from New York specializing in minimal, experimental electronic microsounds.

12k1
12k1 12k1 12k1 12k1 12k1 12k1 12k1 12k1 12k1 12k1 12k1 12k1 12k1 12k1 12k1 12k1 12k1 12k1 12k1 12k1 12k1 12k1 12k1 12k1 12k1 12k1 12k1 12k1

<title>
Badboyonline

<web address>
www.badboyonline.com

<client>
Bad Boy Entertainment

<design company>
Kioken Inc

<programs/software>
Photoshop, Flash.

<number of pages>
n/a

<country of origin>
USA

<work description>
This is the official website for Puff Daddy's Bad Boy label, designed to promote all the new and current releases with videos, audio clips, merchandise, and interactive fans' pages.

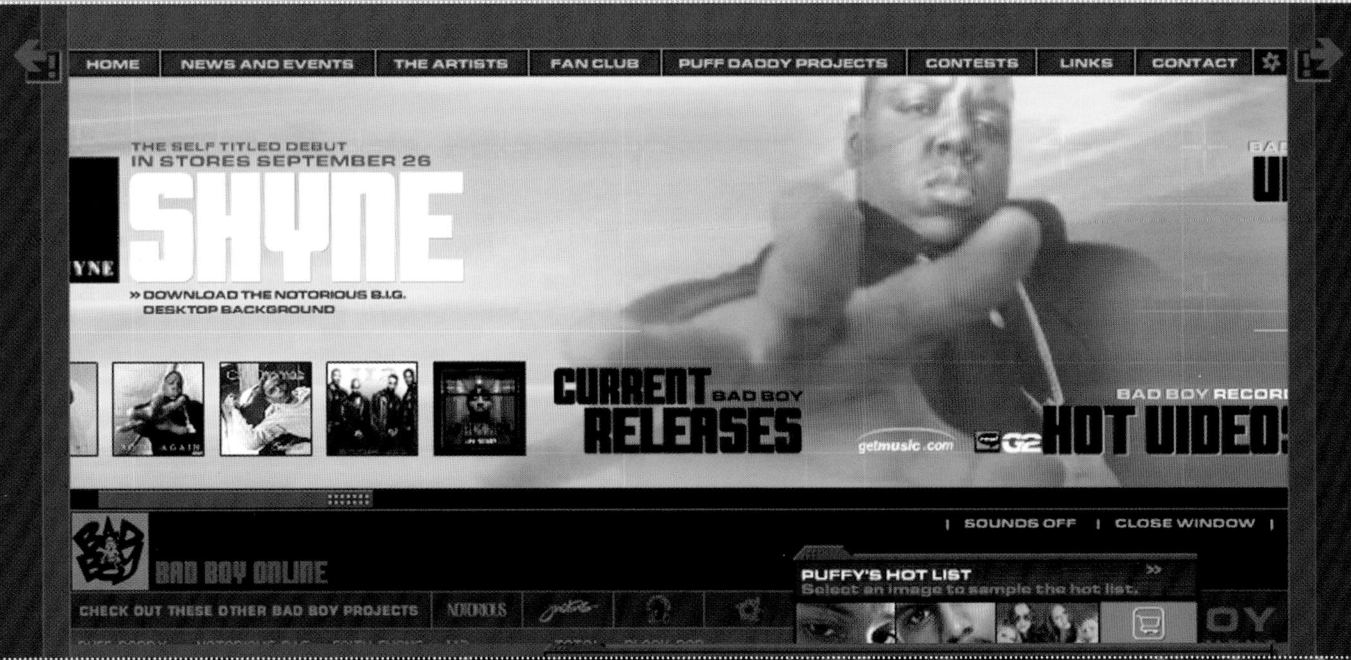
HOME
NEWS AND EVENTS
THE ARTISTS
FAN CLUB
PUFF DADDY PROJECTS
CONTESTS
LINKS
CONTACT
THE SELF TITLED DEBUT
IN STORES SEPTEMBER 26
SHYNE
» DOWNLOAD THE NOTORIOUS B.I.G.
DESKTOP BACKGROUND
CURRENT BAD BOY RELEASES
BAD BOY RECORDS
HOT VIDEOS
getmusic.com
SOUNDS OFF
CLOSE WINDOW
BAD BOY ONLINE
PUFFY'S HOT LIST
Select an image to sample the hot list.
CHECK OUT THESE OTHER BAD BOY PROJECTS

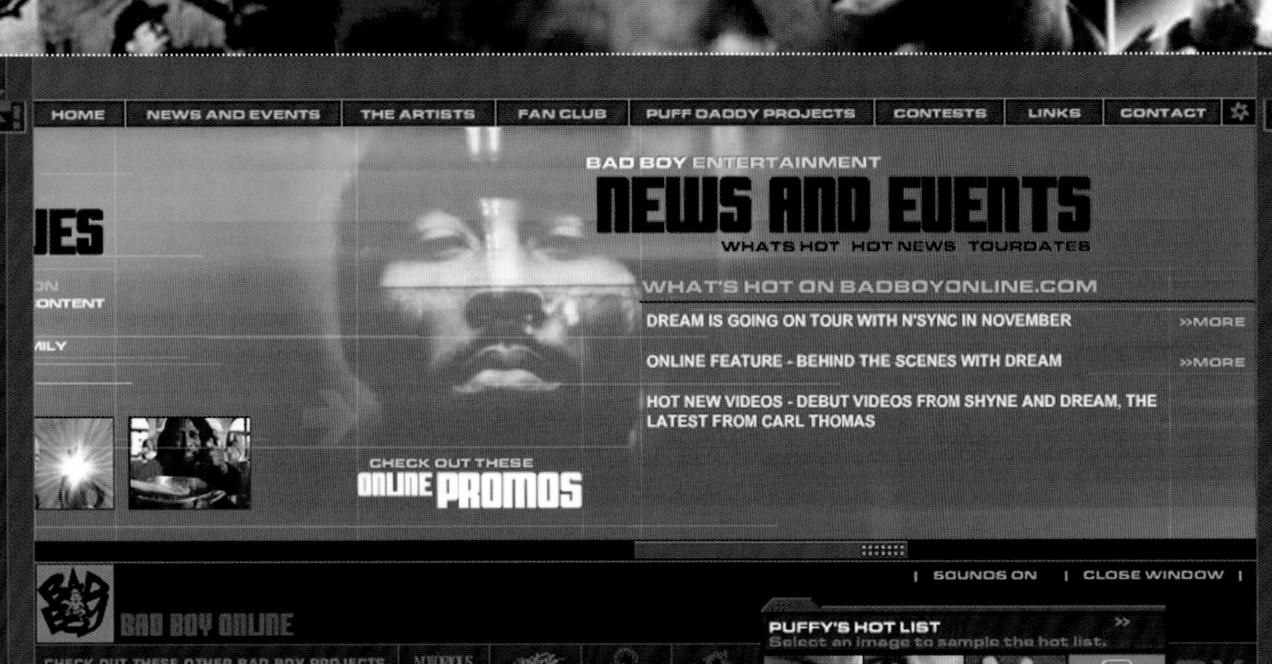
HOME
NEWS AND EVENTS
THE ARTISTS
FAN CLUB
PUFF DADDY PROJECTS
CONTESTS
LINKS
CONTACT
BAD BOY ENTERTAINMENT
NEWS AND EVENTS
WHATS HOT HOT NEWS TOURDATES
WHAT'S HOT ON BADBOYONLINE.COM
DREAM IS GOING ON TOUR WITH N'SYNC IN NOVEMBER
>>MORE
ONLINE FEATURE - BEHIND THE SCENES WITH DREAM
>>MORE
HOT NEW VIDEOS - DEBUT VIDEOS FROM SHYNE AND DREAM, THE LATEST FROM CARL THOMAS
CHECK OUT THESE
ONLINE PROMOS
SOUNDS ON
CLOSE WINDOW
BAD BOY ONLINE
PUFFY'S HOT LIST
Select an image to sample the hot list.
CHECK OUT THESE OTHER BAD BOY PROJECTS

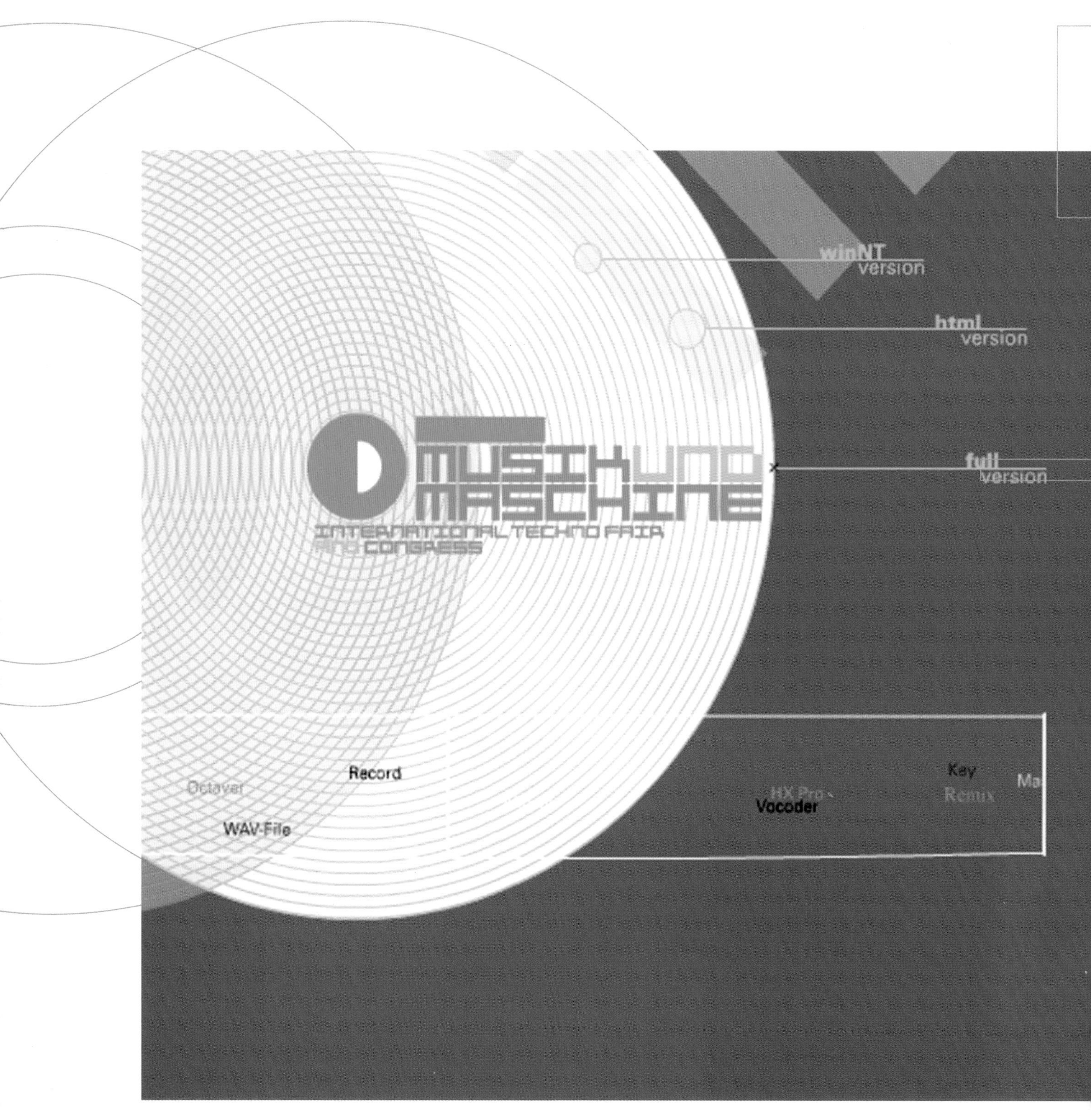

<title>
Musik und Maschine - International Fair and Congress

<web address>
www.musikundmaschine.com

<client>
Musik und Maschine GmbH

<design company>
Realities United

<programs/software>
HTML, Flash

<number of pages>
n/a

<country of origin>
Germany

<work description>
This site provides an interactive and social platform for members of the techno music community.

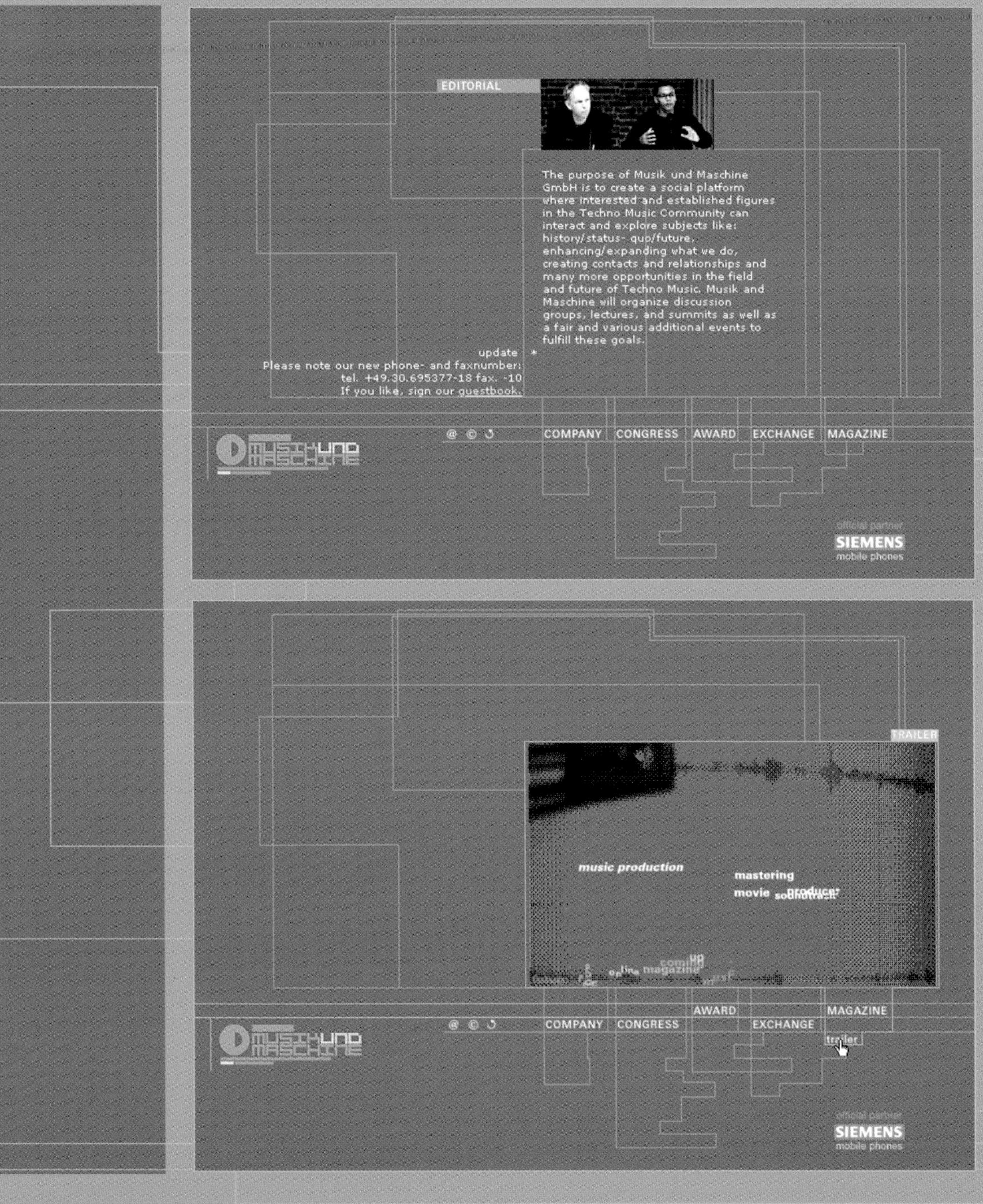
EDITORIAL
The purpose of Musik und Maschine GmbH is to create a social platform where interested and established figures in the Techno Music Community can interact and explore subjects like: history/status- quo/future, enhancing/expanding what we do, creating contacts and relationships and many more opportunities in the field and future of Techno Music. Musik and Maschine will organize discussion groups, lectures, and summits as well as a fair and various additional events to fulfill these goals.
update *
Please note our new phone- and faxnumber:
tel. +49.30.695377-18 fax. -10
If you like, sign our guestbook.
MUSIK UND MASCHINE
COMPANY
CONGRESS
AWARD
EXCHANGE
MAGAZINE
official partner
SIEMENS
mobile phones
TRAILER
music production
mastering
movie
COMPANY
CONGRESS
AWARD
EXCHANGE
MAGAZINE
trailer
official partner
SIEMENS
mobile phones

popstar
onlybasicfeaturesavailablefornow

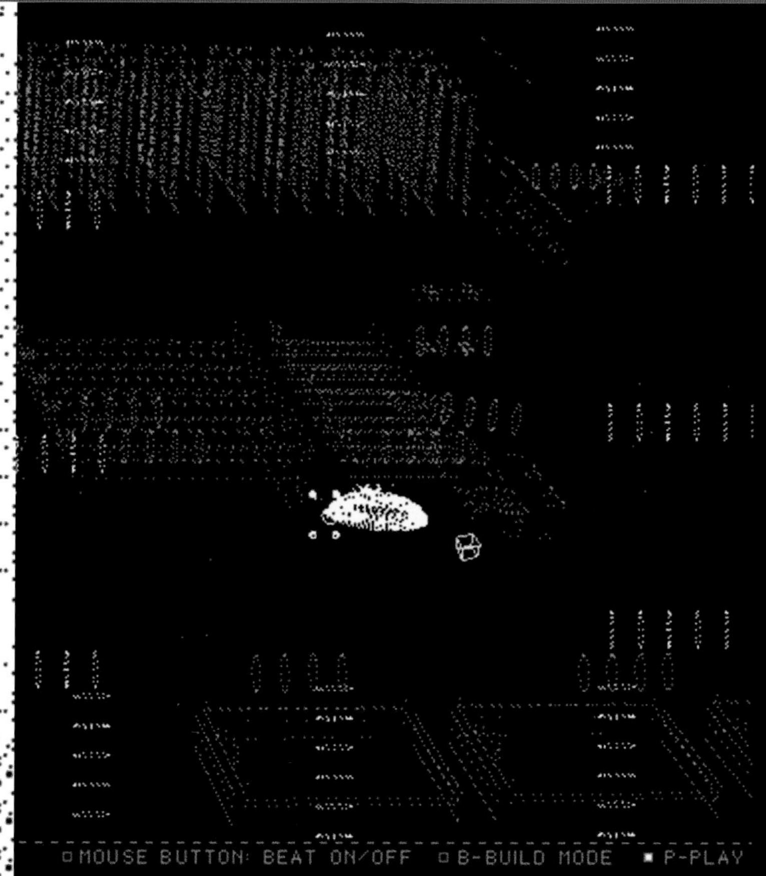
MOUSE BUTTON: BEAT ON/OFF
B-BUILD MODE
P-PLAY

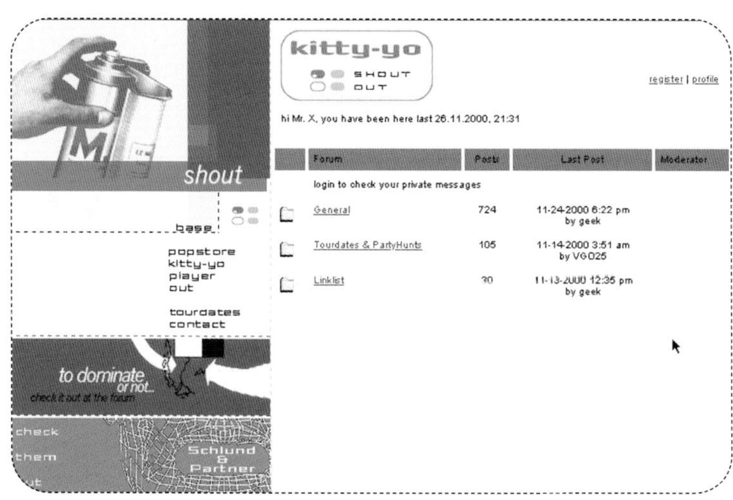

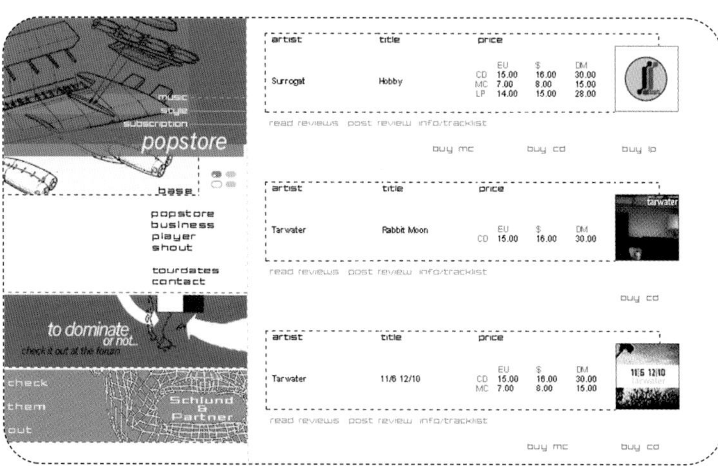

<title>
Kitty-Yo

<web address>
www.kitty-yo.de

<client>
Kitty-Yo

<design company>
Gosub Communications

<programs/software>
Photoshop, Homesite, Director, Shockwave

<number of pages>
30+

<country of origin>
Germany

<work description>
This is the official website for showcasing artists and releases on the Kitty-Yo label.

<title>
sonar2000 - International Festival of Advanced Music and Multimedia Art of Barcelona.

<web address>
www.sonar.es

<client>
Advanced Music

<designer/design company>
Lamosca

<programs/software>
Adobe Photoshop

<number of pages>
40

<country of origin>
Spain

<work description>
The promotional site for the international multimedia advanced music festival in Barcelona provides information with simple iconographic navigation.

sónar 2000

SONAR 2000 LATEST NEWS

ya.com

SONAR'2000 VIRTUAL VERSION

FRIDAY 12PM I SATURDAY 9PM
AT 40 PRINCIPALES

SonarClub 40

14.06.2000 HYMNEN
KARLHEINZ STOCKHAUSEN

Three days and three nights in touch with the most up-to-date developments and featuring the most relevant national and international artists. SONAR presents more than 250 activities: 50 concerts, more than 70 DJs, 90 titles projected at the SonarCinema and 60 works in every multimedia format: interactive capsules, installations, CD-Roms, Net art

SONAR is the obligatory meeting point for an alert public, cutting-edge artists and the most influential professionals from the sectors of music and modern arts.

TICKETS NOW ON SALE I CONCERTS & DJ'S I SONARDAY I SONARNIGHT

<sonar94 <sonar95 <sonar96 <sonar97 <sonar98 <sonar99

sonar2000 > .15th.16th.17th june > Barcelona

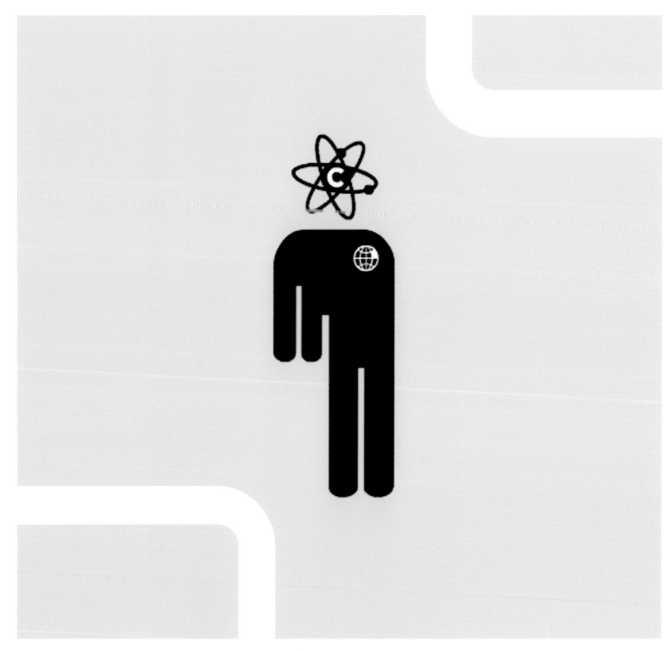

<title>
Caipirinha Productions

<web address>
www.caipirinha.com

<client>
Caipirinha Productions

<designers>
Taylor Deupree (concept, layout)
Aric R. Gutnick (Flash animations)
Michael Edwards (online shop creator)
Andrea Troager (online shop creator)

<programs/software>
Adobe GoLive, Allaire Homesite, Claris Home Page, Flash, Illustrator, Microsoft Visual Interdev, Photoshop, PICO, Secure CRT, UNIX PERL, Vi

<number of pages>
130+

<country of origin>
USA

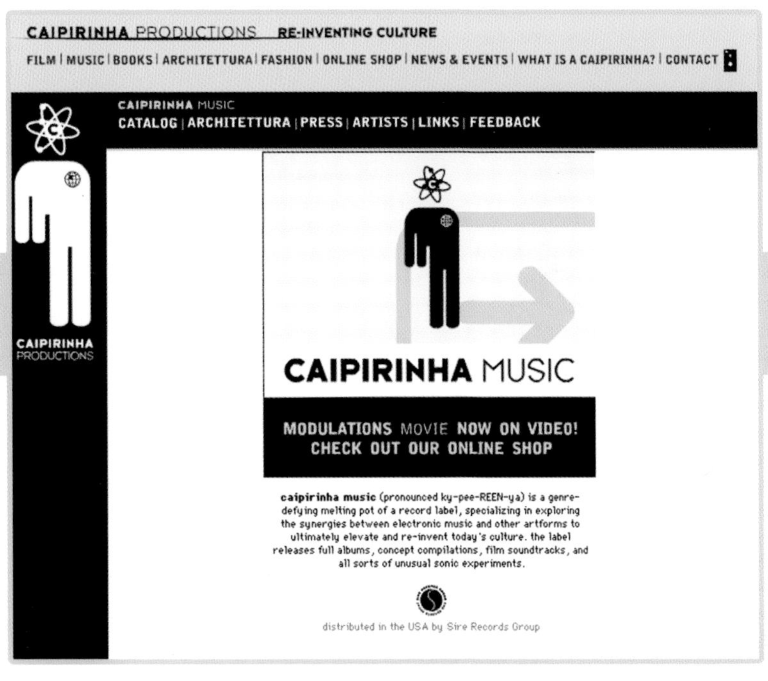

CAIPIRINHA PRODUCTIONS RE-INVENTING CULTURE
FILM | MUSIC | BOOKS | ARCHITETTURA | FASHION | ONLINE SHOP | NEWS & EVENTS | WHAT IS A CAIPIRINHA? | CONTACT
CAIPIRINHA MUSIC
CATALOG | ARCHITETTURA | PRESS | ARTISTS | LINKS | FEEDBACK
CAIPIRINHA PRODUCTIONS
CAIPIRINHA MUSIC
MODULATIONS MOVIE NOW ON VIDEO!
CHECK OUT OUR ONLINE SHOP
caipirinha music (pronounced ky-pee-REEN-ya) is a genre-defying melting pot of a record label, specializing in exploring the synergies between electronic music and other artforms to ultimately elevate and re-invent today's culture. the label releases full albums, concept compilations, film soundtracks, and all sorts of unusual sonic experiments.
distributed in the USA by Sire Records Group

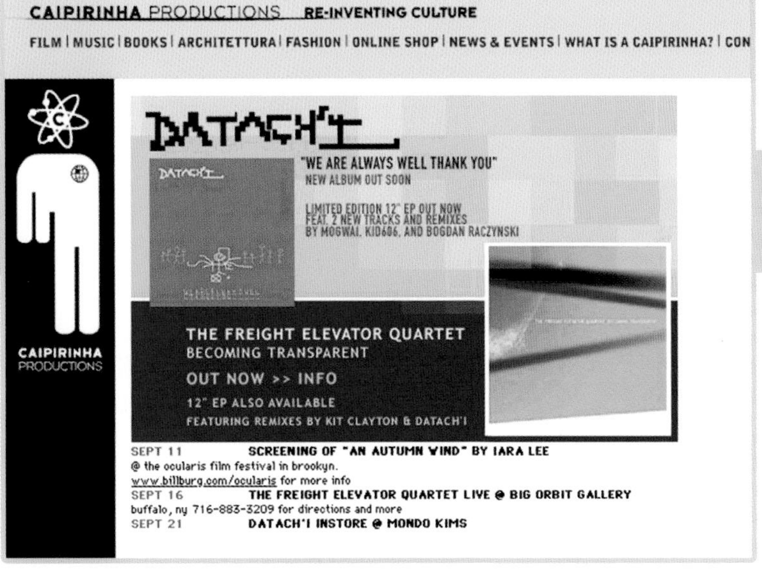

CAIPIRINHA PRODUCTIONS RE-INVENTING CULTURE
FILM | MUSIC | BOOKS | ARCHITETTURA | FASHION | ONLINE SHOP | NEWS & EVENTS | WHAT IS A CAIPIRINHA? | CON
CAIPIRINHA PRODUCTIONS
DATACH'I
"WE ARE ALWAYS WELL THANK YOU"
NEW ALBUM OUT SOON
LIMITED EDITION 12" EP OUT NOW
FEAT. 2 NEW TRACKS AND REMIXES
BY MOGWAI, KID606, AND BOGDAN RACZYNSKI
THE FREIGHT ELEVATOR QUARTET
BECOMING TRANSPARENT
OUT NOW >> INFO
12" EP ALSO AVAILABLE
FEATURING REMIXES BY KIT CLAYTON & DATACH'I
SEPT 11 SCREENING OF "AN AUTUMN WIND" BY IARA LEE
@ the ocularis film festival in brookyn.
www.billburg.com/ocularis for more info
SEPT 16 THE FREIGHT ELEVATOR QUARTET LIVE @ BIG ORBIT GALLERY
buffalo, ny 716-883-3209 for directions and more
SEPT 21 DATACH'I INSTORE @ MONDO KIMS

<work description>

Caipirinha Productions is a multimedia company with activities in film production, music, architecture, and book projects. The Caipirinha record label focuses on electronic music and its synergies with other art forms. The Caipirinha Productions website hosts information about the films and their screening schedules as well as video clips from the films, and audio samples from the CD catalog.

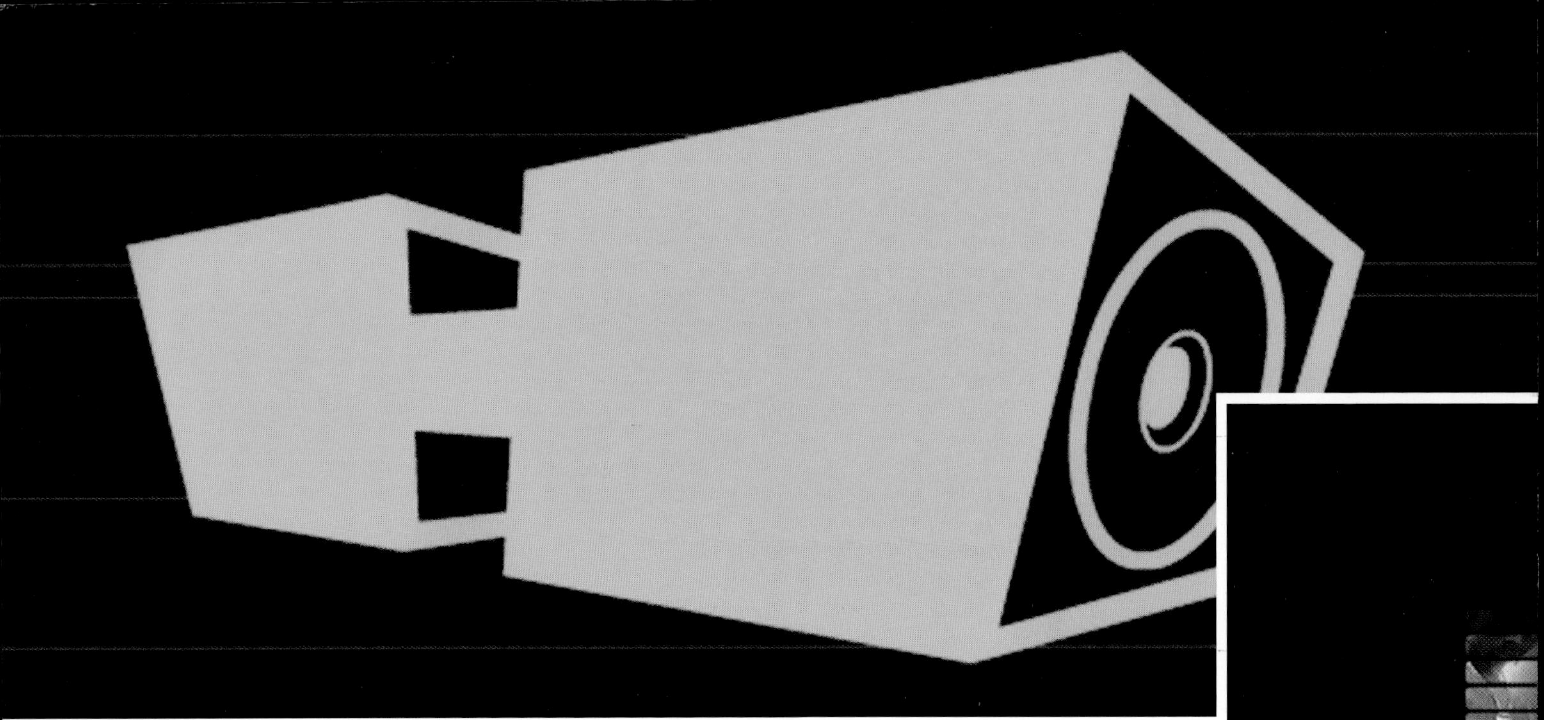

<title>
Hookt.com

<web address>
www.hookt.com

<client>
n/a

<design company>
Oven Digital

<programs/software>
Flash

<number of pages>
about 100

<country of origin>
USA

<work description>
This online magazine showcases hip-hop music, with news, features, webcasts, interactive dialog, and online shopping.

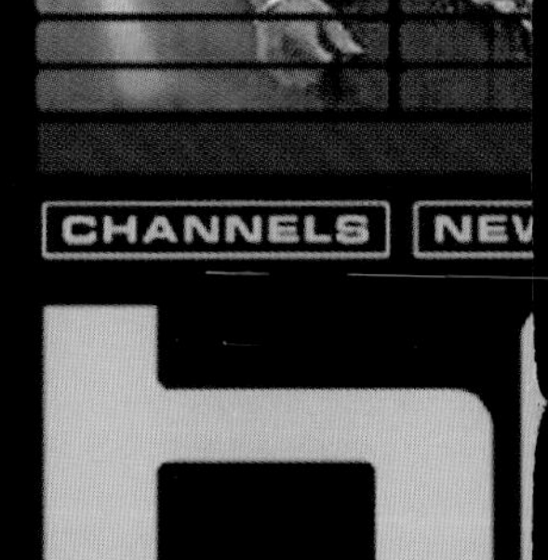

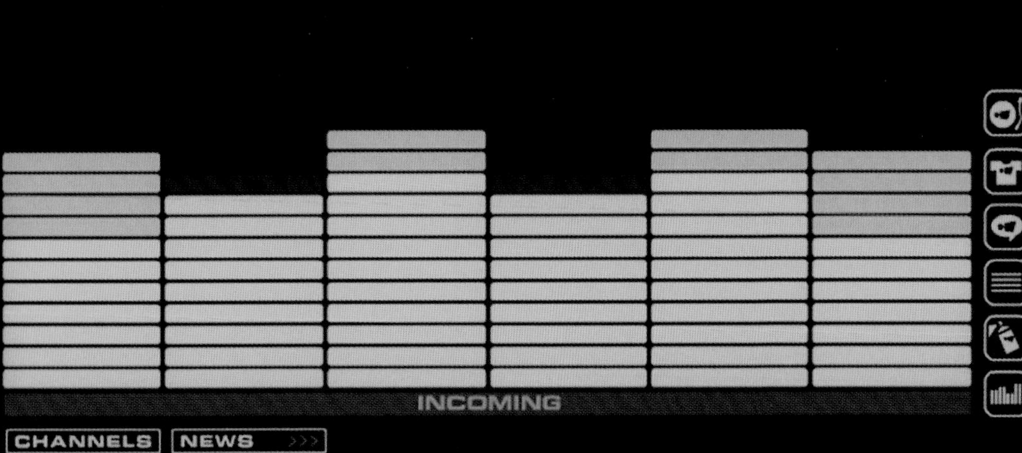

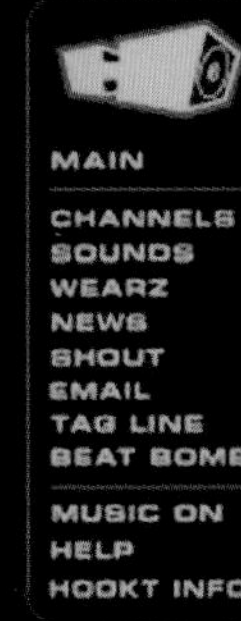

LiL' W
>>>
OOKt ©
HOP

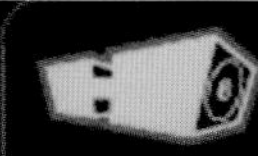
MAIN
CHANNELS
SOUNDS
WEARZ
NEWS
SHOUT
EMAIL
TAG LINE
BEAT BOMB
MUSIC ON
HELP
HOOKT INFO

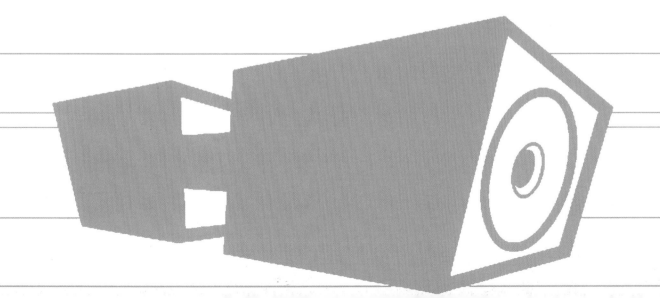

<title>
Urban Sounds

<web address>
www.urbansounds.com

<client>
Urban Sounds

<designer>
Maria Kacmarek

<programs/software>
Adobe Photoshop, BBedit, Adobe Illustrator

number of pages>
200+

<country of origin>
USA

<work description>
Urban Sounds is a collective of writers, web developers, artists, designers, composers, musicians and DJs. The site acts as an online magazine offering an interactive forum for open discussion and the exploration of a broad range of electronic music.

ELECTRONIC MUSIC AND BEYOND

urbansounds

volume 2 > issue 1

the minimal issue

Thumbnail Music || Six artists talk about minimalism >>

Minimalism Towards Transcendence || Tracing the impulse to reduce through the ages >>

Funkstörung || What to expect next from the Munich duo >>

Carl Finlow || Taking electro fast into the future >>

DJ Mixes || Streaming DJ mixes from around the world >>

New Releases || Reviews and audio clips of all our latest picks >>

||| thumbnailmusic SIX ARTISTS TALK ABOUT MINIMALISM

Minimal techno is well-tuned to our cultural moment, encasing repetitive tone fragments in ultra-refined structures both detached and strangely invigorating. But how related are the various strains of minimalism's proliferating series? Urban Sounds asked six practitioners of zero-state music. Interviews and introduction by Philip Sherburne

>> minimalismtowardstranscendence

Tracing the impulse to reduce through the ages. From Eastern religions to high technology, to modernist painting and the Bauhaus, simplicity and necessity rule. By Bryce Churchill

||| funkstörung

Munich's "radio noise"-makers talk about their video project, a new fascination for computers, and what to expect next from their Musik aus Strom label. By Jeff Davis

||| carlfinlow

Proliferating pseudonyms like a professional thief, Leeds-based Voice Stealer Carl Finlow is dragging electro kicking and screaming into the future. By Sean Cooper

Funkstörung

Taking their brand of electronic disruption **to the next level**

features
new releases
dj mixes
links
about us

JEFF DAVIS ||| Munich's Funkstörung crept down into the dance music underground in the early '90s with a six-pack blitz of 12-inches appearing all at once through the Acid Planet, Bunker, and Inter-Ferred Communications labels. Extremely limited prior to a 1999 repress, Acid Planets 11 through 14 and Bunker 24 were fairly basic Lowlands gutter acid, but the Funkstörung LP *Artificial Garbage* hinted at a level of sophistication and ingenuity that would engage increasing numbers of listeners into the latter part of the decade. Through the group's Musik aus Strom label -- begun by Michael Fakesch, a student, and Chris de Luca, owner of Munich's Delerium record store, to release their "favorite music" -- more than a dozen EPs have appeared, packaged in distinctively stamped cardboard sleeves, and including two Funkstörung releases, three solo Fakesch records, a solo de Luca EP, two collaborations between Fakesch and Andre Esterman (as AEMic), and several releases by new or relatively unknown artists. Each release has been a quality outing, with the common thread of musical fracture taking abstraction to new levels while maintaining a subtle melodic balance.

As Funkstörung gained critical acclaim, a diverse spread of artists ranging from Björk to Faust to Wu Tang Clan were courageous enough to commission remixes for the group, with full knowledge that little of their original tracks were likely to remain. The best of the groups's growing catalog of remixes was compiled onto their debut LP, *Additional Productions*, released by Studio !K7 earlier this year. Soon after, !K7 and local support networks organized a limited North American tour, with stops in Miami, Los Angeles, Chicago, and San Francisco, among others. Playing nearly a show a day for just under two weeks, the group's brief summer jaunt was a welcome invasion for a growing legion of supporters who have longed for a live demonstration of the Funkstörung gestalt. Urban Sounds caught up with Fakesch before the group's Cleveland show, and then wrapped up once the tour was complete, to discuss what's on the collective Funkstörung brain and what the future might hold. Photography | Johnathan Haugh.

not simple fl

features
new releases
electro
ambient
downtempo
drum'n'bass
techno + house
experimental + idm
dj mixes
links
about us

not simple floor bangers

urbansounds

<title>
Minus Inc.

<web address>
www.m-nus.com

<client>
Minus Inc.

<design company>
Minus Inc.

<programs/software>
Texteditor, Dreamweaver, Flash, Photoshop, Fireworks

<number of pages>
n/a

<country of origin>
Canada

<work description>
The Minus record company's official website showcases their artists' latest releases. This page features Theorem.

evolve
020100
021200
031300
040500

SWAYZAK VS THEOREM

THE FIRST IN A SERIES OF COLLABORATIONS BETWEEN THEOREM (DALE LAWRENCE) AND LIKE-MINDED PRODUCERS FROM AROUND THE GLOBE, EITHER IN PERSON OR BY REMOTE. SWAYZAK (JAMES AND BROON) RESIDE IN LONDON, ENGLAND, RECORDING FOR THEIR OWN LABEL (SWAYZAK) WITH A PURELY DEEP SOUND BEYOND ANY NARROW DEFINITION.

THE ORIGINAL SOURCE SOUNDS BEHIND THX1 WERE CREATED BY THEOREM IN DETROIT, AND THEN ARRANGED AND PRODUCED BY THE SWAYZAK DUO IN LONDON. NOT A REMIX, YET NOT YOUR ORDINARY COLLABORATION, AS YOU ARE ABOUT TO HEAR...

THESE TRACKS WERE RECORDED BETWEEN FEBRUARY AND MAY OF 1999.

AVAILABLE NOW.

[A1] BREAK IN AT APT. 285

[B1] BAD HAIR DAY
[B2] UNHERLUFERLICK

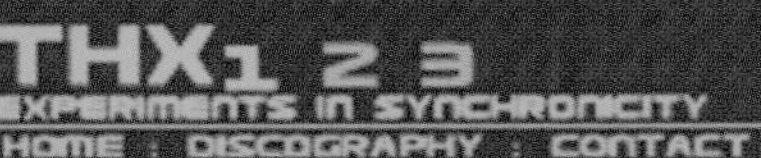

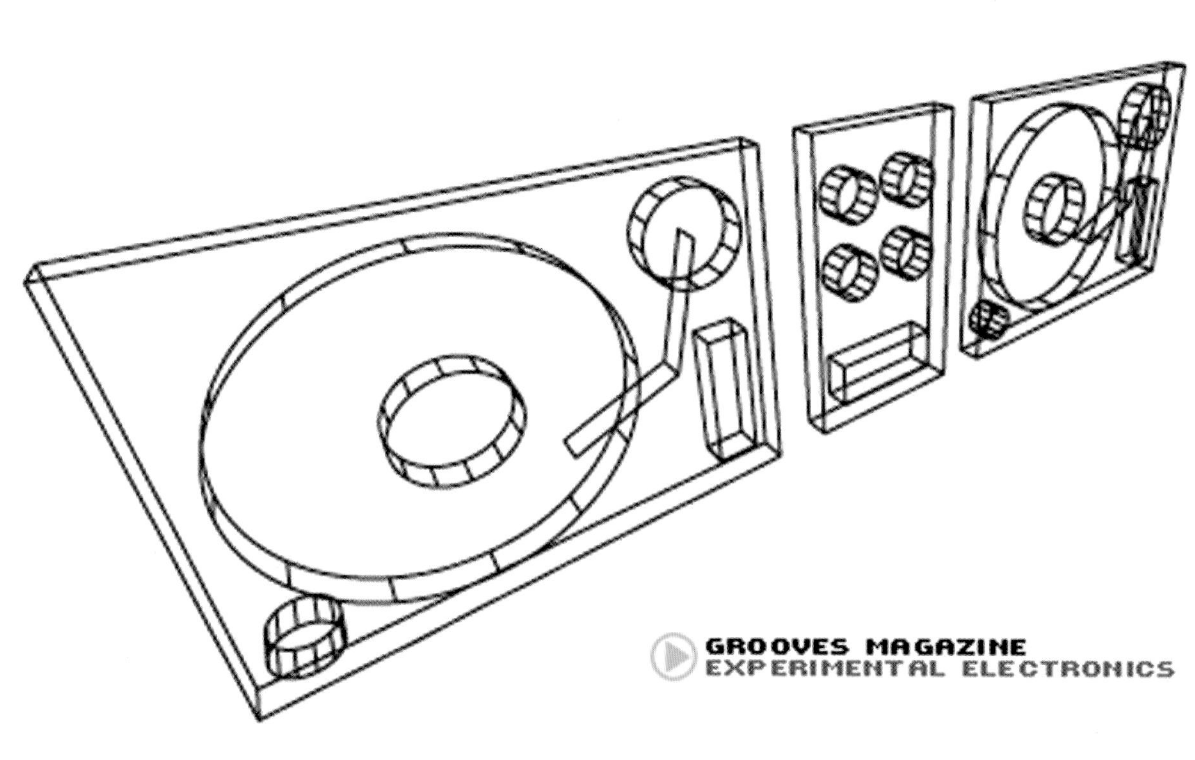

<title>
Grooves Magazine:
Experimental Electronics

<web address>
www.groovesmag.com

<client>
Grooves Magazine

<designer>
Brian Rachielles

<programs/software>
Adobe Photoshop,
Adobe Illustrator

<number of pages>
n/a

<country of origin>
USA

<work description>
This site carries news, articles and reviews on the experimental electronic music scene.

://currently---->

AIR KING @ RESFEST 2000 - For the second year in a row, Air King creates the music and sound design for a ResFest winner. Read about **Corduroy Kitchen**'s award-winning CD-ROM at ResFest 2000. And listen to some of our mp3 samples from the CD at airkingsound.com.

AIR KING @ GALLERY 16 - We've just scored a new installation by Amy Franceschini of Future Farmers which will open 9-14 @ Gallery 16 in SF and run through 10-31.

GET YOUR *AUTOPILOT* - SF's best independent record store, Aquarius Records (1055 Valencia St.) is now carrying Air King's *Autopilot*. Look for it in the Experimental section (A-D) or order online @ aquariusrecordsSF.com.

Read more about Autopilot...

NEW MP3s - check out our collection of air king mp3s. Updated weekly, this archive contains highlights from our multimedia and installation work, with a few bonus tracks tossed in for good measure.

CALL US : 415.648.3713
EMAIL US: autopilot@airkingsound.com

<title>
Air King Sound

<web address>
www.airkingsound.com

<client>
Air King Sound

<designer>
Thomas Muer
(with help from Future Farmers)

<programs/software>
Photoshop, Illustrator, Dreamweaver, BBedit

<number of pages>
about 10

<country of origin>
USA

<work description>
This site promotes the work of Air King Sound, a San Francisco-based music and sound design studio specializing in original audio content for film and installations.

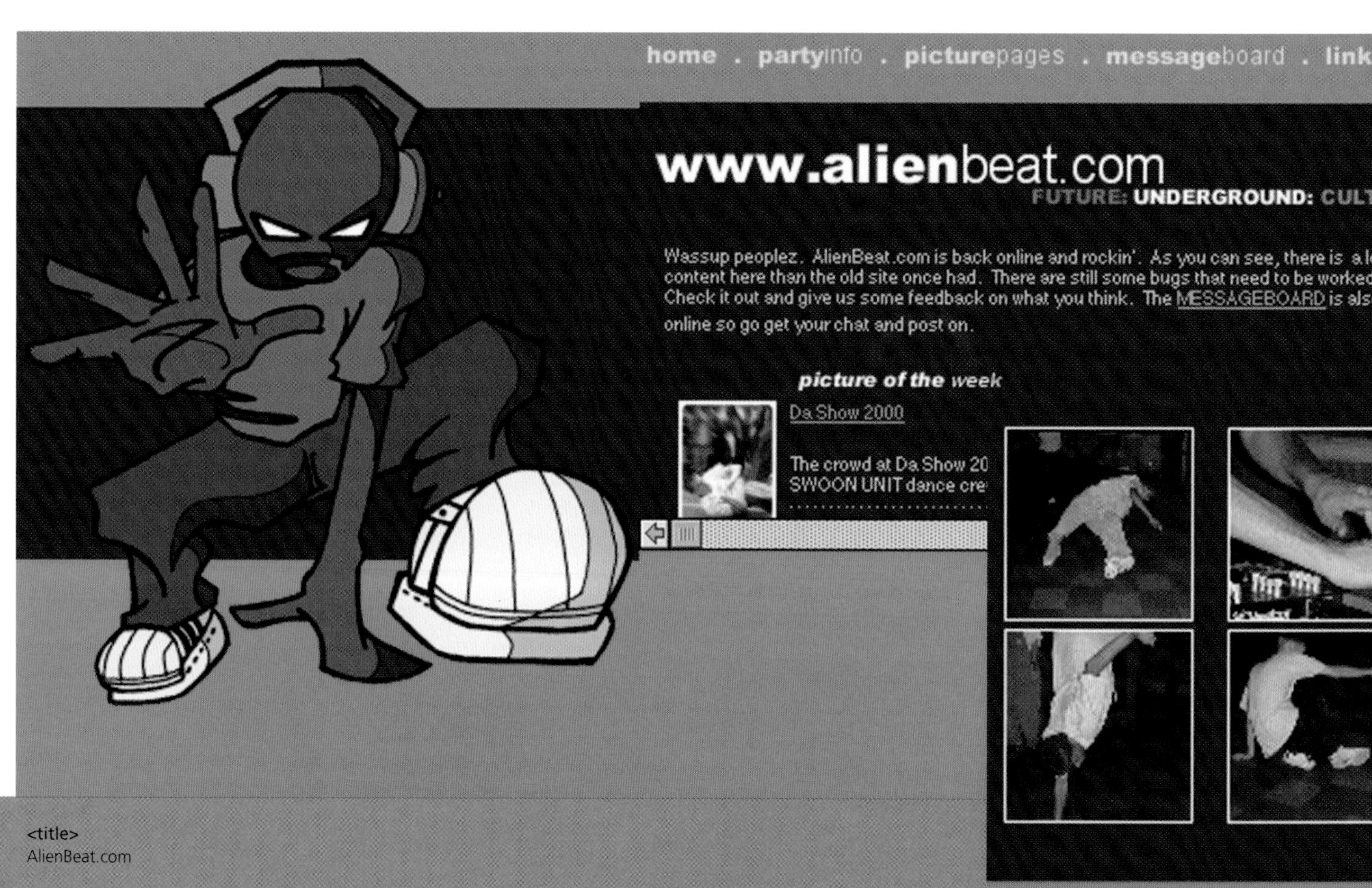

home . partyinfo . picturepages . messageboard . links
www.alienbeat.com
FUTURE: UNDERGROUND: CULT
Wassup peoplez. AlienBeat.com is back online and rockin'. As you can see, there is a lo
content here than the old site once had. There are still some bugs that need to be worked
Check it out and give us some feedback on what you think. The MESSAGEBOARD is also
online so go get your chat and post on.
picture of the week
Da Show 2000
The crowd at Da Show 20
SWOON UNIT dance cre

<title>
AlienBeat.com

<web address>
www.alienbeat.com

<client>
AlienBeat Productions

<designer>
Sam Paye

<illustrator>
Jonathan Lowe

<design company>
Pixl Studios

<programs/software>
Paintshop Pro, Photoshop, Flash, Frontpage, Notepad

<number of pages>
30+

<country of origin>
USA

Links

Local Scene
- Sonic Boom
- Wicked Smille
- DJ Jedi
- Johnny Blaze
- Fresh
- Carolina Spins
- Release
- Club Mythos

Hip-Hop/B-Boys/Graffiti
- Breakdance.com
- 12oz Prophet
- Style Elements Crew
- Rock Steady Crew
- Invisibl Scratch Picklz
- 1200 Hobos
- B-Boy.Com
- Hip-Hop.com
- Art of BreakDancing
- Writing Wall
- MadGraff

Clothing
- Tribal Gear
- ESDJCO
- ECKO
- Jnco
- Droog
- FreshJive
- BC Ethic

DJs, MCs, & Crews

Kleen
JameZ
ElectroniQ
Child
Swoon
Unit
EyEKonn

<work description>
AlienBeat.com promotes underground dance and DJ crews in North Carolina, providing, news on events and releases, information, photos and general communication.

●KOMPAKT

● SHOP & MAILORDER ● LABEL ● DISTRIBUTION

● SHOP & MAILORDER ● LABEL ● DISTRIBUTION ● KOMPAKT

●KOMPAKT

BY RENAMING DELIRIUM INTO KOMPAKT IN THE BEGINNING OF 1998, IT WAS POSSIBLE TO MANAGE THE PROBLEM WITH THE CONFUSING DJUNGLE OF NAMES, LOGOS, STORE, LABELS ETC. BY GIVING A LONG OVERDUE TRADEMARK AND BRAND TO THE MEANWHILE INTERNATIONALLY KNOWN COLOGNE MINIMAL SOUND. UNDER THE SAME ROOF AS THE ALREADY KNOWN LABELS PROFAN AND STUDIO 1, KOMPAKT COMPRISES NOT ONLY LABEL AND RECORD STORE. DUE TO THE CONSTANTLY RISING NUMBER OF NEWCOMERS AND NEW TALENTS AND THE NECESSITY TO OFFER THE UTMOST FREEDOM FOR RELEASES OF WEIRD, EXPERIMENTAL SOUNDS, IT SEEMED ONLY CONSEQUENT ENOUGH TO FOUND KOMPAKT DISTRIBUTION. STRICTLY FOLLOWING THE MOTTO: "FROM THE CREATOR DIRECTLY ON TO THE TURN-TABLES", KOMPAKT DISTRIBUTION SUPPLIES NATIONAL AND INTERNATIONAL WHOLSALERS AND RETAILERS WITH FRESHLY-MADE HOME-PRODUCTIONS. MOREOVER, SPECIAL CARE IS DEDICATED TO THE COMPREHENSIVE BACK CATALOGUE THAT HAS BEEN DEVELOPED OVER THE YEARS.

DISCOGRAFIE

● KOM 001	JÜRGEN PAAPE	TRIUMPH	12"
● KOM 002	DETTINGER	BLOND	12"
● KOM 003	JÜRGEN PAAPE	GLANZ	12"
● KOM 004	M. MAYER	17&4	12"
● KOM 005	JOACHIM SPIETH	ABI 99	12"
● KOM 006	DETTINGER	PUMA	12"
● KOM 007	SCHAEBEN & VOSS	DICHT DRAN	12"
● KOM 008	BENJAMIN WILD	KRONBERG	12"
● KOM 009	REINHARD VOIGT	ROBSON PONTE	12"
● KOM 010	DIVERSE	TOTAL 1	DOLP
● KOM 011	DUBSTAR	SHINING THROUGH	12"
● KOM 012	DETTINGER	TOTENTANZ	12"
● KOM 013	SASCHA FUNKE	CAMPUS	12"
● KOM 014	GEBR. TEICHMANN	AUS DER FERNE	12"

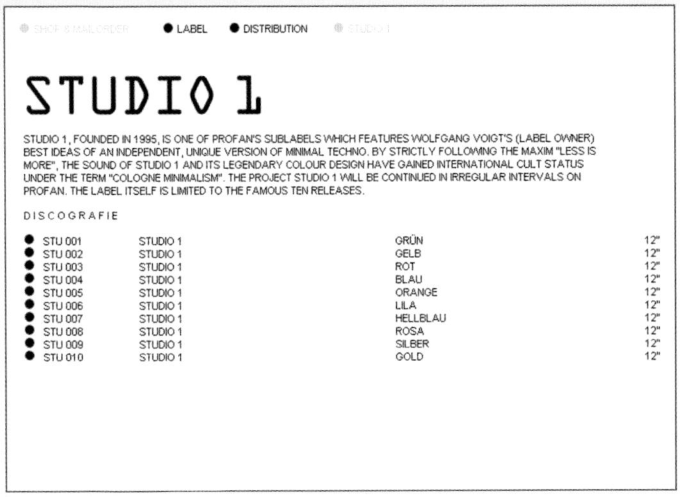

● SHOP & MAILORDER ● LABEL ● DISTRIBUTION ● STUDIO 1

STUDIO 1

STUDIO 1, FOUNDED IN 1995, IS ONE OF PROFAN'S SUBLABELS WHICH FEATURES WOLFGANG VOIGT'S (LABEL OWNER) BEST IDEAS OF AN INDEPENDENT, UNIQUE VERSION OF MINIMAL TECHNO. BY STRICTLY FOLLOWING THE MAXIM "LESS IS MORE", THE SOUND OF STUDIO 1 AND ITS LEGENDARY COLOUR DESIGN HAVE GAINED INTERNATIONAL CULT STATUS UNDER THE TERM "COLOGNE MINIMALISM". THE PROJECT STUDIO 1 WILL BE CONTINUED IN IRREGULAR INTERVALS ON PROFAN. THE LABEL ITSELF IS LIMITED TO THE FAMOUS TEN RELEASES.

DISCOGRAFIE

● STU 001	STUDIO 1	GRÜN	12"
● STU 002	STUDIO 1	GELB	12"
● STU 003	STUDIO 1	ROT	12"
● STU 004	STUDIO 1	BLAU	12"
● STU 005	STUDIO 1	ORANGE	12"
● STU 006	STUDIO 1	LILA	12"
● STU 007	STUDIO 1	HELLBLAU	12"
● STU 008	STUDIO 1	ROSA	12"
● STU 009	STUDIO 1	SILBER	12"
● STU 010	STUDIO 1	GOLD	12"

<title>
Kompakt Schallplatten

<web address>
www.kompakt-net.de

<client>
Kompakt

<design company>
7inch/Bianca Strauch

<programs/software>
n/a

<number of pages>
200+

<country of origin>
Germany

<work description>
This site represents the Kompakt label, providing news, information, and online record distribution.

重

BULLETIN BOARD | HEAVY NEWS | JOBS AT HEAVY | VOTE FOR HEAVY AT WIRED MAG

HEAVY RADIO
OPEN

NEW THIS WEEK
heavy music
HEAVY

HEAVY MUSIC
BEASTIE BOYS

music: the diablo pro
photography: stephanie

HEAVY SUMMER

SETTINGS | HELP | GET ON THE LIST | CONTACT

BEHIND THE MUSIC
SNN
BLISSTER
HALL OF FAME
AMERICAN SUCK COUNTDOWN
HEAVYTV
Heavy.com

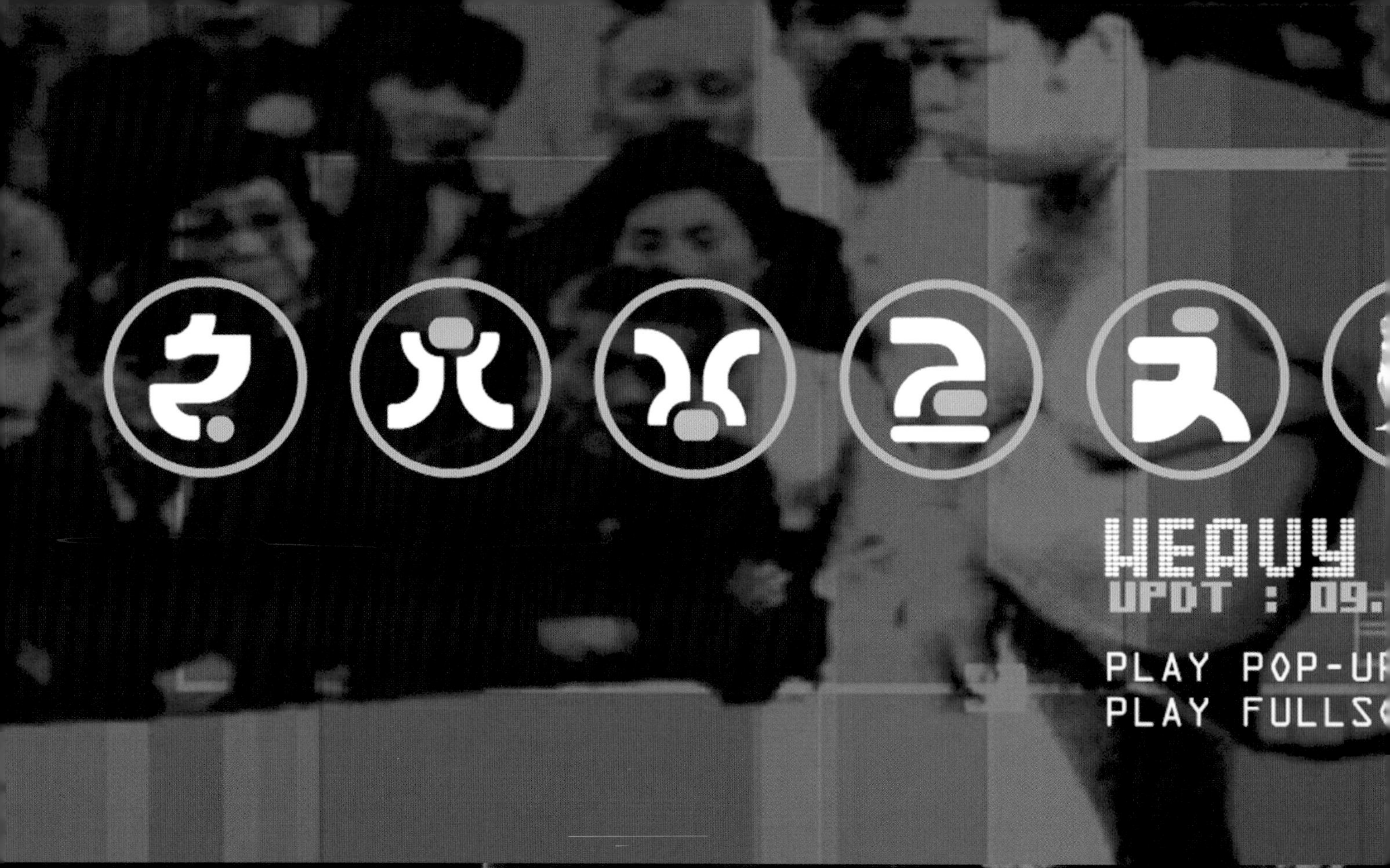

HEAVY

UPDT : 09.

PLAY POP-UP

PLAY FULLSC

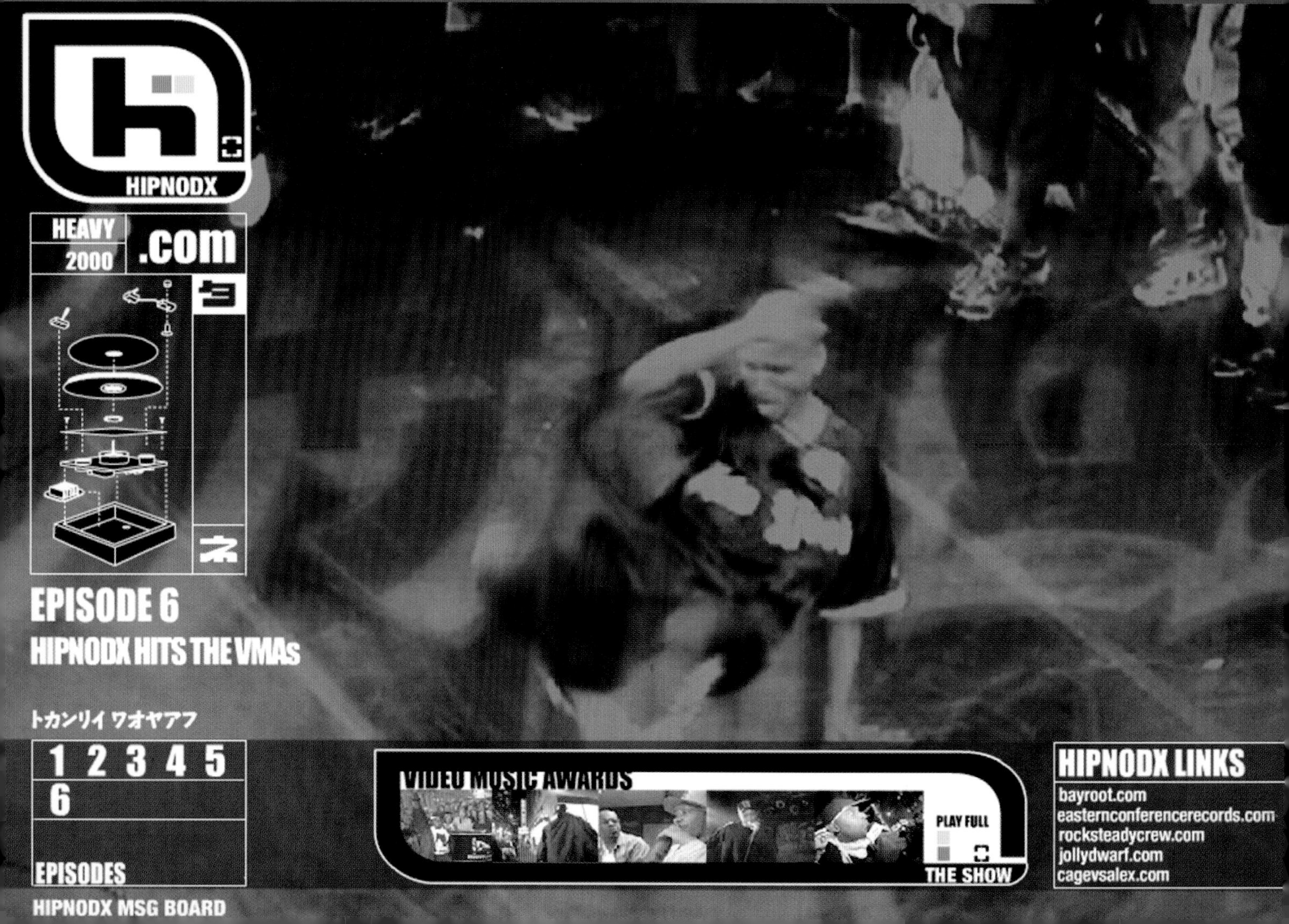

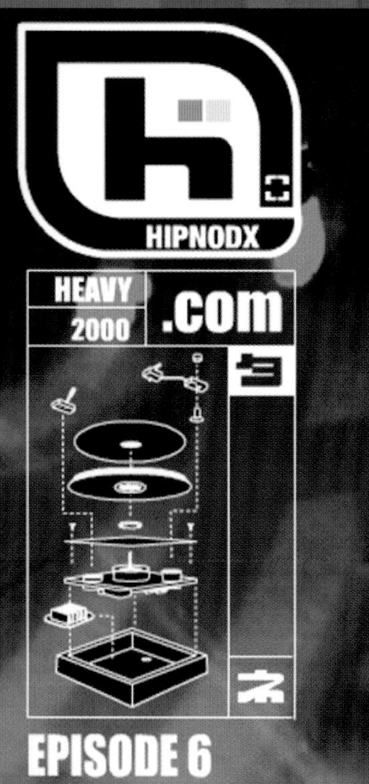

EPISODE 6

HIPNODX HITS THE VMAs

トカンリイ ワオヤアフ

1 2 3 4 5
6

EPISODES

HIPNODX MSG BOARD

HIPNODX LINKS

bayroot.com
easternconferencerecords.com
rocksteadycrew.com
jollydwarf.com
cagevsalex.com

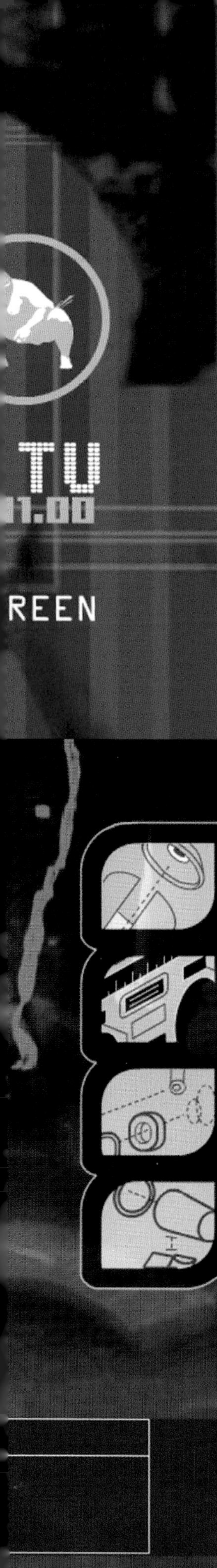

<title>
Heavy.com

<web address>
www.heavy.com

<client>
n/a

<design company>
Heavy

<programs/software>
Flash, PHP, Photoshop, Illustrator, Finalcut Pro, After Effects, Streamline, Protools, Soundedit, Peak, BBedit, Anarchie, Media Cleaner Pro, Sorenson Video, QDesign Sound

number of pages>
n/a

<country of origin>
USA

<work description>
This site offers animation, video clips, news, information, merchandise, and sounds from Heavy's hiphop catalog.

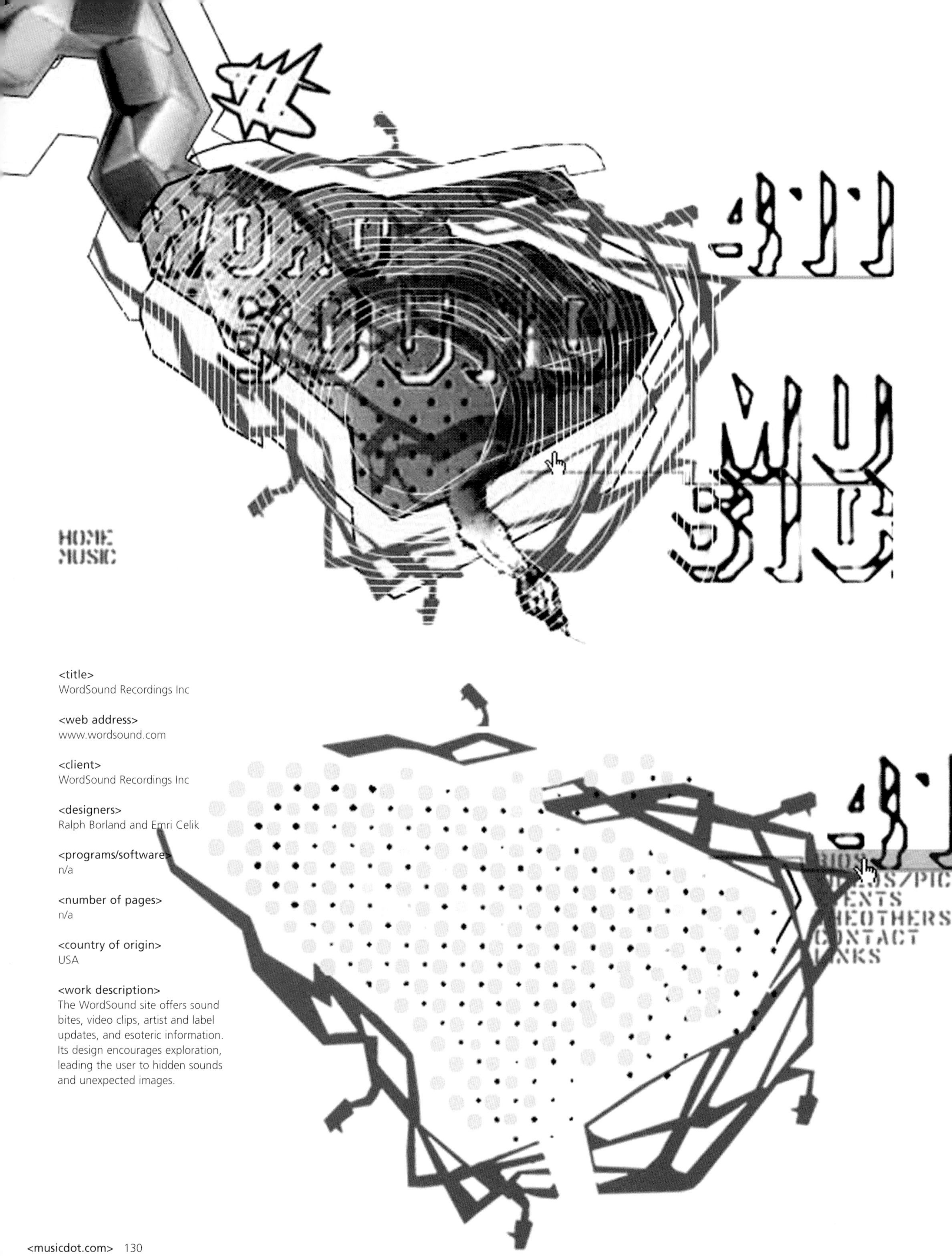

<title>
WordSound Recordings Inc

<web address>
www.wordsound.com

<client>
WordSound Recordings Inc

<designers>
Ralph Borland and Emri Celik

<programs/software>
n/a

<number of pages>
n/a

<country of origin>
USA

<work description>
The WordSound site offers sound bites, video clips, artist and label updates, and esoteric information. Its design encourages exploration, leading the user to hidden sounds and unexpected images.

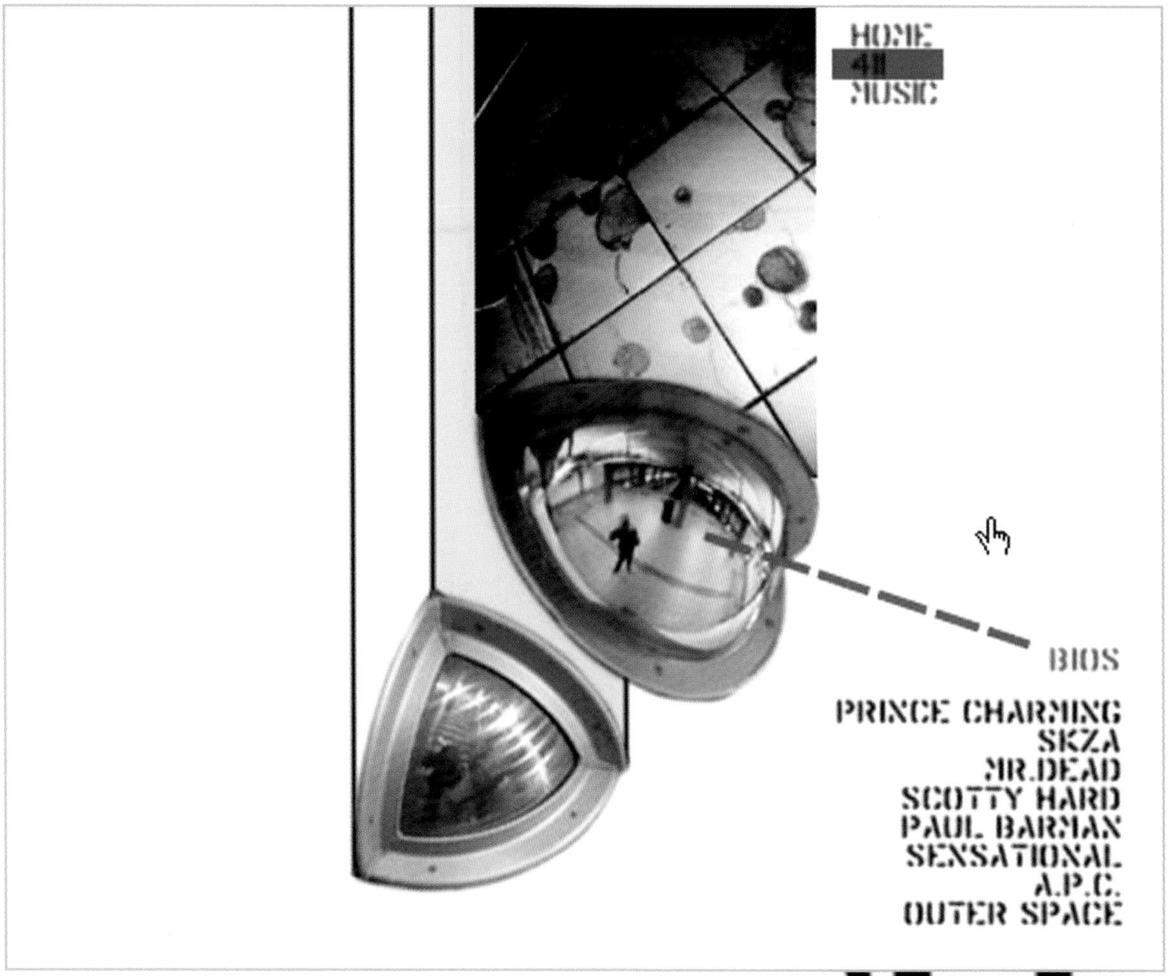

HOME
4ll
MUSIC

BIOS

PRINCE CHARMING
SKZA
MR.DEAD
SCOTTY HARD
PAUL BARMAN
SENSATIONAL
A.P.C.
OUTER SPACE

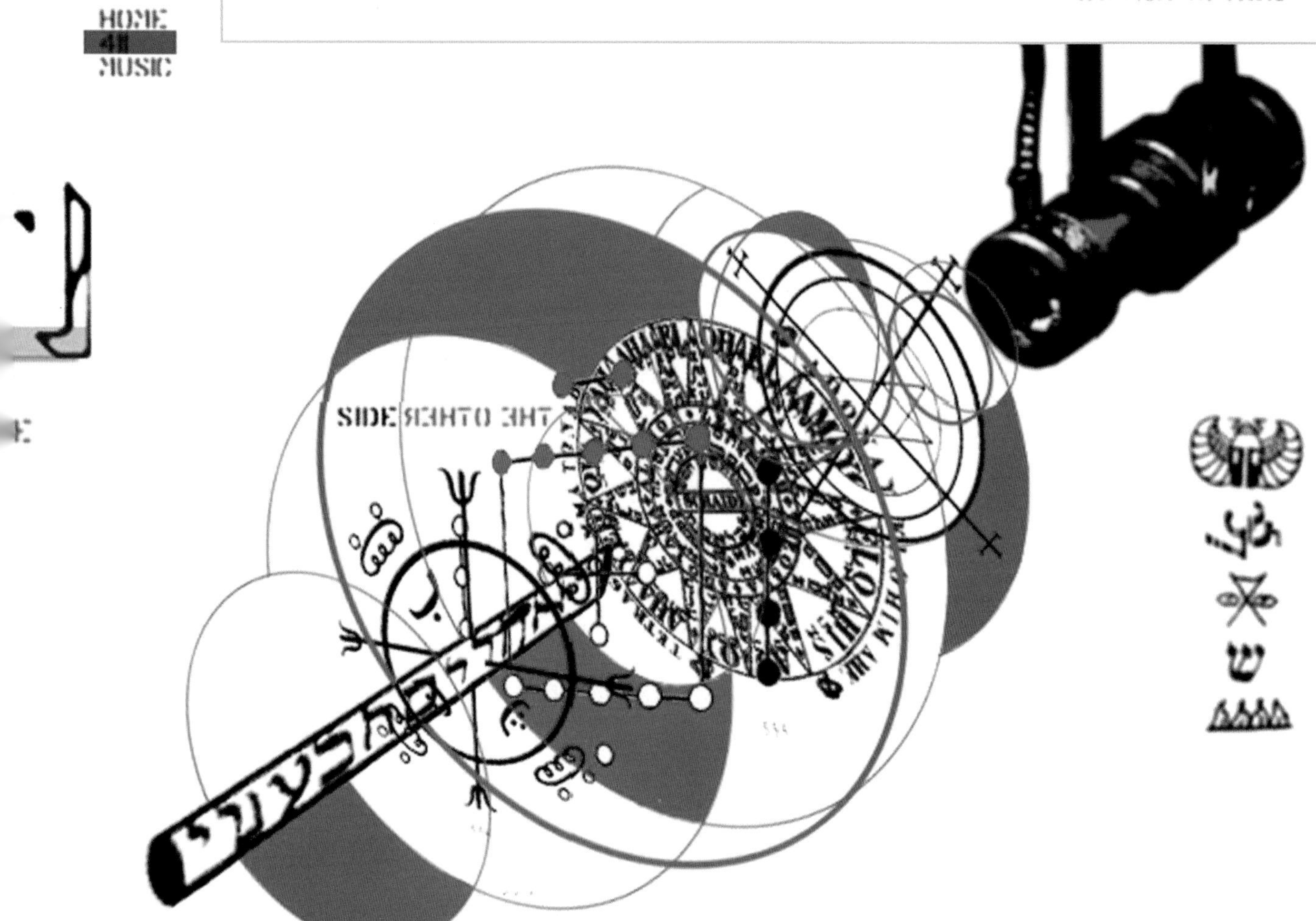

HOME
4ll
MUSIC

SIDE ƎHTO ƎHT THE OTHER SIDE

<title>
Hefty Records

<web address>
www.heftyrecords.com

<client>
Hefty Records

<design company>
sQUARELABS

<programs/software>
Flash, Photoshop

<number of pages>
n/a

<country of origin>
USA

<work description>
Promotional site for the Hefty record label.

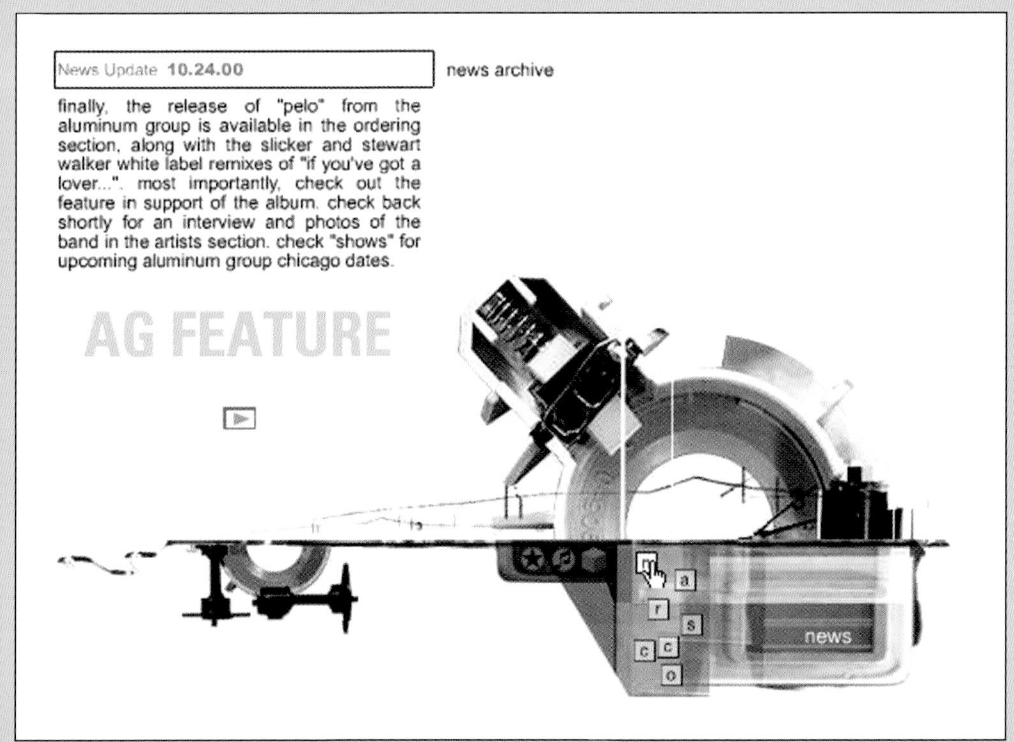

News Update 10.24.00
news archive
finally, the release of "pelo" from the aluminum group is available in the ordering section, along with the slicker and stewart walker white label remixes of "if you've got a lover...". most importantly, check out the feature in support of the album. check back shortly for an interview and photos of the band in the artists section. check "shows" for upcoming aluminum group chicago dates.
AG FEATURE
news

IA#002

A GRAPE DOPE

aka: JOHN HERNDON
location: CHICAGO, ILLINOIS

LIMITED TO 750 COPIES

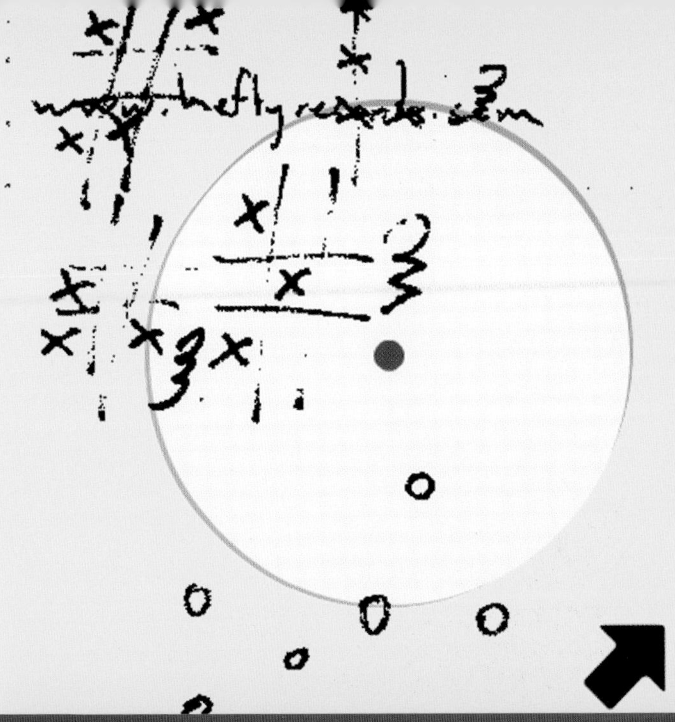

IA#001

SAVATH+SAVALAS

aka: SCOTT HERREN
location: ATLANTA, GEORGIA

S+S LIMITED TO 700 COPIES

HEFTY!

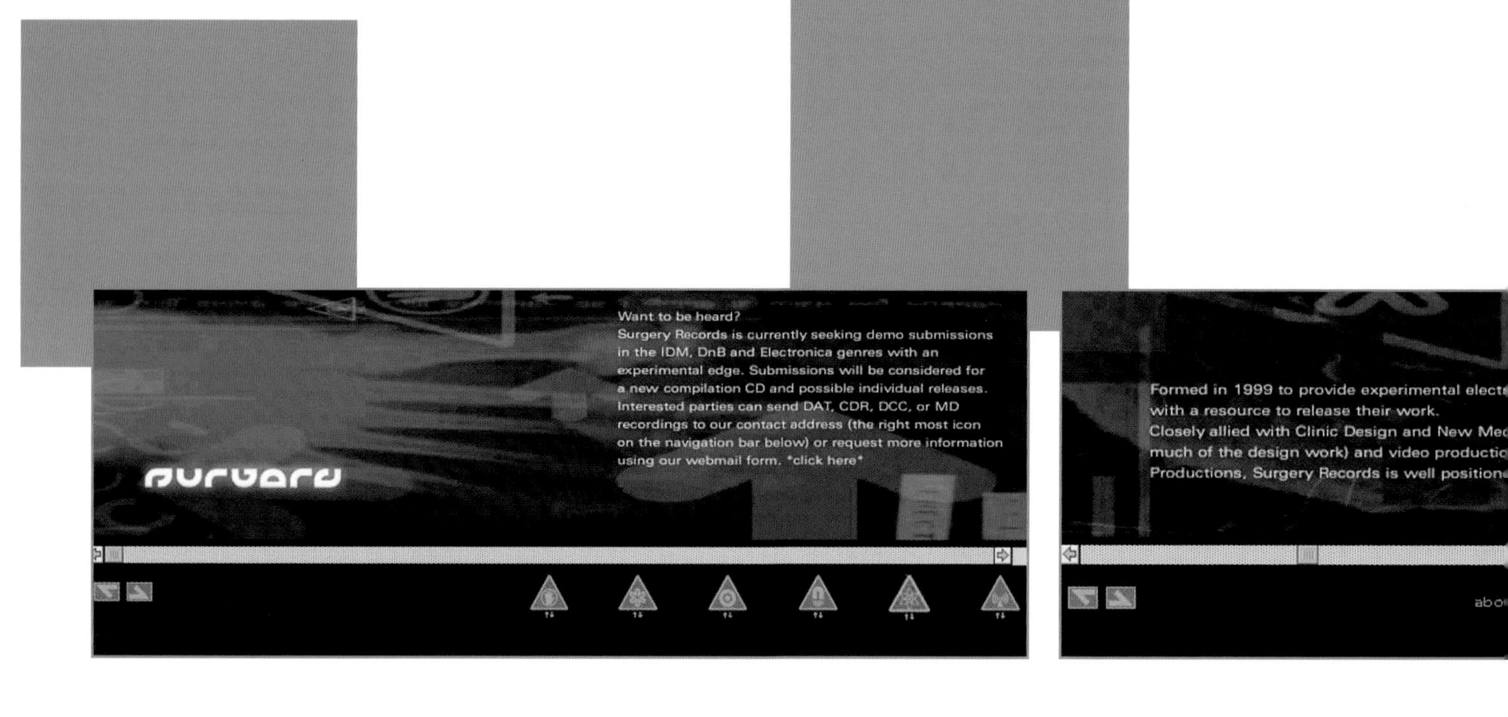

Want to be heard?
Surgery Records is currently seeking demo submissions in the IDM, DnB and Electronica genres with an experimental edge. Submissions will be considered for a new compilation CD and possible individual releases. Interested parties can send DAT, CDR, DCC, or MD recordings to our contact address (the right most icon on the navigation bar below) or request more information using our webmail form. *click here*
Formed in 1999 to provide experimental
with a resource to release their work.
Closely allied with Clinic Design and New
much of the design work) and video
Productions, Surgery Records is well

Surgery Records main studio is a state of the art, fully digital, hard disk based system, based around a Yamaha O2R digital console with numerous synthesisers/samplers and FX units. (Click image to visit our GearHead pages.)

<title>
Surgery Records PTY LTD

<web address>
www.surgeryrecords.com.au

<client>
Surgery Records PTY LTD

<design company>
Surgery Records PTY LTD
(Ian Hamilton@clinicdesign.com.au)

<programs/software>
Photoshop, Dreamweaver, Notepad

<number of pages>
5

<country of origin>
Australia

<work description>
This site promotes Surgery Records, an experimental electronic label, offering catalog information, merchandise, and music samples.

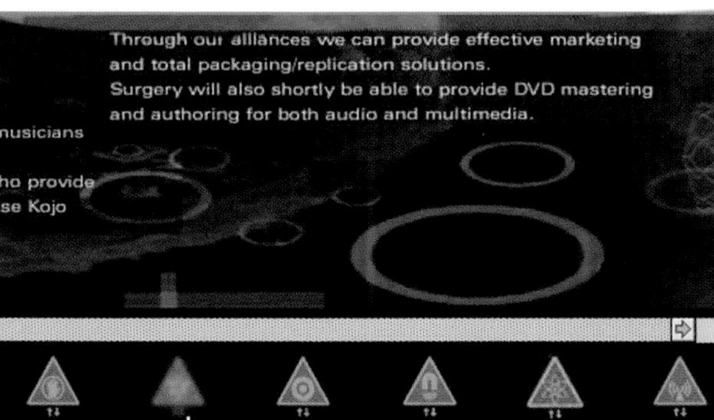

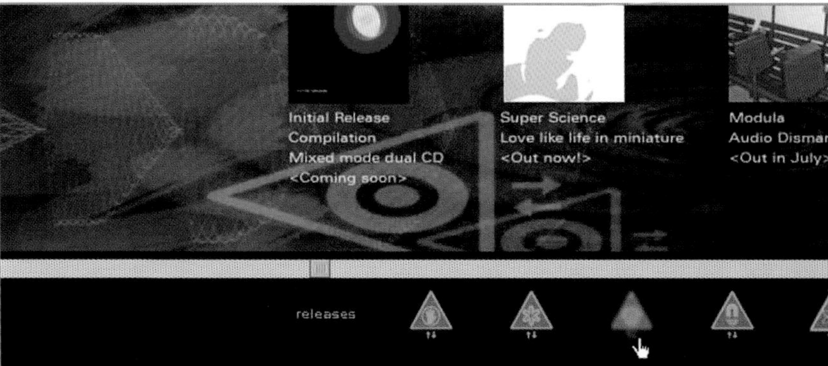

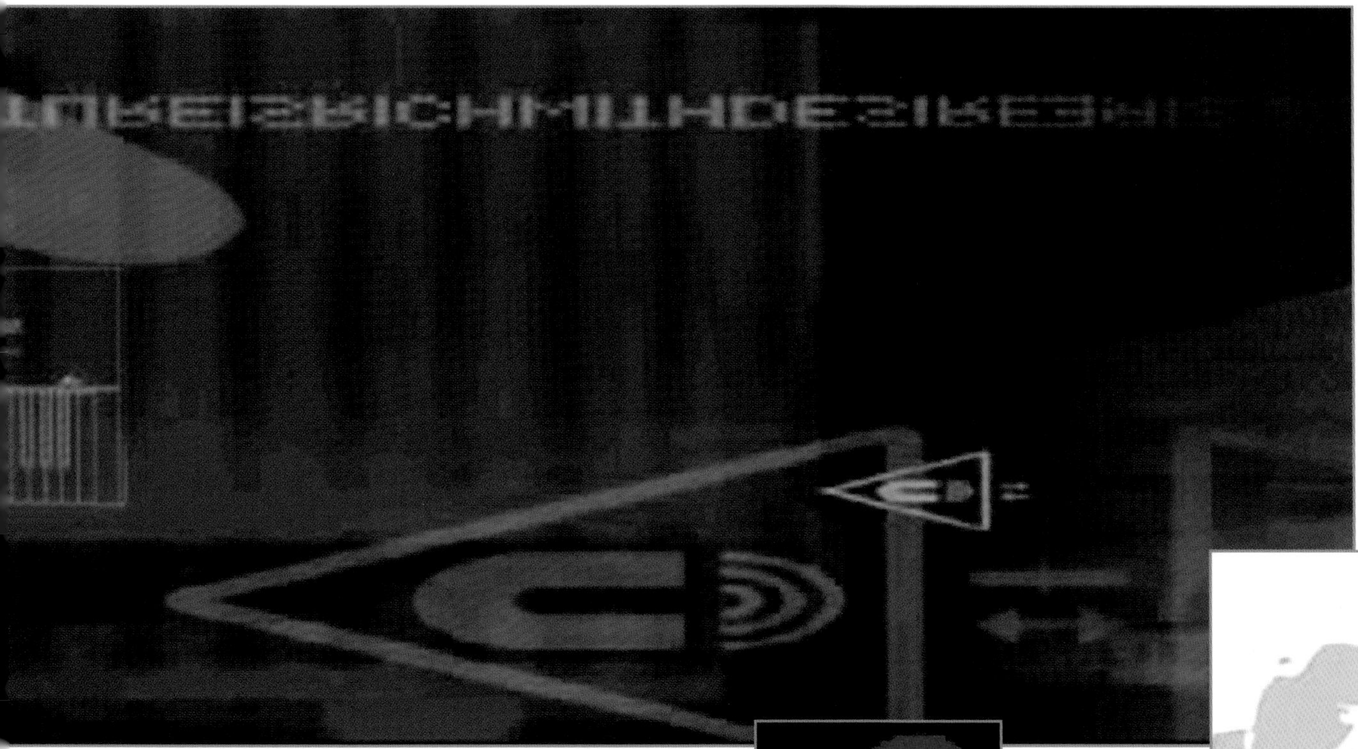

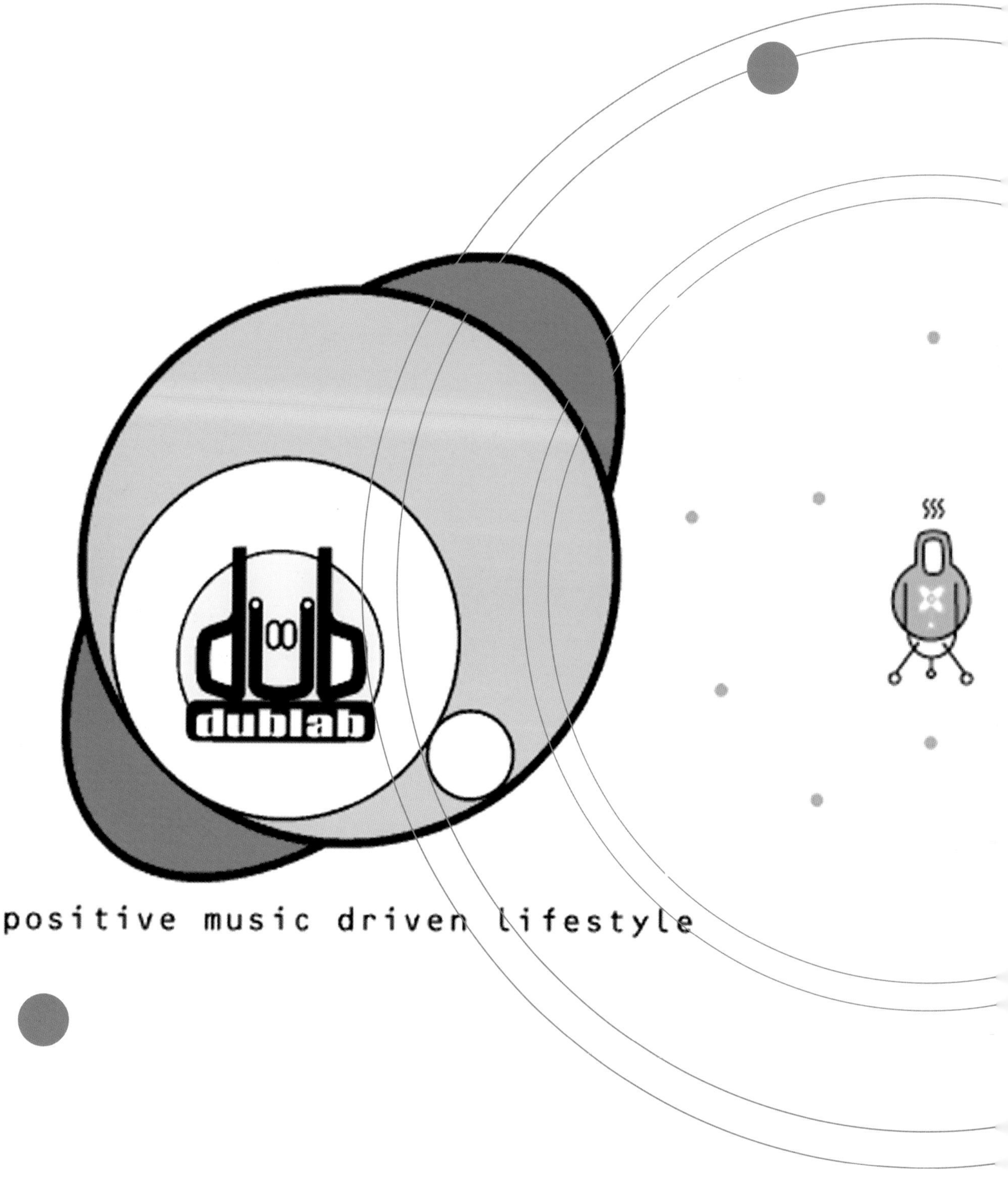

dub
dublab

positive music driven lifestyle

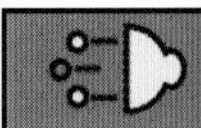

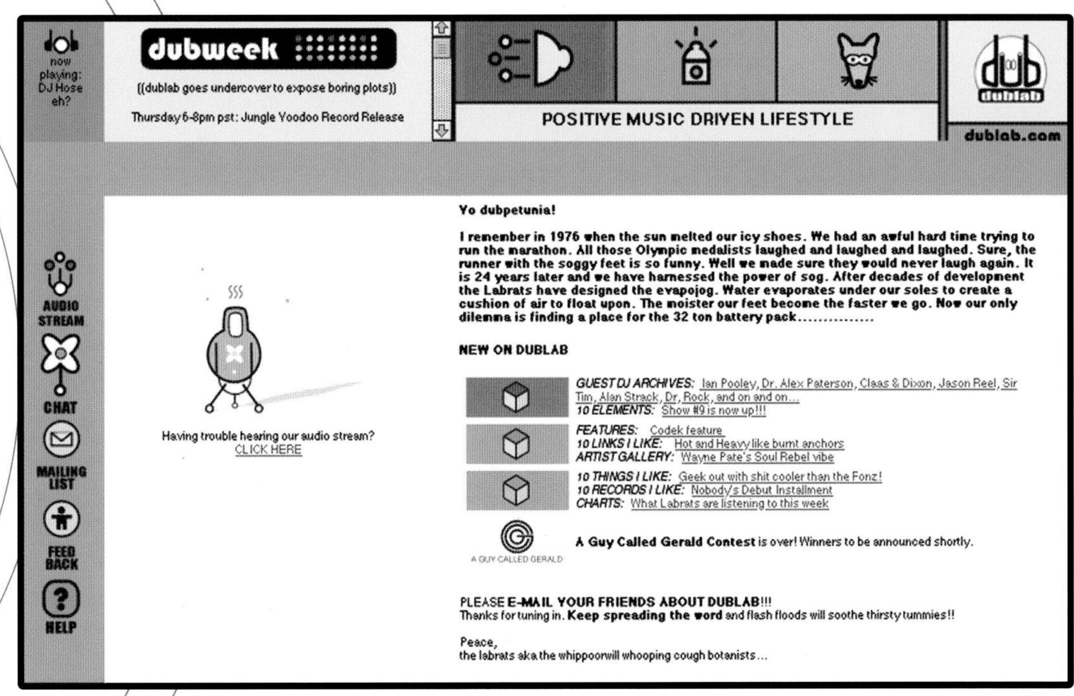

now playing: DJ Hose eh?
dubweek
[(dublab goes undercover to expose boring plots)]
Thursday 6-8pm pst: Jungle Yoodoo Record Release
POSITIVE MUSIC DRIVEN LIFESTYLE
dublab
dublab.com
AUDIO STREAM
CHAT
MAILING LIST
FEED BACK
HELP
Having trouble hearing our audio stream?
CLICK HERE
Yo dubpetunia!
I remember in 1976 when the sun melted our icy shoes. We had an awful hard time trying to run the marathon. All those Olympic medalists laughed and laughed and laughed. Sure, the runner with the soggy feet is so funny. Well we made sure they would never laugh again. It is 24 years later and we have harnessed the power of sog. After decades of development the Labrats have designed the evapojog. Water evaporates under our soles to create a cushion of air to float upon. The moister our feet become the faster we go. Now our only dilemma is finding a place for the 32 ton battery pack...............
NEW ON DUBLAB
GUEST DJ ARCHIVES: Ian Pooley, Dr. Alex Paterson, Claas & Dixon, Jason Reel, Sir Tim, Alan Strack, Dr, Rock, and on and on...
10 ELEMENTS: Show #9 is now up!!!
FEATURES: Codek feature
10 LINKS I LIKE: Hot and Heavy like burnt anchors
ARTIST GALLERY: Wayne Pate's Soul Rebel vibe
10 THINGS I LIKE: Geek out with shit cooler than the Fonz!
10 RECORDS I LIKE: Nobody's Debut Installment
CHARTS: What Labrats are listening to this week
A GUY CALLED GERALD
A Guy Called Gerald Contest is over! Winners to be announced shortly.
PLEASE E-MAIL YOUR FRIENDS ABOUT DUBLAB!!!
Thanks for tuning in. Keep spreading the word and flash floods will soothe thirsty tummies!!
Peace,
the labrats aka the whippoorwill whooping cough botanists...

<title>
Dublab.com
(positive.music.driven.lifestyle)

<web address>
www.dublab.com

<client>
Dublab

<design company>
Team Auro

<programs/software>
Dreamweaver, Fireworks, Photoshop, Illustrator, Flash

<number of pages>
400+

<country of origin>
USA

<work description>
The Dublab site offers an internet radio dedicated to the growth of a new, positive, music-driven culture and lifestyle.

<title>
Mezzmusic.com

<web address>
www.mezzmusic.com

<client>
The Mezzanine

<designer/design company>
n/a

<programs/software>
Adobe Photoshop, Illustrator, ImageReady, Premiere, RealProducer Plus, Windows media on-demand producer, Dreamweaver, Flash, Cold Fusion Studio, Audio Catalyst, Wavelab

<number of pages>
50+

<country of origin>
UK

<work description>
This site offers online music sales, news on dance events, reviews, and multi-channel webcasting.

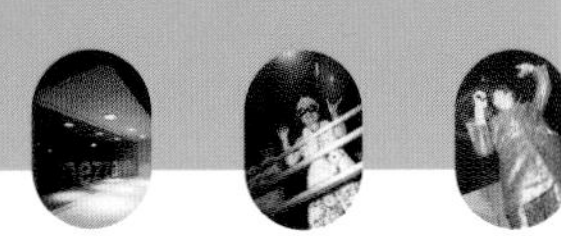

<title>
a-musik

<web address>
www.a-musik.com

<client>
a-musik, sonig, sieben, entenpfuhl, mouse on mars

<design company>
Covarpa, Constantin Rothkopf

<programs/software>
Simpletext, Pagespinner, Gifbuilder, Snapz Pro, Photoshop, Bryce, Cinema, Quicktime, JDK and Visual Basic

<number of pages>
43

<country of origin>
Germany

<work description>
First published in late 1995 to promote the a-musik label and shop, the original site design was based upon one screenshot of a MacOs 7.5 desktop and a scan of the first record released by a-musik. Now information is gathered from several databases, and the site features animations, project descriptions, and the homepages of related labels. The shop can be visited through a quicktime-panorama.

from here you also have acess to
'sieben' label by a-musik and entenpfuhl
a-musik.com/estible different projects from around a-musik
a-musik.com/parable send us photos of your stereo equipment.
a-musik.com/eliness a-musik.com/puters a-musik.com/a a-musik.com/bat a-musik.com/mensal

Imagine there would be a large room inside this room a tracking system with wich all movements inside could be registred, connected to a workstation, running a program and sending its outputs to six videobeams, which all points to the six walls of this room.

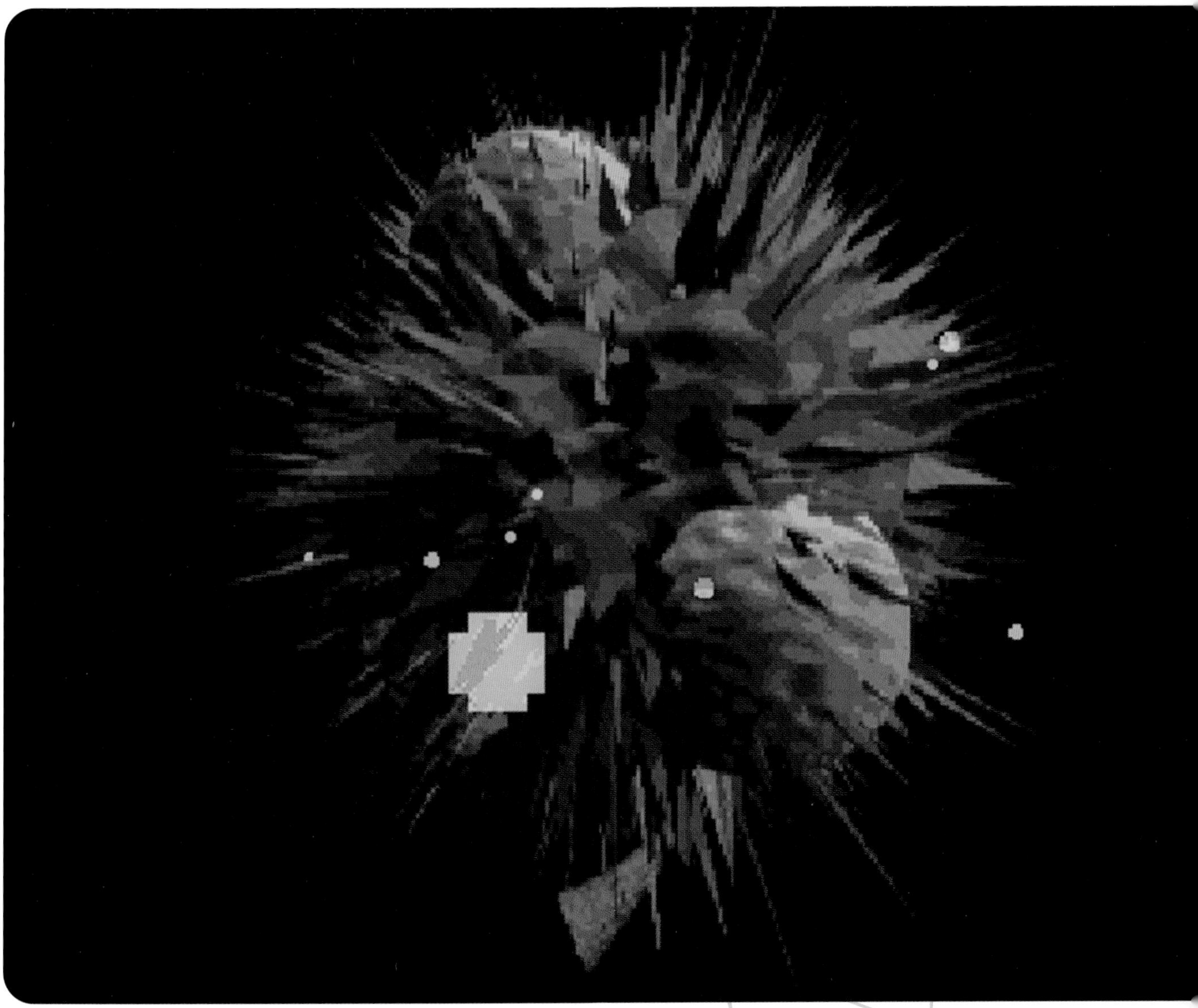

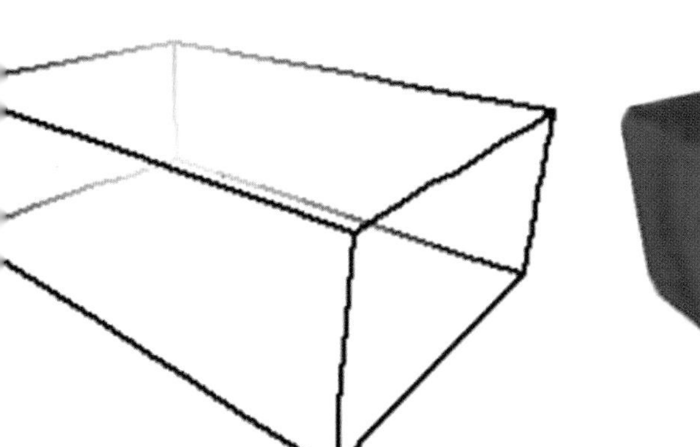

Taking physics
one can think of the volume of the room as filled by a (parametric) liquid, and the walls as build out of a (parametric) elastical material (e.g.rubber). Every movement inside the room creates a wave inside the liquid and deforms its confinements.

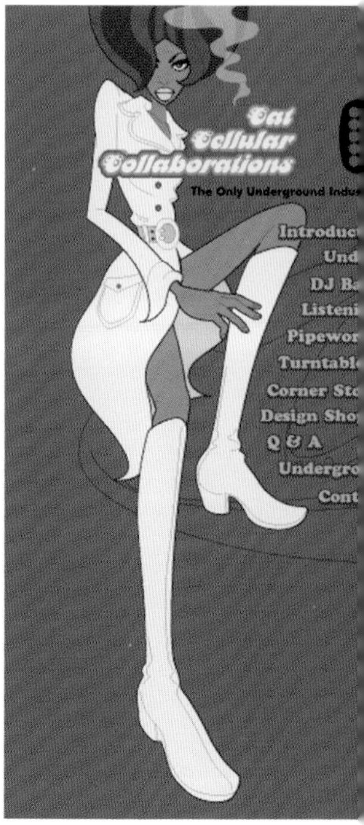

Cat
Cellular
Collaborations
The Only Underground Indus

Introduc
Und
DJ Ba
Listeni
Pipewor
Turntable
Corner Sto
Design Shop
Q & A
Undergro
Cont

Coming in
2000

Cat
Cellular
Collaborations
The Ultimate Sound Pool

Enter

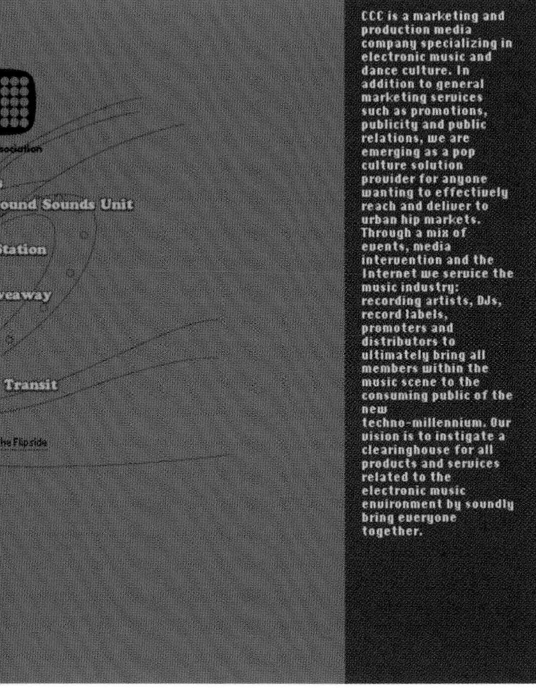

<title>
Cat Cellular Collaborations

<web address>
www.catcellular.com

<client>
Pipeworks Media

<design company>
Cat Cellular

<programs/software>
Photoshop, Illustrator

<number of pages>
11

<country of origin>
USA/Japan

<work description>
This is an online calling card for Cat Cellular Collaborations, who provide general marketing services for urban electronic music and dance culture.

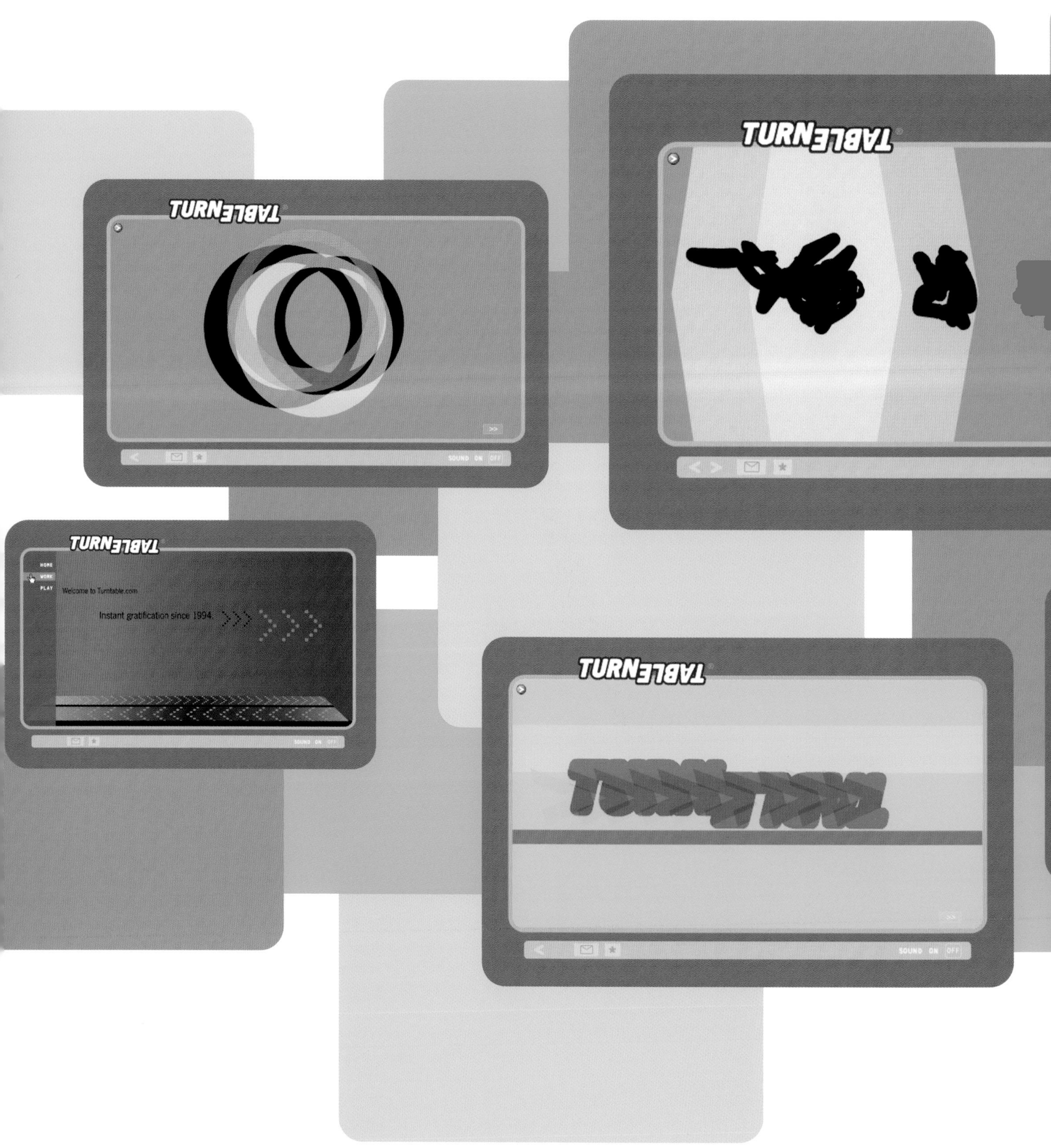
HOME
WORK
PLAY
Welcome to Turntable.com
Instant gratification since 1994.
SOUND ON OFF

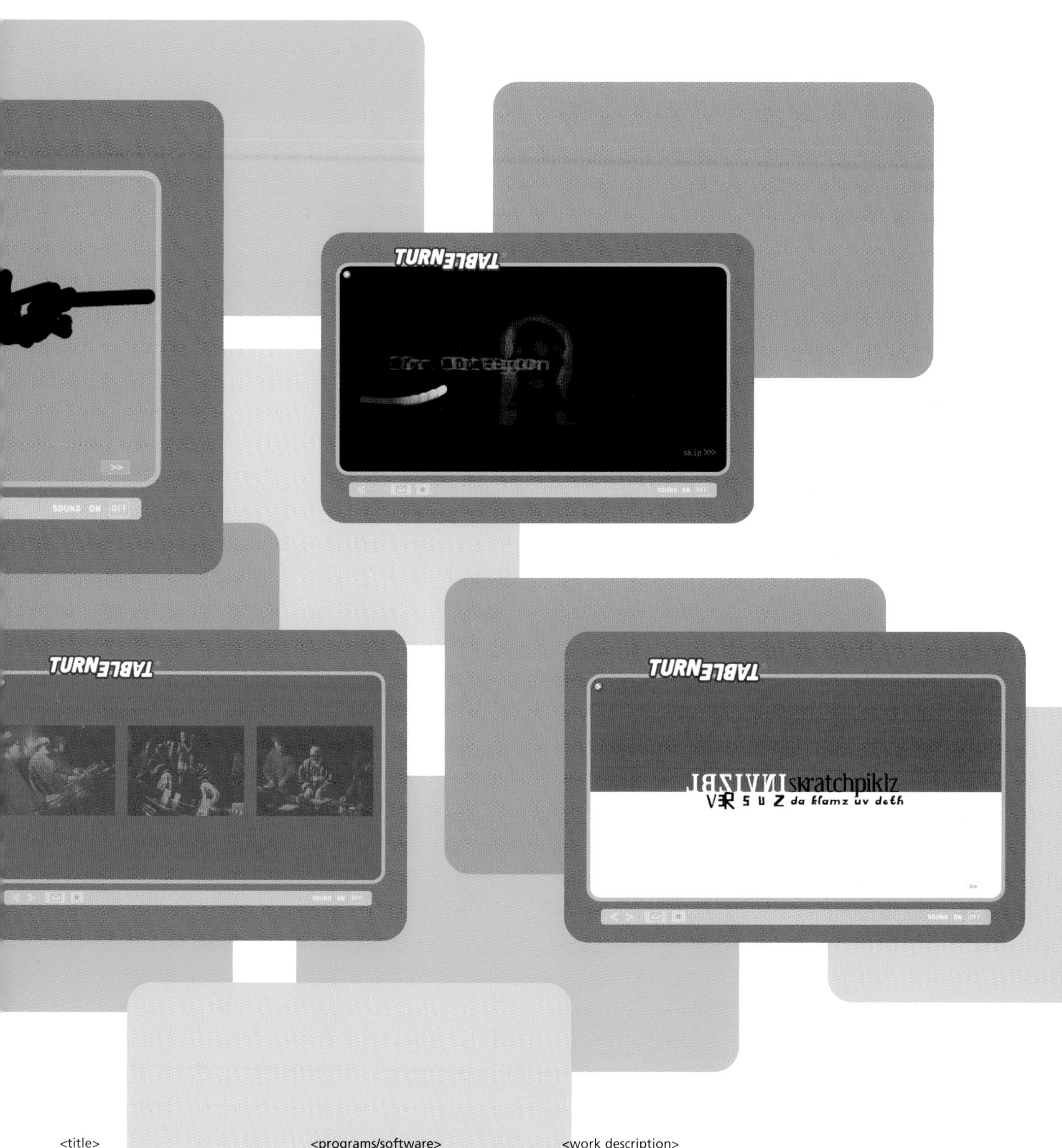

<title>
Turntable.com

<web address>
www.turntable.com

<client>
Turntable

<design company>
Turntable

<programs/software>
Flash, IE, NN, Freehand, Illustrator, Fireworks, Dreamweaver, After Effects, Quicktime, Font Reverse, MacOS, NT

<number of pages>
n/a

<country of origin>
USA

<work description>
This site represents Turntable, a digital design development and strategic consulting firm based in Northern California.

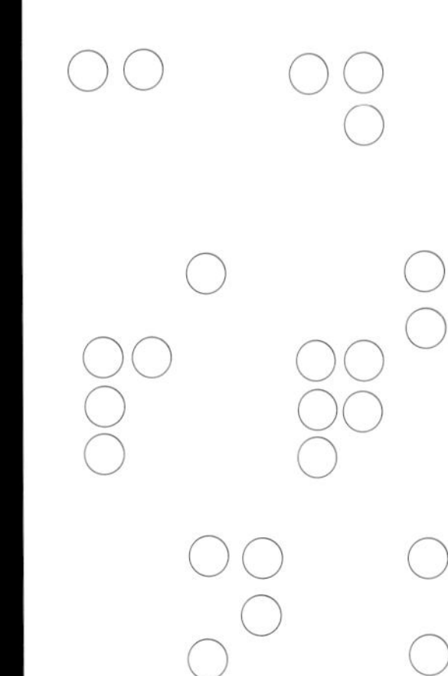

<title>
SKAM Records

<web address>
www.skam.co.uk

<client>
SKAM Records

<design company>
Bubble Media

<programs/software>
Macromedia, Dreamweaver, Flash

<number of pages>
constantly changing

<country of origin>
UK

<work description>
This site represents the SKAM record label with audio clips, online shopping from their catalog, and news on releases.

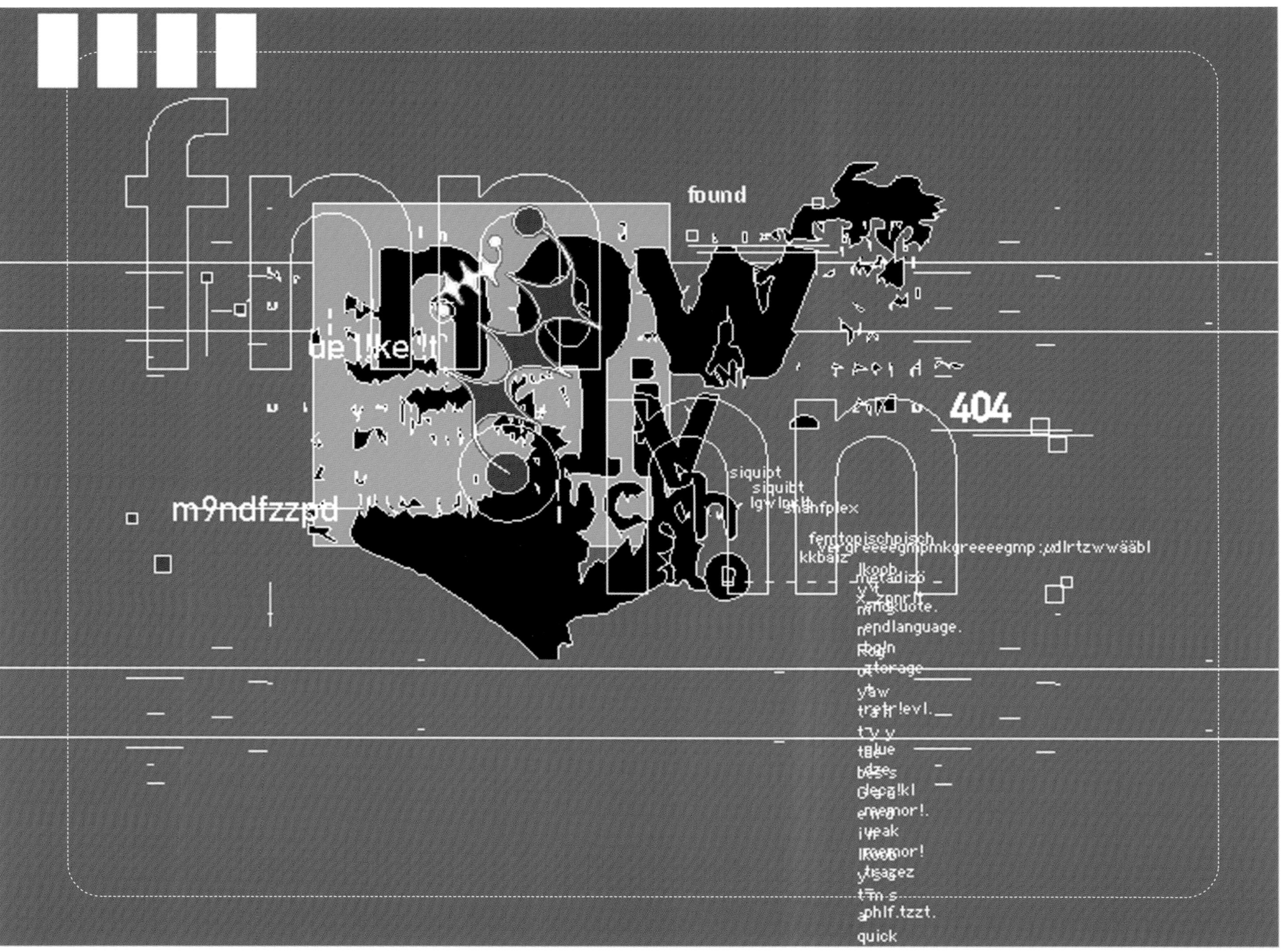
found
404
m9ndfzzpd
siquipt
siquipt
endlanguage.
yaw
quick

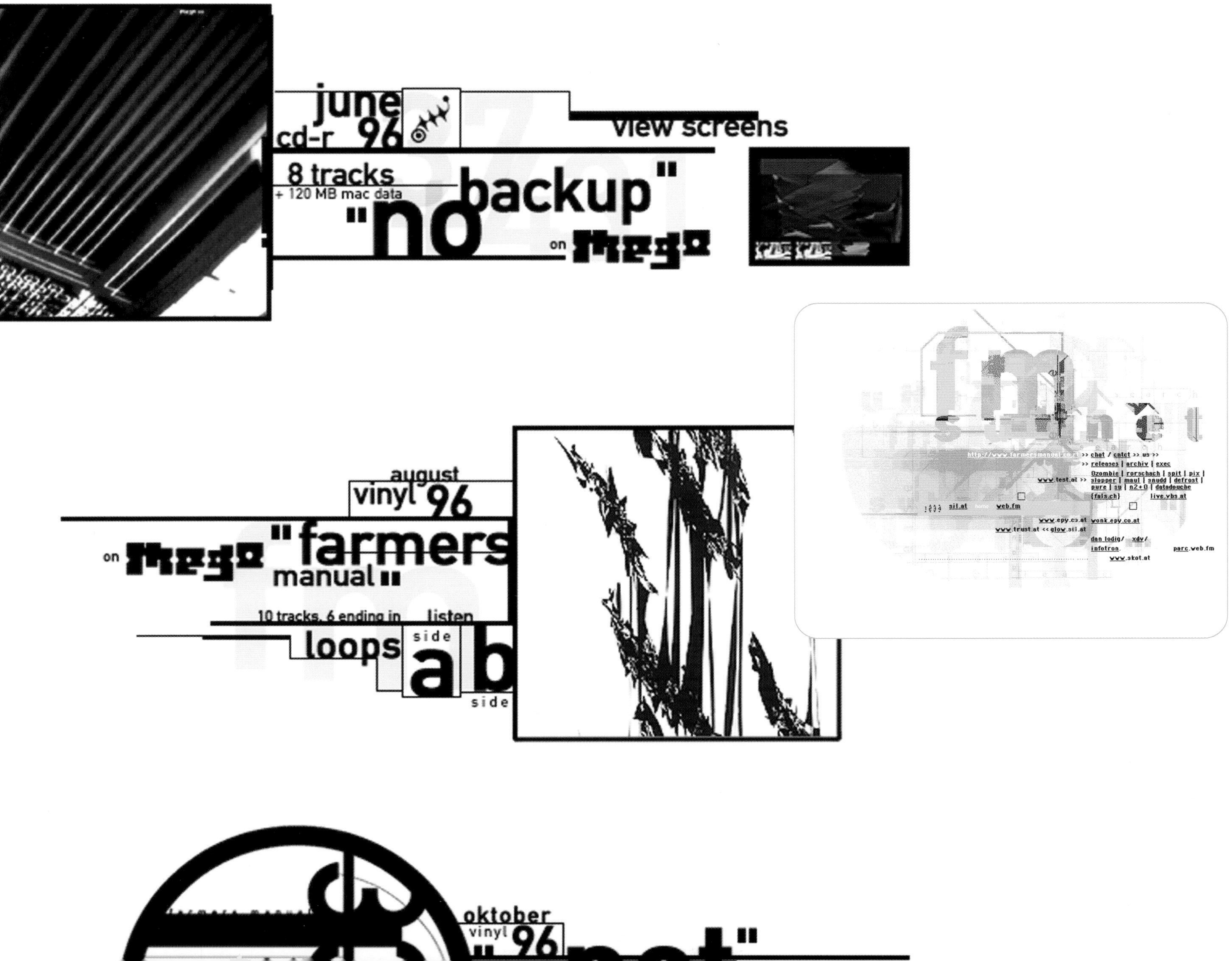
june
cd-r 96
view screens
8 tracks
+ 120 MB mac data
"no backup"
on Mego
august
vinyl 96
on Mego "farmers manual"
10 tracks, 6 ending in loops
listen
side a b side
oktober
vinyl 96

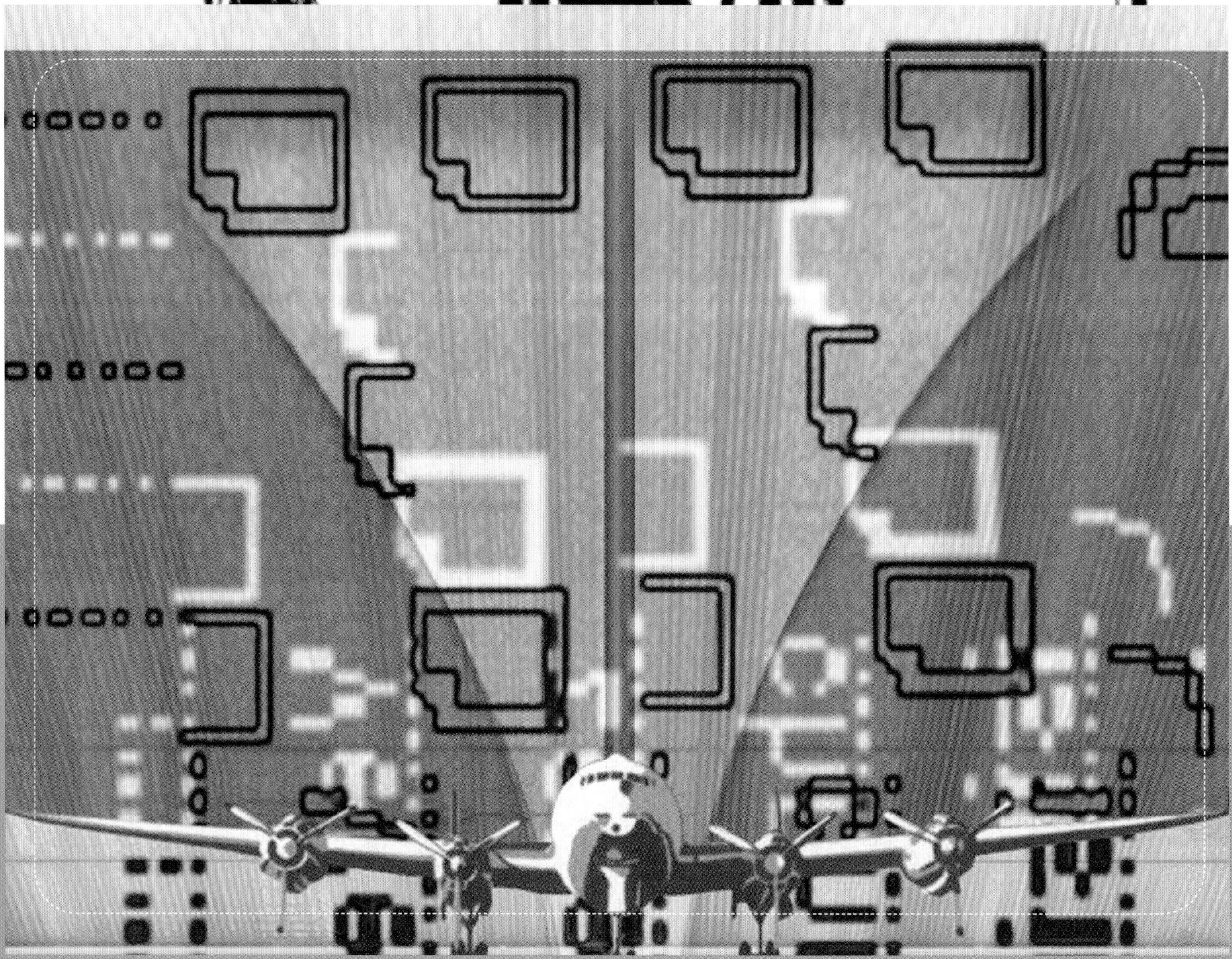

<title>
Farmers Manual

<web address>
www. farmersmanual.co.at

<client>
n/a

<design company>
Snudd, Hiaz, FM

<programs/software>
n/a

<number of pages>
about 50

<country of origin>
Austria

<work description>
This is the homepage for the esoteric, electronic music label, Farmers Manual.

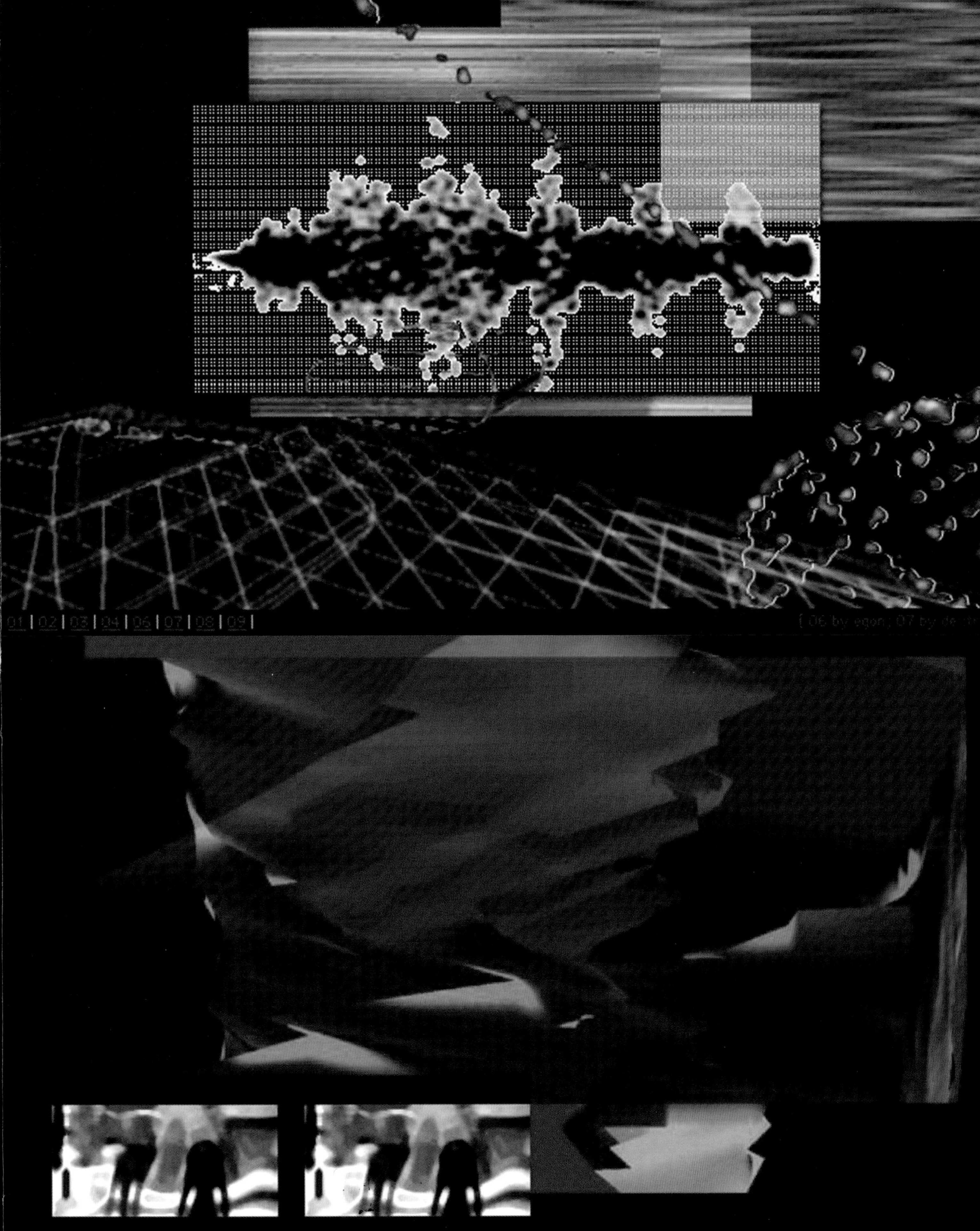
01 | 02 | 03 | 04 | 06 | 07 | 08 | 09 |
[06 by egon ; 07 by

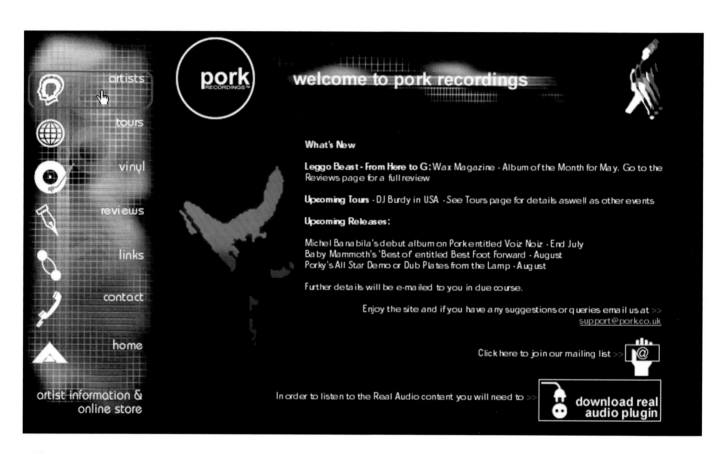

artists
tours
vinyl
reviews
links
contact
home
artist information & online store

pork RECORDINGS™

welcome to pork recordings

What's New

Leggo Beast - From Here to G: Wax Magazine - Album of the Month for May. Go to the Reviews page for a full review

Upcoming Tours - DJ Burdy in USA - See Tours page for details aswell as other events

Upcoming Releases:

Michel Banabila's debut album on Pork entitled Voiz Noiz - End July
Baby Mammoth's 'Best of' entitled Best Foot Forward - August
Porky's All Star Demo or Dub Plates from the Lamp - August

Further details will be e-mailed to you in due course.

Enjoy the site and if you have any suggestions or queries email us at >> support@pork.co.uk

Click here to join our mailing list >>

In order to listen to the Real Audio content you will need to >> download real audio plugin

<title>
Pork Recordings

<web address>
www.pork.co.uk

<client>
Pork Recordings

<design company>
Interactive Web

<programs/software>
Actinic Catalog

<number of pages>
15-20

<country of origin>
UK

<work description>
This site provides information, promotion and online sales for Pork Recordings, a primarily electronic instrumental label, and for Pork Song music publishing.

pork
RECORDINGS™

WWW.SANRIOT.COM

© 1848, 2000 COMATONSE RECORDINGS

いらっしゃいませ

Welcome SANRIOT! This site now a REVOLUTION for new product of friends such as T-SHIRT.
Let us introduce some TradeMARX in SANRIOT of COMATONSE RECORDINGS lands !
They are names Hello Karl, Rosas Lucksome, Badtz Marukusu and Mazushii-chan !

Let's HOME-ing | CATALOG-ing | ORDER-ing | IIMEIRU-ing: sanriot@comatonse.com

© 1848, 2000 COMATONSE RECORDINGS 1097-B 54th Street, Oakland CA 94608-3018 USA

<title>
Sanriot

<web address>
www.sanriot.com

<client>
Sanriot

<designer>
Terre Thaemlitz

<programs/software>
Texteditor, Photoshop

<number of pages>
25

<country of origin>
USA/Japan

<work description>
This site represents the Sanriot label and offers music, merchandise, and information.

<title>
Comatonse Recordings

<web address>
www.comatonse.com

<client>
Comatonse Recordings

<designer>
Terre Thaemlitz

<programs/software>
Texteditor, Photoshop

<number of pages>
380+

<country of origin>
USA/Japan

<work description>
This site represents the Comatonse record label and production house.

COMING SOON
eureka!

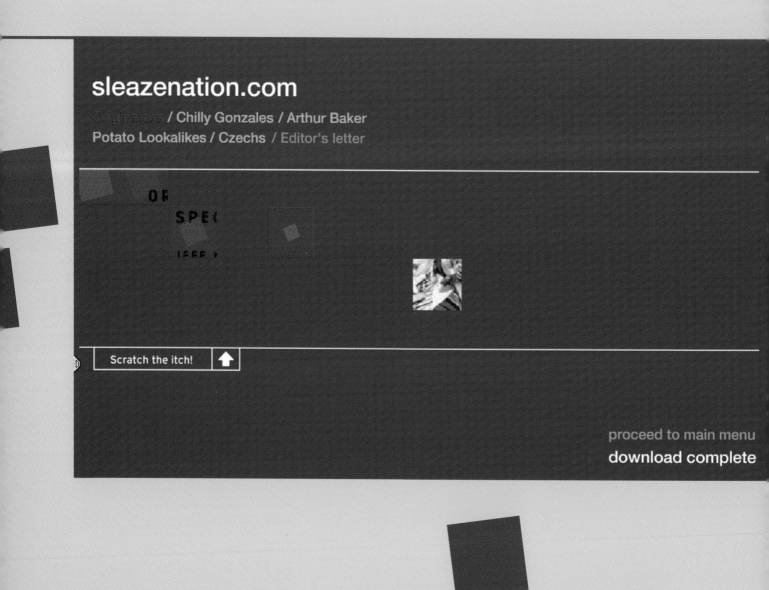

sleazenation.com

Originators / Chilly Gonzales / Arthur Baker
Potato Lookalikes / Czechs / Editor's letter

Scratch the itch!

proceed to main menu
download complete

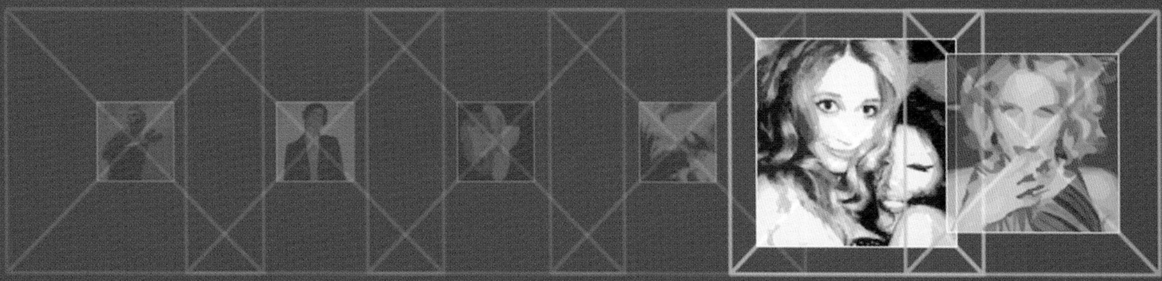

THOUGHT HONESTY AMUSEMENT

SLEAZENATION MAGAZINE IS PUBLISHED 12 TIMES A YEAR BY SWINSTEAD PUBLISHING TERMS AND CONDITIONS

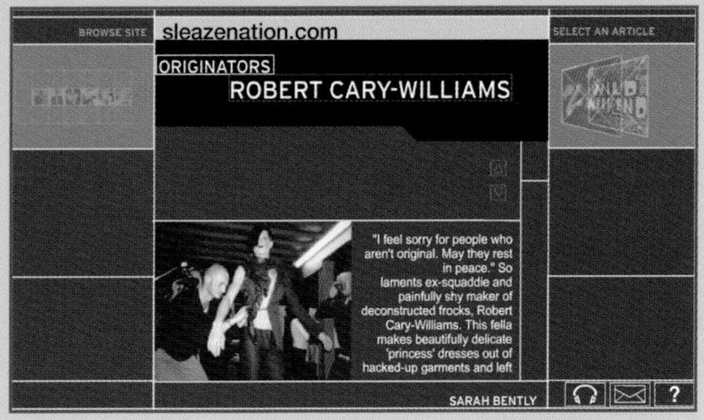

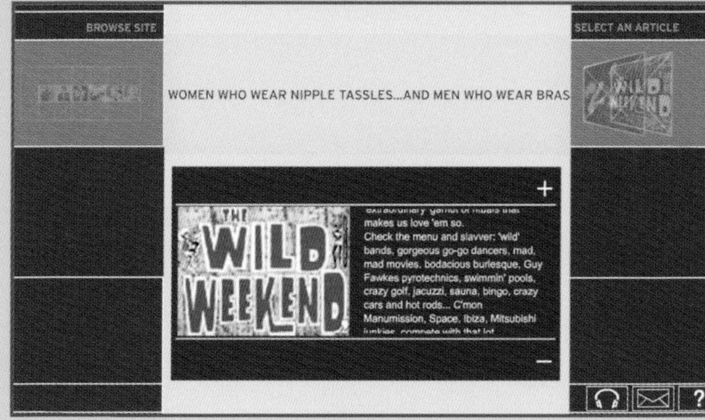

<title>
Sleazenation.com

<web address>
www.sleazenation.com

<client>
Sleazenation magazine

<design company>
Sleazenation in-house design team

<programs/software>
Flash

<number of pages>
20-30

<country of origin>
UK

<work description>
The award-winning Sleazenation.com was first launched in 1999 following the success of the Sleazenation free club fanzine. Relaunched in 2000, the site still has a strong fashion, style and design content and also offers music, online shopping, animations, videos, and live events.

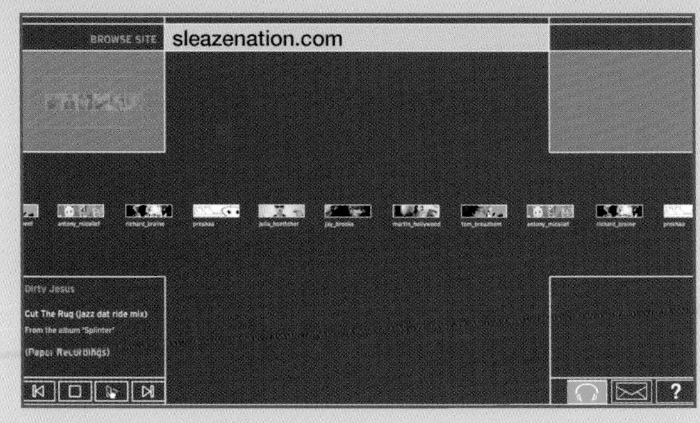

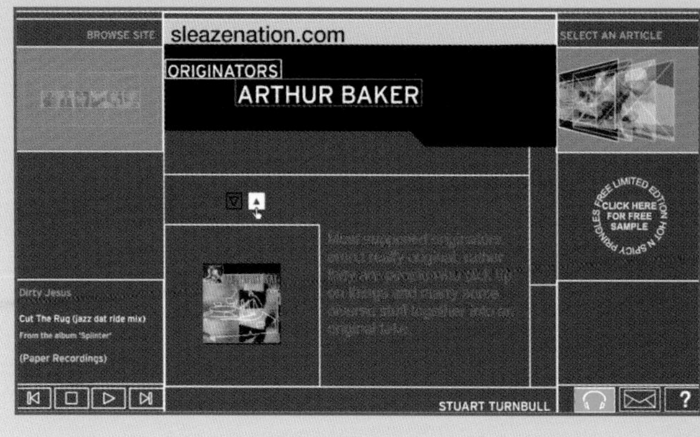

NOVEMBER ISSUE
ON SALE FROM
27TH OCTOBER

FREE CD
WITH THIS MONTHS ISSUE

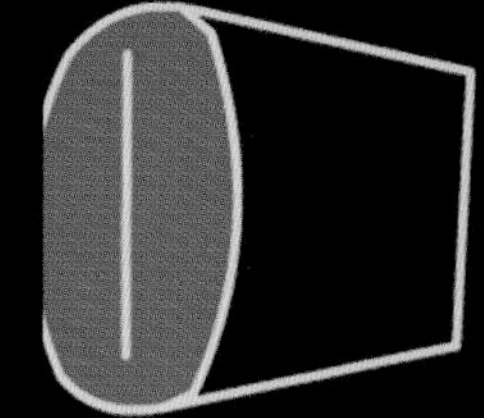

<title>
Blacklist Music Online

<web address>
www.blacklistonline.com

<client>
Blacklist Music

<designer>
Riad Hoesin

<design company>
Neopolitan Entities

<programs/software>
Adobe Photoshop, Flash, Dreamweaver, RealProducer, Gold Wave

BLACKLIST ONLINE . COM

<number of pages>
16

<country of origin>
Canada

<work description>
This site showcases the talents of all the artists under the Blacklist record label.

BLACKLIST ONLINE . CO

CLOSE THIS WINDOW

BLACKLISTONLINE.COM

GUESTBOOK

CONTACT LINKS AWARDS MAILING LIST SITE DESIGN MUSIC OFF

MOTION

the newly launched motionlive.com

UBAD

MANIFEST

POWER

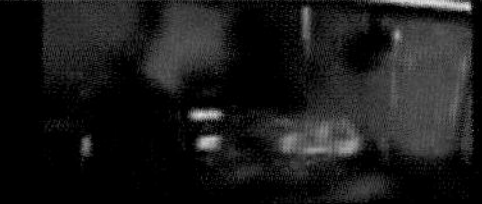

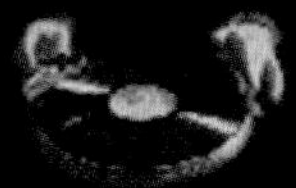

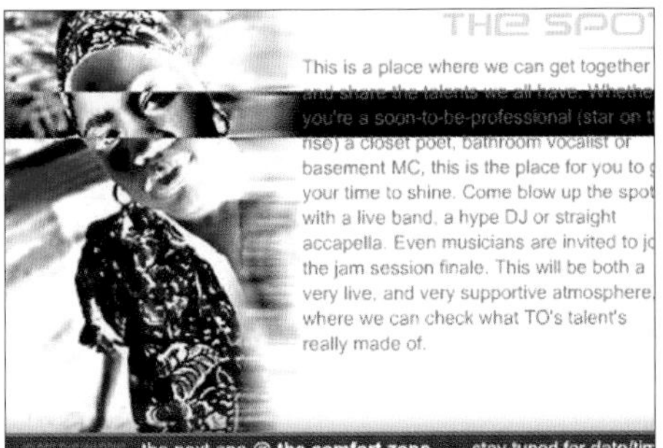

<title>
Hydrogen Dukebox

<web address>
www.hydrogendukebox.com

<client>
Hydrogen Dukebox

<design company>
Kleber Design Ltd

<programs/software>
Photoshop, Flash,
Freehand, BBedit.

<number of pages>
n/a

<country of origin>
UK

<work description>
This site is designed to promote the record label Hydrogen Dukebox.

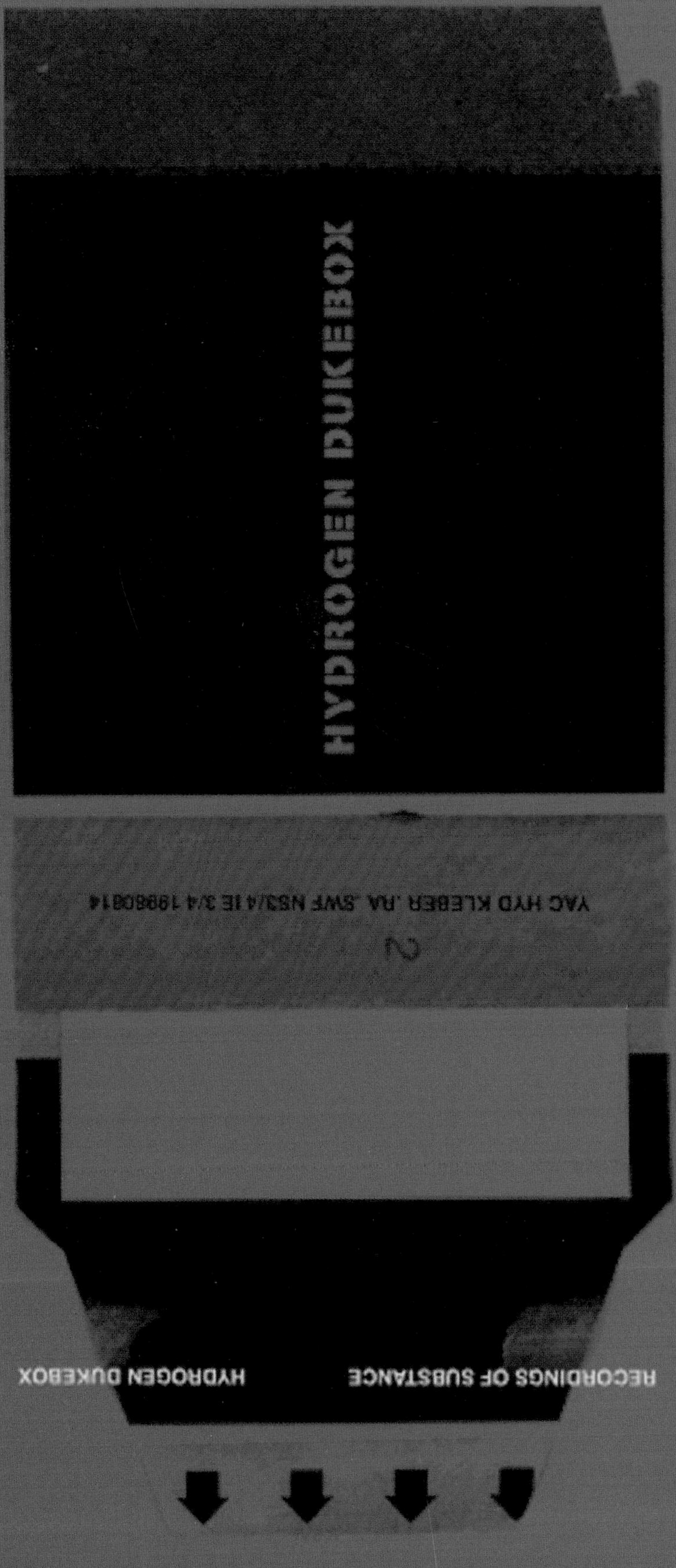

This is hydrogendukebox.com

Hydronews.
Hydroevents.
Hydroinfo.
Hydrocatalog.
Recordings of substance.
Hydromart.
Gasbox.

HYDROGEN
DUKEBOX

<stereo>

substance

NEWS EVENTS RELEASES ARTISTES
MAIL ORDER HYD/DUK GASBOX

<title>
Holzplatten

<web address>
www.holzplatten.de

<client>
n/a

<design company>
Bastian

<programs/software>
BBedit, Photoshop, Flash, Transmit

<number of pages>
300

<country of origin>
Germany

<work description>
Information site and online store for the record label Holtzplatten.

HOLZPLATTEN :: T-SHIRT

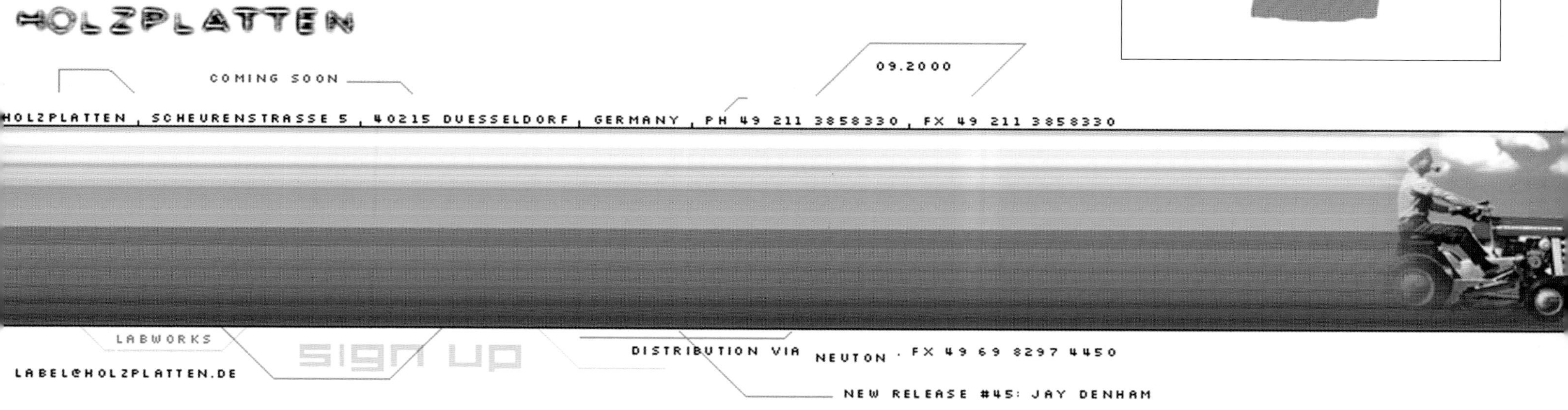

HOLZPLATTEN

COMING SOON

09.2000

HOLZPLATTEN , SCHEURENSTRASSE 5 , 40215 DUESSELDORF , GERMANY , PH 49 211 3858330 , FX 49 211 3858330

LABWORKS

sign up

DISTRIBUTION VIA NEUTON · FX 49 69 8297 4450

NEW RELEASE #45: JAY DENHAM

LABEL@HOLZPLATTEN.DE

COMING SOON

09.2000

KAZUMI , SCHEURENSTRASSE 5 , 40215 DUESSELDORF , GERMANY , PH 49 211 3858330 , FX 49 211 3858330

LABWORKS

sign up

DISTRIBUTION VIA NEUTON . FX 49 69 8297 4450

LABEL@KAZUMI.DE

UT NOW

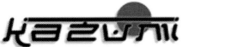

Fidel's cigar bar in association with pork

FUNKYWORMHOLE
every thursday @ the space, leeds.

GOOD SHIT monthly fridays @ gypsy moth
humberside university.

full flava
numerous events across hull and leeds.

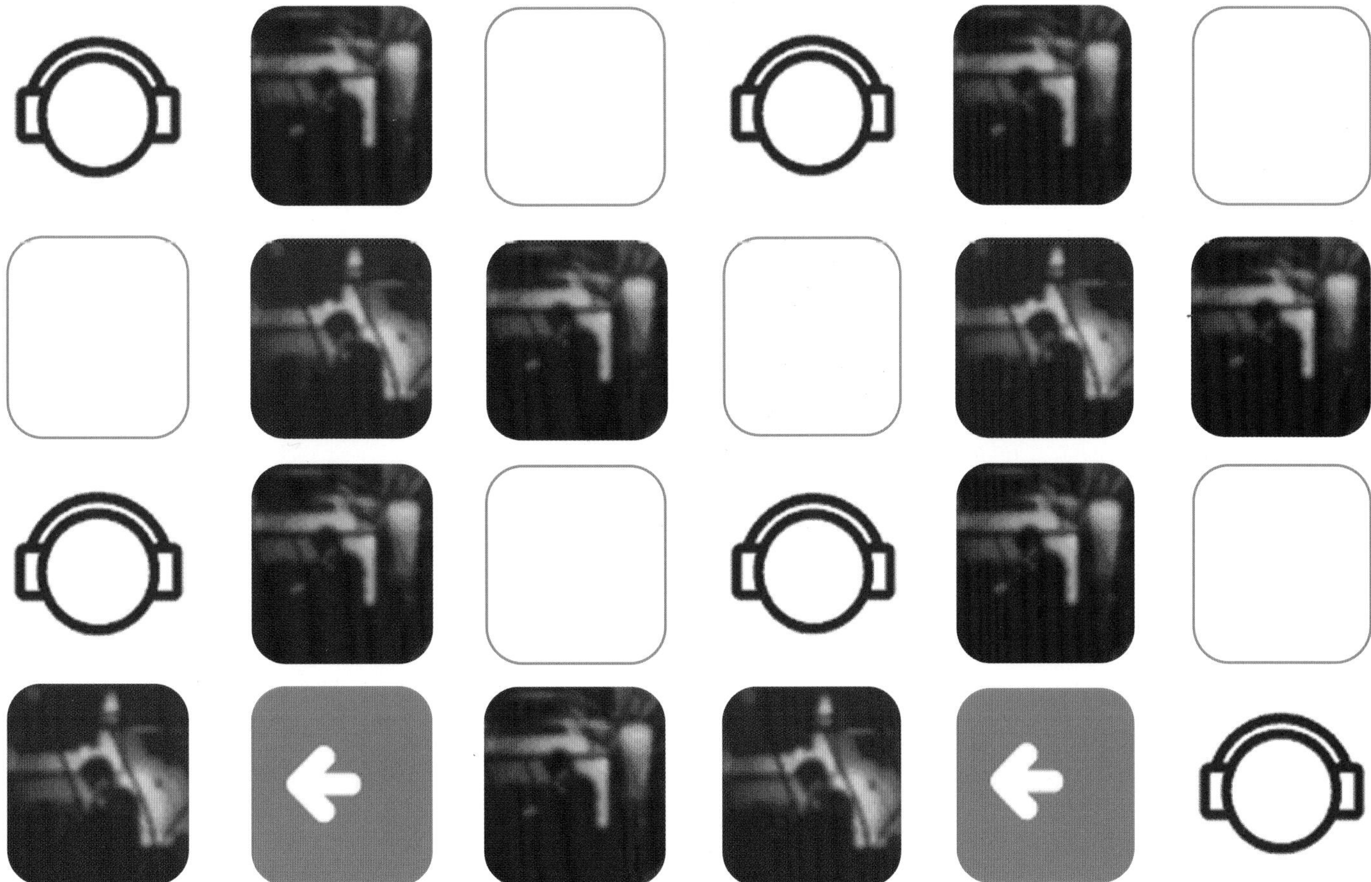

<title>
LAMP - Mark Hall

<web address>
www.thelamp.demon.co.uk

<client>
LAMP

<designer>
Gill Patchett

<programs/software>
Dreamweaver, Photoshop, Acrobat

<number of pages>
6

<country of origin>
UK

<work description>
This site promotes music, exhibitions and events in and around a gallery/club in the north of England.

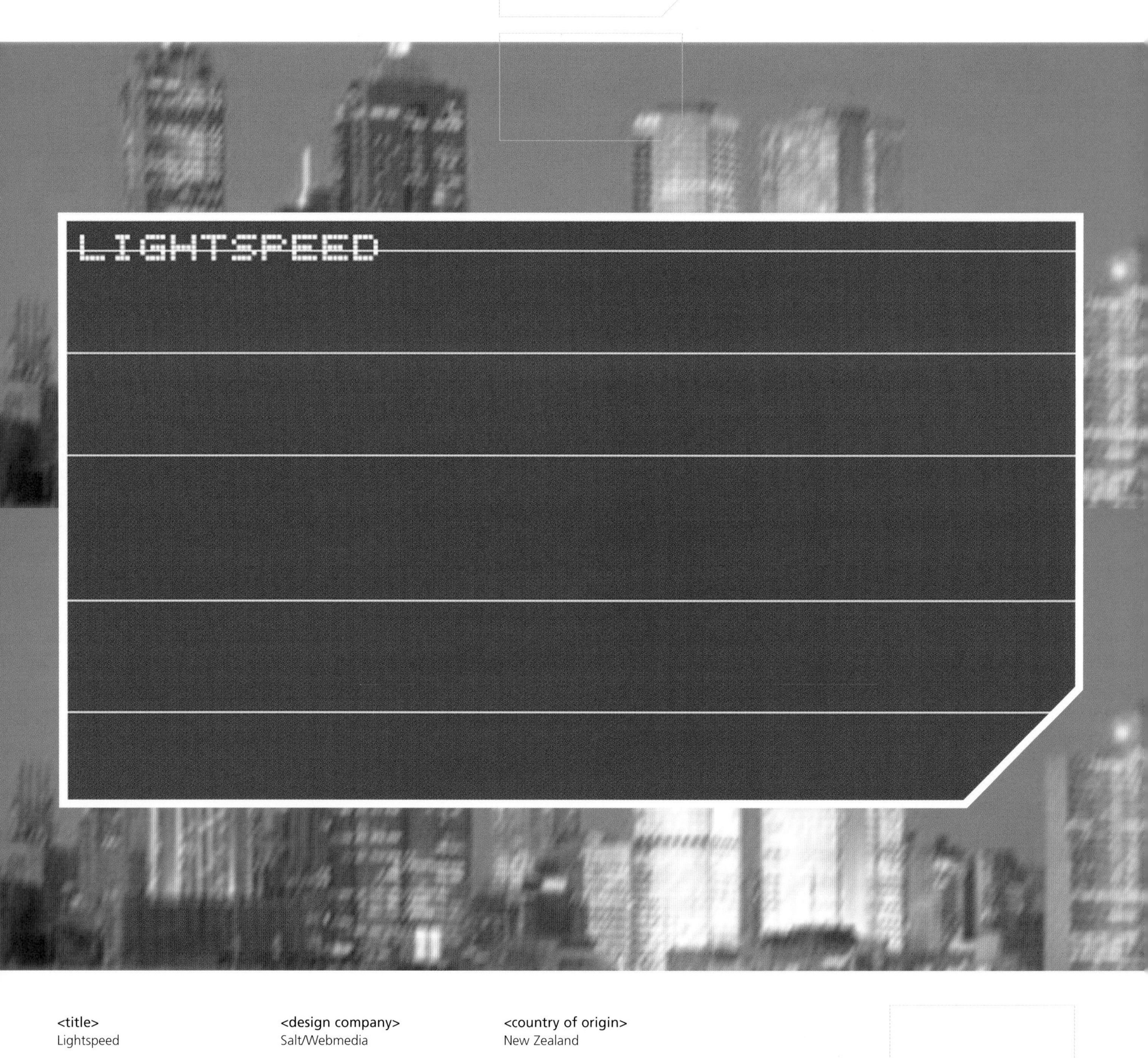

<title>
Lightspeed

<web address>
www.lightspeed.co.nz

<client>
Lightspeed Productions

<design company>
Salt/Webmedia

<programs/software>
Flash, Photoshop, PHP, Freehand

<number of pages>
varies

<country of origin>
New Zealand

<work description>
Homesite for Lightspeed Productions, a company who tour the world's top house-DJs throughout Australiasia.

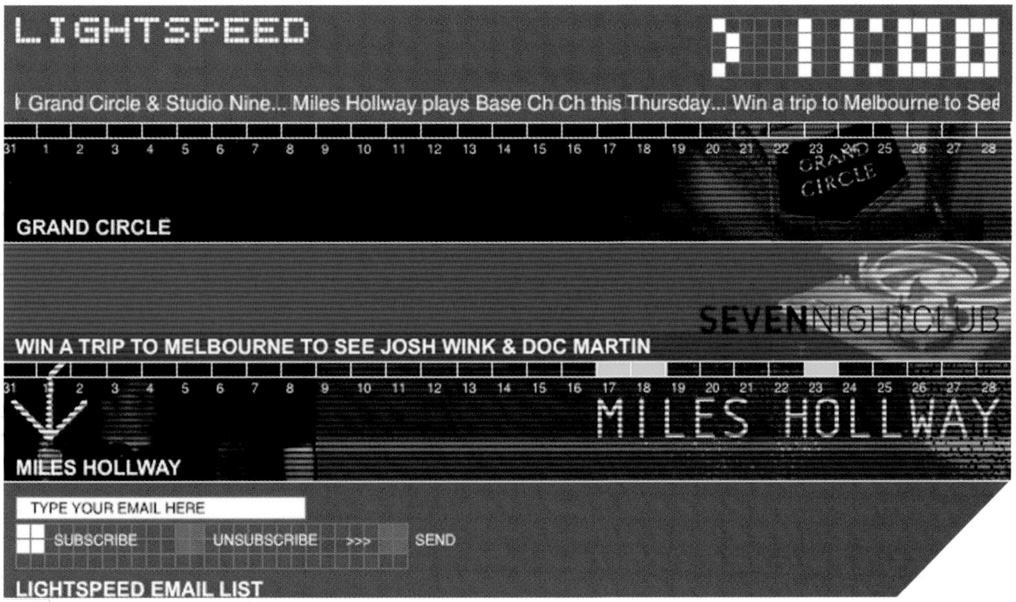
LIGHTSPEED
11:00
Grand Circle & Studio Nine... Miles Hollway plays Base Ch Ch this Thursday... Win a trip to Melbourne to See
31 1 2 3 4 5 6 7 8 9 10 11 12 13 14 15 16 17 18 19 20 21 22 23 24 25 26 27 28
GRAND CIRCLE
SEVENNIGHTCLUB
WIN A TRIP TO MELBOURNE TO SEE JOSH WINK & DOC MARTIN
MILES HOLLWAY
MILES HOLLWAY
TYPE YOUR EMAIL HERE
SUBSCRIBE
UNSUBSCRIBE
>>>
SEND
LIGHTSPEED EMAIL LIST

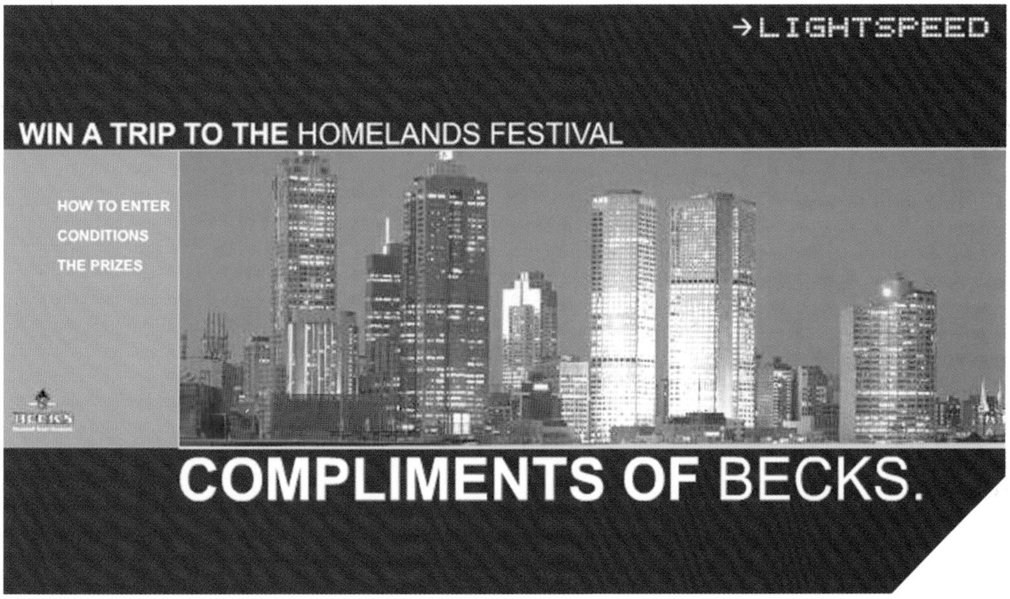
→LIGHTSPEED
WIN A TRIP TO THE HOMELANDS FESTIVAL
HOW TO ENTER
CONDITIONS
THE PRIZES
COMPLIMENTS OF BECKS.

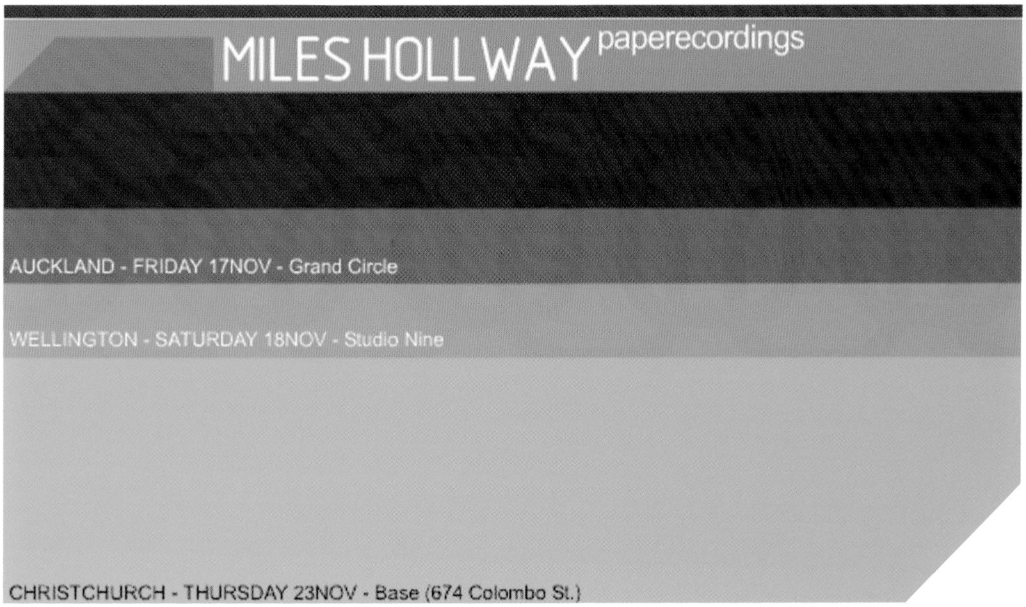
MILES HOLLWAY paperecordings
AUCKLAND - FRIDAY 17NOV - Grand Circle
WELLINGTON - SATURDAY 18NOV - Studio Nine
CHRISTCHURCH - THURSDAY 23NOV - Base (674 Colombo St.)

<title>
Positiva Records

<web address>
www.postivarecords.com

<client>
EMI/Chrysalis

<designers>
Ash Richards, Sam Collett

<design company>
Lateral Net Ltd.

<programs/software>
Adobe Photoshop, Adobe GoLive, BBedit

<number of pages>
varies

<country of origin>
UK

<work description>
The promotional site for Postiva Records carries press-releases, a discography, and advance audio and video clips.

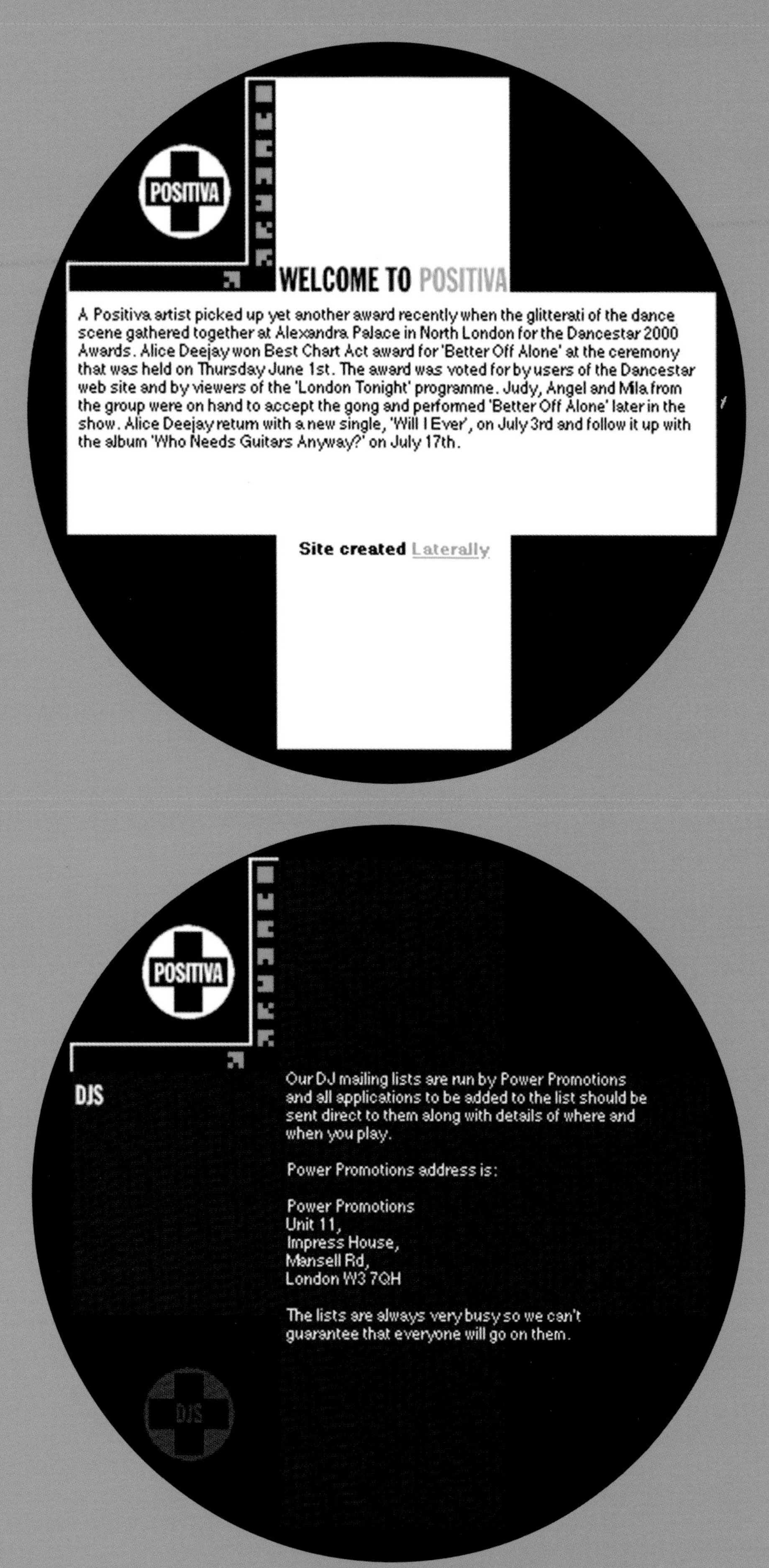
POSITIVA
WELCOME TO POSITIVA
A Positiva artist picked up yet another award recently when the glitterati of the dance scene gathered together at Alexandra Palace in North London for the Dancestar 2000 Awards. Alice Deejay won Best Chart Act award for 'Better Off Alone' at the ceremony that was held on Thursday June 1st. The award was voted for by users of the Dancestar web site and by viewers of the 'London Tonight' programme. Judy, Angel and Mila from the group were on hand to accept the gong and performed 'Better Off Alone' later in the show. Alice Deejay return with a new single, 'Will I Ever', on July 3rd and follow it up with the album 'Who Needs Guitars Anyway?' on July 17th.
Site created Laterally
POSITIVA
DJS
Our DJ mailing lists are run by Power Promotions and all applications to be added to the list should be sent direct to them along with details of where and when you play.
Power Promotions address is:
Power Promotions
Unit 11,
Impress House,
Mansell Rd,
London W3 7QH
The lists are always very busy so we can't guarantee that everyone will go on them.
DJS

<title>
Theralite Records

<web address>
www.theralite.avalon.hr

<client>
Theralite Records

<design company>
Indigo Designs

<programs/software>
Homesite, Photoshop

<number of pages>
30+

<country of origin>
Croatia

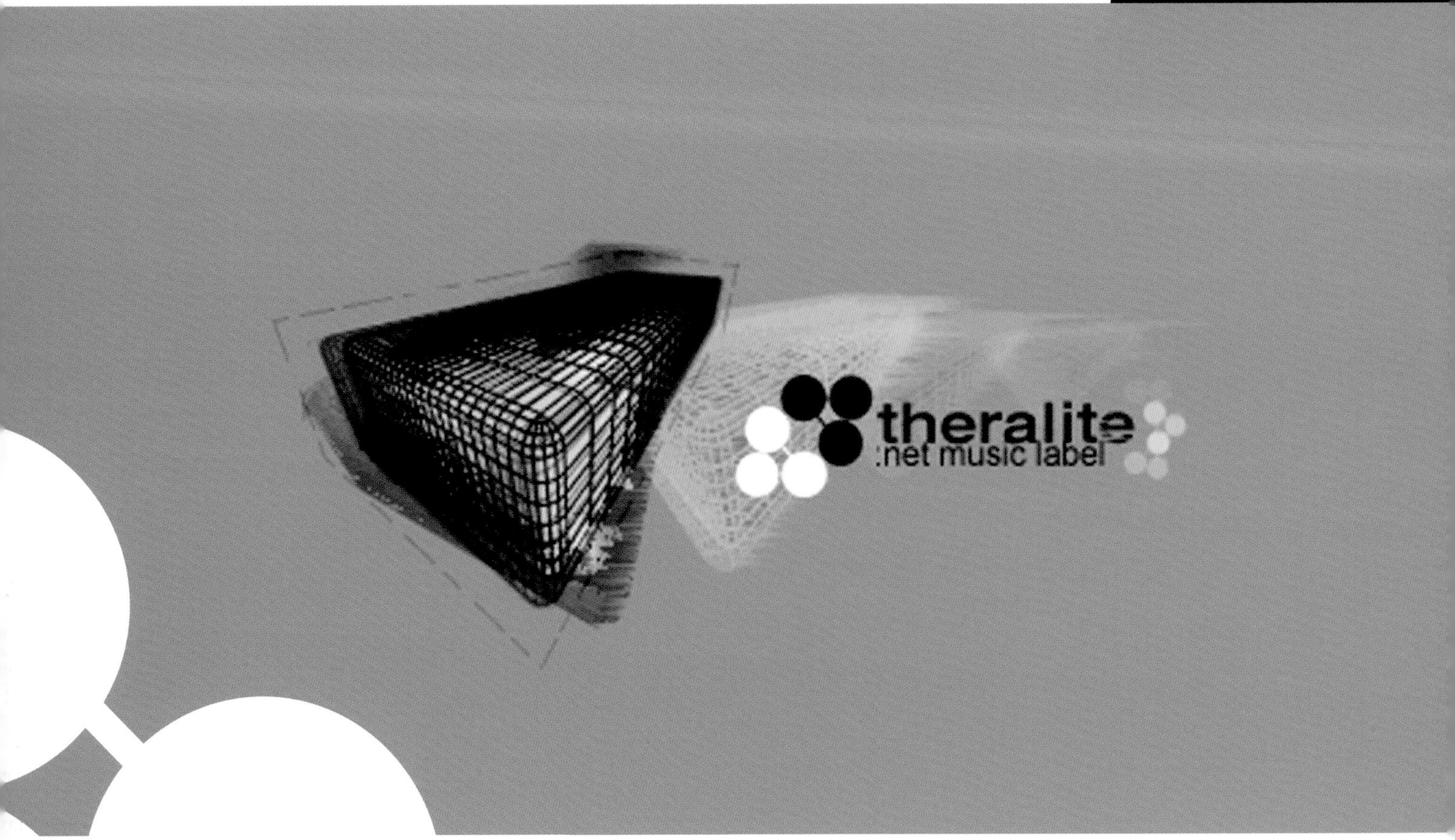

<work description>
Theralite is an online record label that offers freely downloadable music. It gathers artists from all over the world and helps them to distribute their music over the internet to reach the widest possible audience.

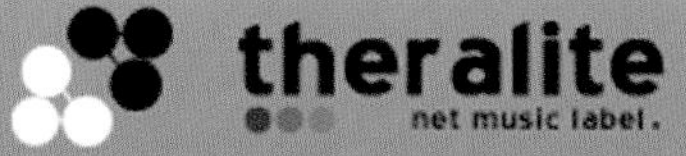
theralite
net music label.

da phonque never stops.

what do we represent:

we are a collective of musicians that intensively use computers to create electronic music in a wide range of styles.

we are a net music label. all our works are free to download from our site, we don't require any kind of payment for the tracks.

although free our music is subject to all copyright laws. for each release we retain all copyrights. unauthorized publishing of our music on cd compilations (audio or mp3) is prohibited!

if you don't know how to play our music on your computer take a look at our small **how-to-play** guide. and if you have any comments or questions? don't hesitate, feel free, mail us!

news headlines:

[09.07.2000]
new style fusion from villbe
scene.org spaceless
we're taking a summer break
more news...

latest release:

THER A012
VILLBE
Secret Identity
128kbps MP3

site help:

netscape 4.5+ in 800*600 highly recommended.
use the top right bar to navigate the site.

get info about new releases:

send a blank email to:
announce-subscribe@theralite.avalon.hr

3981 WebTracker
since: 10.03.2000

ultraphonq design by indigo
welcome image by shale

our site is hosted by
AVALON
www.avalon.hr

<title>
Plug Research Records

<web address>
www.plugresearch.com

<client>
Plug Research Records

<design company>
Sutekh/ Context Free Media

<programs/software>
Dreamweaver, Photoshop

<number of pages>
35

ABOUT
NEWS
ARTISTS
RELEASES
BOOKINGS
CONTACT
LINKS

PLUG RESEARCH RADIO

CD :
PR250006CD. 27075-2 CD. UPC# 612651002526

2x12" VINYL
PR250006LP. 27075-6 VINYL. UPC#: 612651002519

11 ALL-NEW TRACKS
W & P BY: JEREMY DOWER
PUBLISHED BY: PLUG RESEARCH

JEREMY DOWER

SENTIMENTAL DANCE MUSIC FOR COU-PLES

more information, more fun:
WWW.PLUG RESEARCH.COM

DESIGNED BY LOWCULTURE.COM
ANIMATED BY JAMES REITANO@FLOATINGSPACE

SKIP INTRO

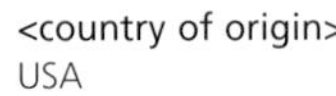

<country of origin>
USA

<work description>
The Plug Research Records label official site offers news on releases, artists, bookings, and webcasts.

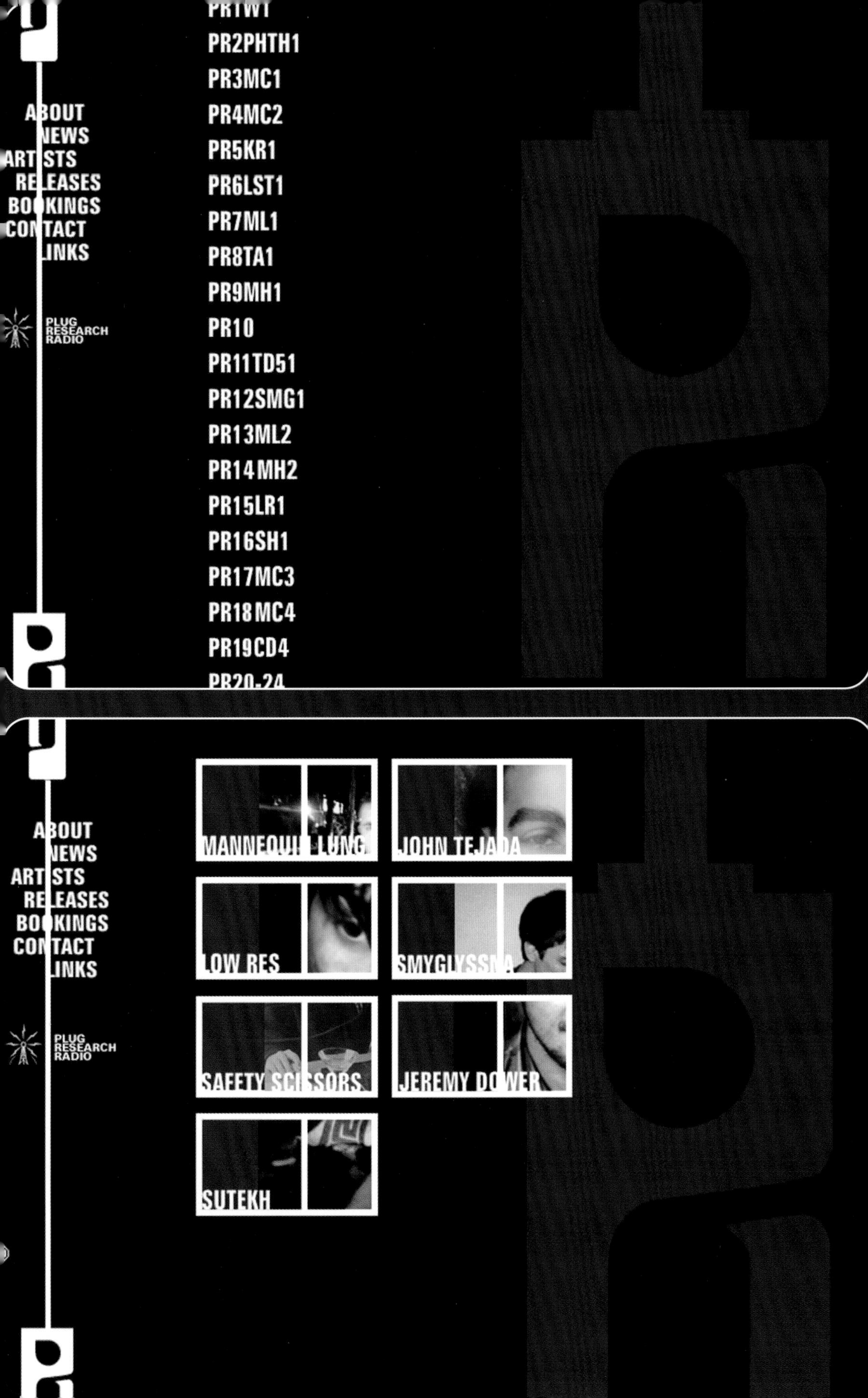
ABOUT
NEWS
ARTISTS
RELEASES
BOOKINGS
CONTACT
LINKS
PLUG RESEARCH RADIO
PR2PHTH1
PR3MC1
PR4MC2
PR5KR1
PR6LST1
PR7ML1
PR8TA1
PR9MH1
PR10
PR11TD51
PR12SMG1
PR13ML2
PR14MH2
PR15LR1
PR16SH1
PR17MC3
PR18MC4
PR19CD4
ABOUT
NEWS
ARTISTS
RELEASES
BOOKINGS
CONTACT
LINKS
PLUG RESEARCH RADIO
JOHN TEJADA
LOW RES
SAFETY SCISSORS
SUTEKH

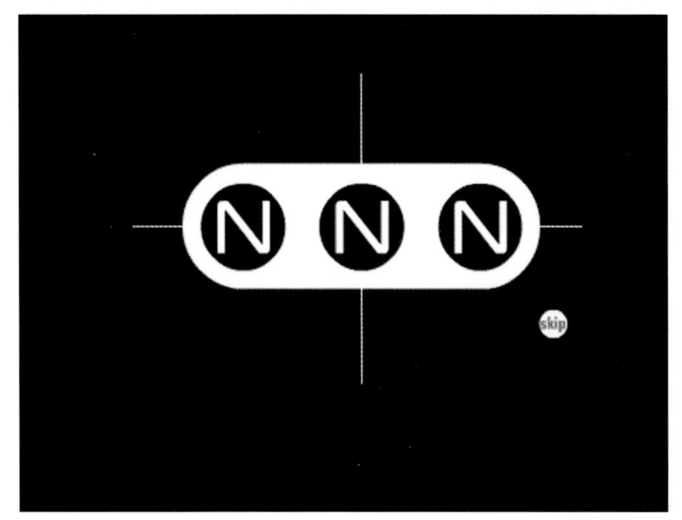
N N N
skip

LUMICON

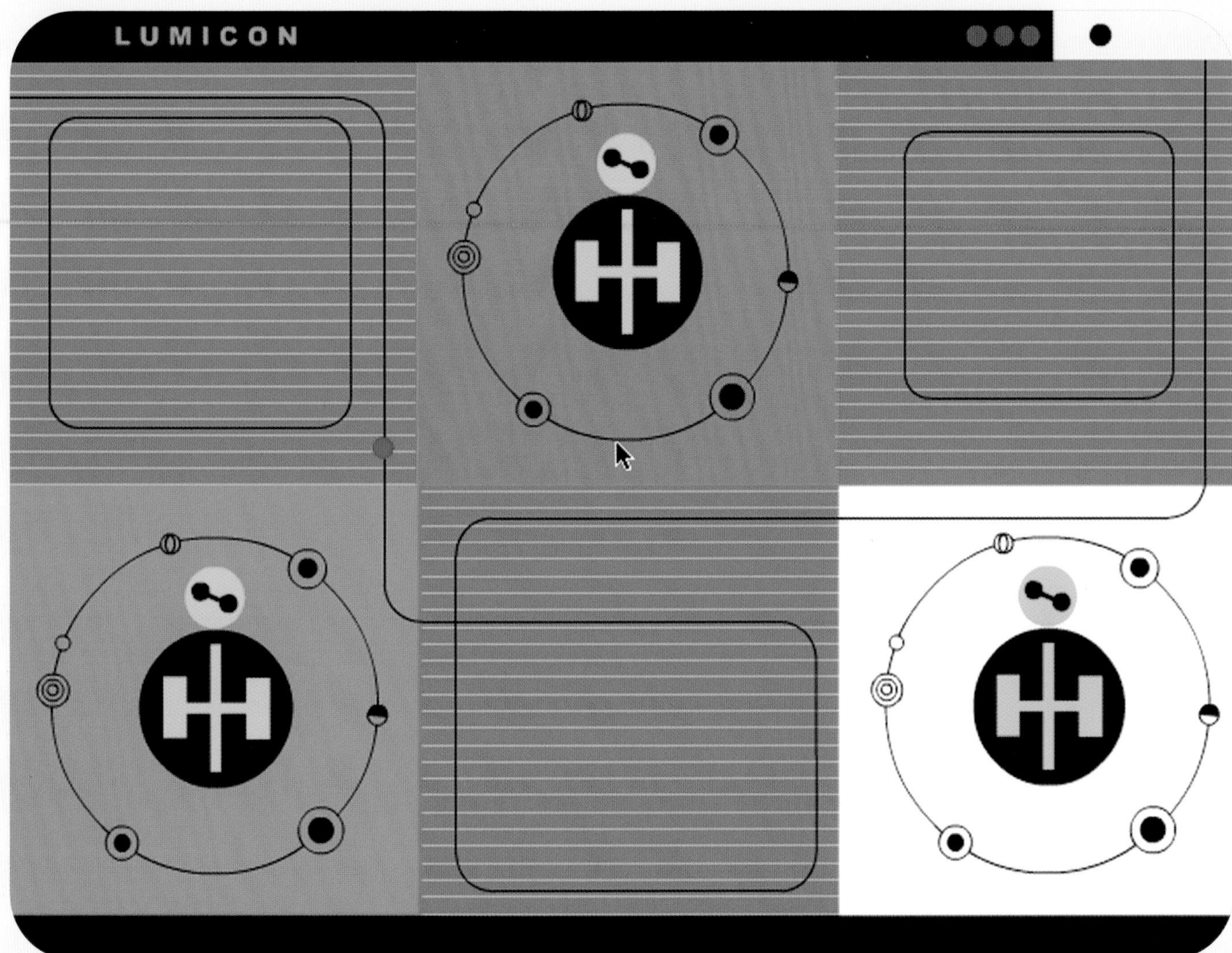

<title>
Monocrom/Lumicon

<web address>
www.monocrom.de
www.lumicon.de

<client>
Monocrom gbr

<design company>
Monocrom gbr

<programs/software>
Macromedia Flash, Dreamweaver, Fireworks, Kinetix, Adobe Photoshop

<number of pages>
16

<country of origin>
Germany

<work description>
Interlinked promotional sites for the web design company monocrom. These sites are self-generated art projects designed with animation and sound integration.

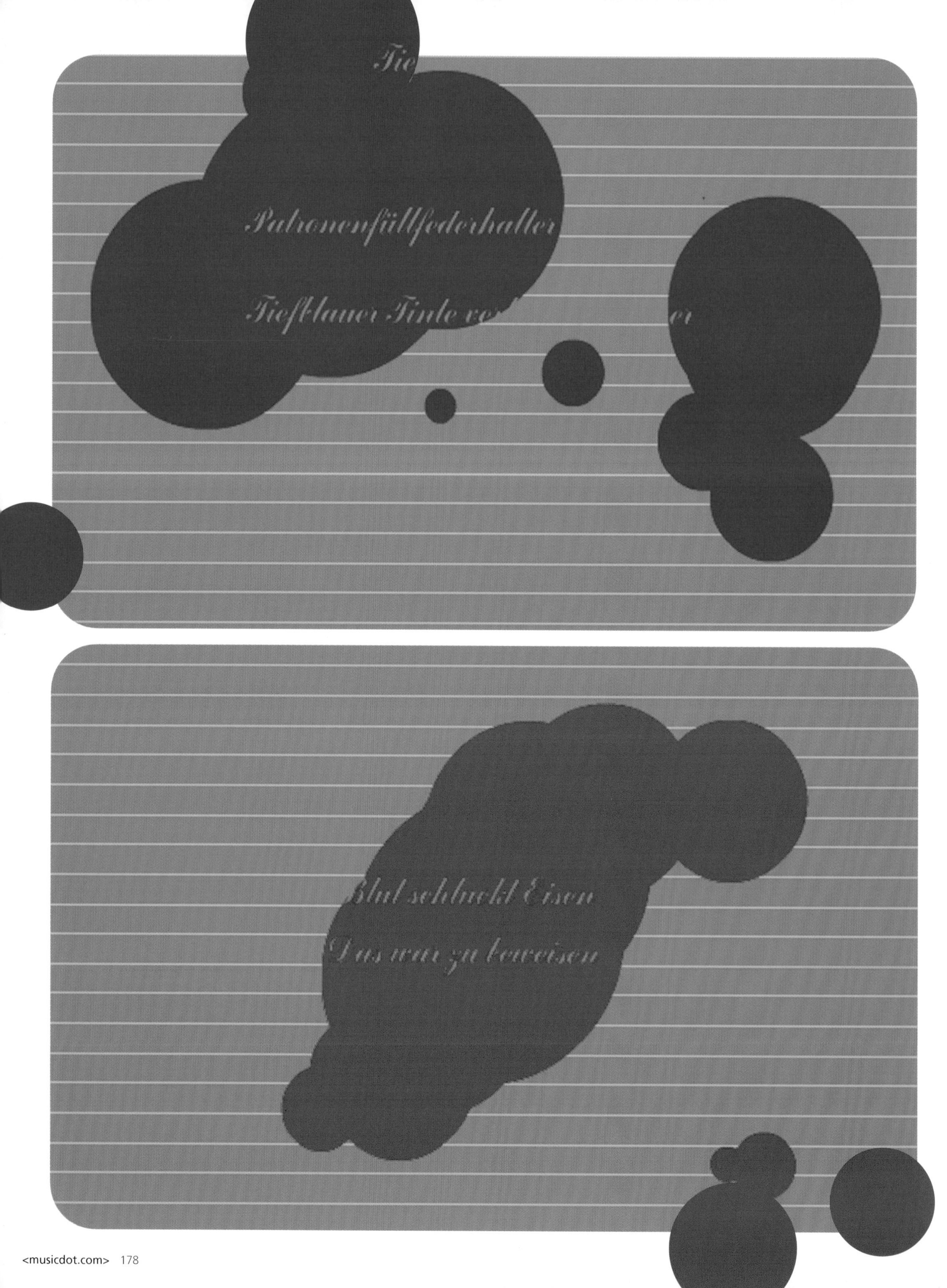
Tie
Patronenfüllfederhalter
Tiefblauer Tinte ve
er
Blut schlucht Eisen
Das war zu beweisen

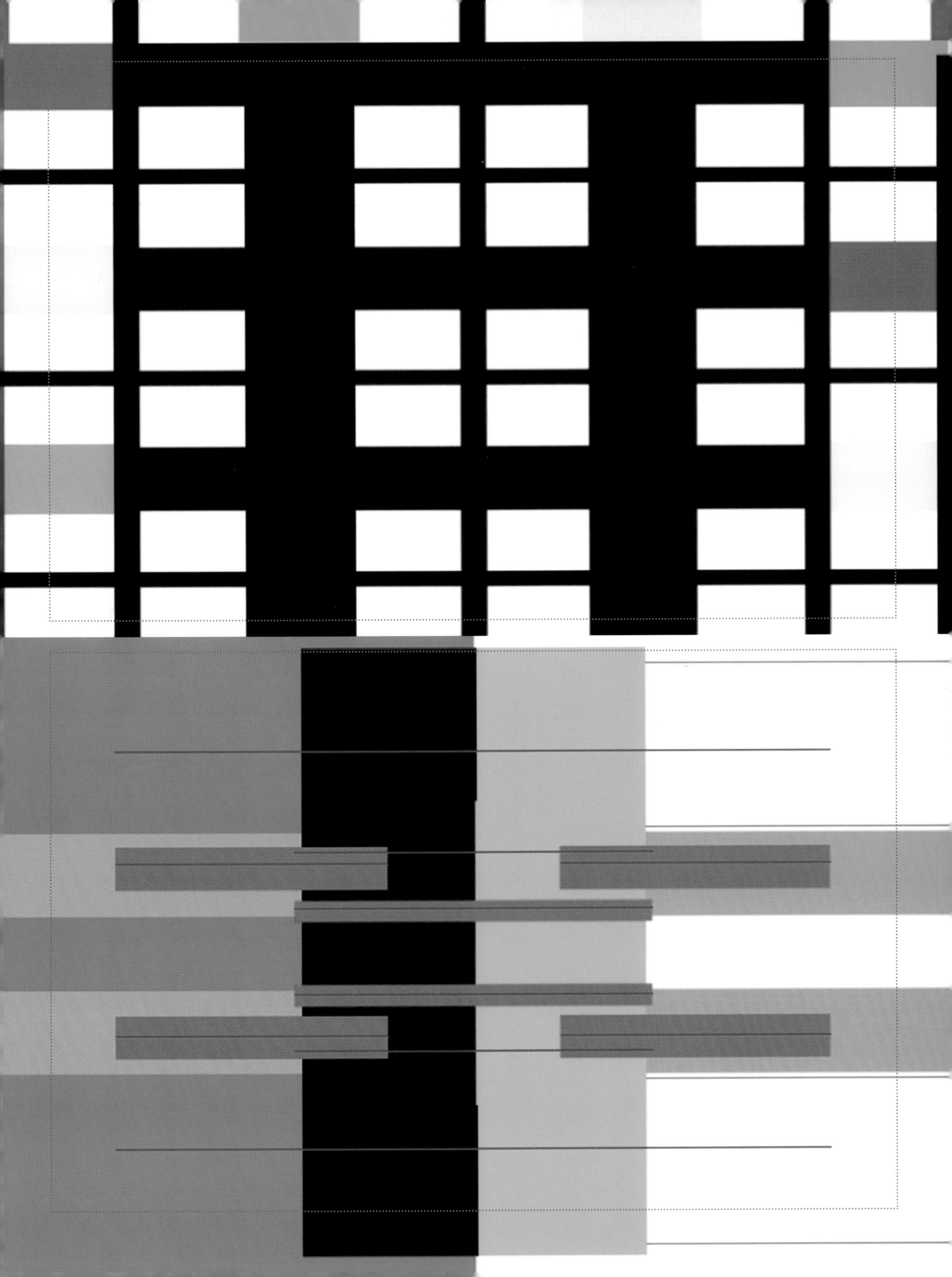

<index>

page entries refer to captions

(clients, designers and design companies are listed)

<U>

<W>

<X>